Doris,

Thank you for all of the years
of support + believing that this
book would come to fruition.

In Christian Hope,

Hope in the Age of
Climate Change

Hope in the Age of Climate Change

Creation Care This Side of the Resurrection

Chris Doran

CASCADE *Books* · Eugene, Oregon

HOPE IN THE AGE OF CLIMATE CHANGE
Creation Care This Side of the Resurrection

Cascade Books
An Imprint of Wipf and Stock Publishers
199 W. 8th Ave., Suite 3
Eugene, OR 97401

www.wipfandstock.com

Unless otherwise indicated, Scripture quotations are from the New Revised Standard Version Bible, copyright © 1989 National Council of the Churches of Christ in the United States of America. Used by permission. All rights reserved worldwide.

Scripture quotations marked NIV are taken from the Holy Bible, New International Version®, NIV®. Copyright © 1973, 1978, 1984, 2011 by Biblica, Inc.™ Used by permission of Zondervan. All rights reserved worldwide. www.zondervan.com The "NIV" and "New International Version" are trademarks registered in the United States Patent and Trademark Office by Biblica, Inc.™

Scripture quotations marked ESV are from ESV® Bible (The Holy Bible, English Standard Version®), copyright © 2001 by Crossway, a publishing ministry of Good News Publishers. Used by permission. All rights reserved

PAPERBACK ISBN: 978-1-4982-9702-8
HARDCOVER ISBN: 978-1-4982-9704-2
EBOOK ISBN: 978-1-4982-9703-5

Cataloguing-in-Publication data:

Names: Doran, Chris.

Title: Hope in the age of climate change : creation care this side of the resurrection / Chris Doran.

Description: Eugene, OR : Cascade Books, 2017 | Includes bibliographical references and index.

Identifiers: ISBN 978-1-4982-9702-8 (paperback) | ISBN 978-1-4982-9704-2 (hardcover) | ISBN 978-1-4982-9703-5 (ebook)

Subjects: LCSH: Creation. | Ecotheology. | Human ecology—Religious aspects—Christianity.

Classification: BT695.5 .D67 2017 (print) | BT695.5 .D67 (ebook)

Manufactured in the U.S.A.   04/27/17

To my students who hope for a better tomorrow

Contents

Acknowledgments

No book is truly written by one person. So many ideas, thoughts, comments, and suggestions, both intentional and unintentional, shape a way a person thinks and ultimately writes down those thoughts for others to read. I am unequivocally grateful to all of those who contributed whether they knew it or not along the way. I am particularly thankful to the following folks who contributed directly in ways that assisted this project coming to fruition. First, thank you to the National Endowment for the Humanities for funding the Rethinking the Land Ethic Summer Institute at which I was a summer scholar in 2011. That summer gave me the time and the creative juices through interdisciplinary dialogue to brainstorm many of the central themes that appear in these pages. Thank you, Kelsey Patrick, for being the first person to read through and comment upon some of the work that eventually turned into this book. Thank you, Breanna Abram, for giving the drafts of some of these chapters a serious read even when they were nowhere near finished. Thank you to those in my SUST 592 course that was the first class to read a draft of this work from the beginning to end. Your thoughtful engagement with the material encouraged me to finish this project. Thank you, Daniel Spencer, for accepting the task of reading through drafts of the entire project and giving such wonderful feedback. This book is better because of your comments. Thank you, Caleb Clanton, my dear brother, for encouraging me to believe that I had good enough ideas to get onto paper. It is a gift that I cannot properly repay. And finally, thank you to my wife Amy, for always allowing me the freedom to pursue that which I believe is important. I would not have finished this without your faithful and enduring love that has made me a better person and a more thoughtful scholar.

Introduction

In January 2015, my wife and I took an extended vacation (for us at least) as a way to start off my first ever institutionally supported sabbatical leave. During that trip, we spent time scuba diving. While I am not entirely proficient at the intricacies of the sport, I enjoy diving very much. Being underwater with flora and fauna that are so incredibly disconnected from my everyday above-water existence allows me to reflect upon life in ways that I would not normally consider. For example, during this particular trip there were many moments when I was surrounded by thousands of fish, turtles, and the various creatures that inhabit a coral reef, some that I was very cognizant of and others that I was not. I was in awe of all of the life that was suddenly around me and lived daily in the ocean whether I was aware of their existence or not. This scene in the middle of the Indian Ocean made me reflect deeply upon the story of Job and his revelation when taken up in the whirlwind. In response to Job's demand for God to explain why he is suffering unfairly, God gives Job an in-depth tour of creation, showing him creatures that Job had neither seen nor could even fathom. As I circled various underwater rocks and coral formations, I could not help thinking of myself in my own personal whirlwind 60 feet or so below the ocean's surface. On one of our last dives, I encountered one of the most fascinating creatures. An octopus was attached to a coral formation camouflaged so well against the surface of the rock that my wife could not make out what I was pointing at so vigorously. As the current changed, the tip of our dive guide's fin passed ever so closely to the octopus and the creature changed from the multiple colors that allowed it to blend in with the color of the rocks to a vivid white and then two seconds later returned to its elaborate camouflaged pattern. It is one thing to see that sort of thing in a nature documentary on television; it is quite another to see it from only a few feet away.

At one point during Job's whirlwind tour, God points to the massive creatures called Behemoth and Leviathan and describes them in exquisite poetic detail. It is as if God wants Job to be in awe of what God has created.

In one of my underwater jaunts I was looking intently at some fish within a coral reef when my dive guide began to bang furiously on her tank with a metal pointer to get our attention. I looked up and for the next 30 to 45 seconds I was spellbound by the sight of another of God's "leviathans"—a whale shark. This particular whale shark was still a juvenile of only about 10 to 12 feet, but it was magnificent nonetheless. (Whale sharks are the largest fish on the planet; adults can get to be 40 to 50 feet long and live 70 to 100 years.) One can only imagine that Job was equally breathless when he saw some of God's most spectacular creatures.

My reflections on these amazing underwater creatures led me to consider Job's response at the end of his whirlwind encounter. In a short soliloquy Job admits that he was wrong to demand answers for his question because he ultimately has no comprehension of the plan that God has for the universe. Job concludes with the enigmatic confession, "therefore I despise myself, / and repent in dust and ashes."[1] The story of Job is compelling because the audience knows that Job is blameless even though his friends do not: he is truly being treated unfairly, by the fiat of God, too. This makes Job's response in the end, though, even more incredible. Job drops his righteous demand for justice and testifies to a reality that he believes is far more significant. God is the Creator and Job is the creature; he now realizes that fact existentially and accepts his place in the universe. If the narrative ends at this point without the restoration of Job's fortune and bestowal of more children, as many scholars believe was the original ending, then Job's pronouncement is even more startling. To gain humility, to know one's proper place in the universe, is fundamentally important to having a relationship with God and the rest of God's creation.

Something else, however, brought me to the other side of the world (I live in California). In 2011 I saw a documentary entitled *The Island President*. It tells the story about how rising sea levels due to climate change are eventually going to submerge the archipelago nation of the Maldives and force the relocation of nearly 300,000 citizens. And with that relocation, a culture and way of life that has existed for more than 2,000 years will abruptly come to an end. The ongoing submergence and resulting relocation is not something that will happen in the distant future, but likely in the next 50 to 100 years. Most of the Maldives is only about three to four feet above sea level, making it the planet's lowest-lying nation. Towns on some islands are already experiencing considerable beach erosion that will eventually prevent habitation from continuing. Government officials, including former President Mohamed Nasheed, have attempted to prepare for this by

1. Job 42:6.

attempting to purchase land in Australia, India, and Sri Lanka, but to no avail. It is the most tragic sort of "Not In My BackYard" (NIMBY) problem. No one wants 300,000 people to be dispossessed, but Australia, India, and Sri Lanka have their own national concerns to worry about.

The situation is even more tragic, though, as the rising sea level around the Maldives is not a consequence of the activities of the Maldivian people. The cause is the historical burning of fossil fuels by the world's developed nations, especially the United States, Australia, and many member nations of the European Union. However, in the face of certain disaster and the loss of their way of life, the Maldivian people are resolute. The Maldives has pledged to become carbon neutral by 2019.[2] While this pledge may end up being more symbolic than practical, it shines a bright light upon countries like the United States, China, India, and member nations of the European Union who will not do the same nor participate meaningfully in the relocation schemes that will be necessary to relocate Maldivians and the millions of other climate refugees around the planet that will need new homes in the coming years.

How could it be that the historical economic and technological development of people on the other side of the world could cause an island nation to go underwater? What climate change and its numerous consequences are teaching humans more radically than perhaps ever before is that life on this planet is interdependently connected. The more sophisticated our economies and technologies become, the more we impact places on this planet that we may have never seen or even heard about. As a citizen of the United States, I now must confront the stark reality that what I do everyday as I live my "normal" American life affects the rest of the globe. My actions not only impact the lives of humans and nonhumans now, but will continue to do so into the distant future. What I eat everyday affects people, the land, and farm creatures. How I get to work just to do my job is a calculation in fossil-fuel management. My flight to the Maldives for a "much-needed" vacation has consequences far beyond what my savings account now shows. As a Christian, all of these things should matter because they either shape me into the likeness of Christ[3] or distort me into the image of our worldly culture. In the American context especially, Christians often fail to reflect upon how the daily events of our normal lives shape us. And this lack of reflection upon the "normal" life that our government and various corporations encourage us to live has caused many American Christians to discount

2. United Nations Framework Convention on Climate Change, "Copenhagen Accord," 9.

3. E.g., 1 Cor 11:1; 2 Cor 3:18; Eph 4:15; 2 Pet 3:18.

how their actions are part of the interdependent web of life God created on this planet.

Presupposition #1: Climate Change Is Happening

There are three presuppositions that I take seriously and ask the reader to grant before moving forward. The first is this: climate change is occurring, and it is primarily caused and further exacerbated by human economic development, particularly the historical and current burning of hydrocarbons, or fossil fuels, by developed nations and now the accelerated burning of these by developing nations. The evidence for anthropogenic climate change is overwhelming and has been so for quite a while.[4] We are participants in the most substantial planetary geoengineering effort in the history of human civilization. We are in the midst of the Anthropocene Era whether we care to admit it or not.[5] All that is left to be determined is the magnitude of the consequences of past human activity that are already locked into the climate and the mitigation and adaptation efforts that help us prepare for a vastly uncertain future. The rising sea level that is causing the beach erosion of the Maldives is just one dramatic example of the new reality we confront. Unfortunately, however, far too few American Christians are convinced by the immense amount of scientific evidence of this.[6]

So why are so many American Christians unconcerned about the consequences of climate change and human responsibility for it? There are naive assertions that some believe, like: How could rising sea levels really wipe out part of the planet if God promised not to flood the Earth ever again? Some even use the Noah story to claim that anthropogenic climate change is not possible because if the great flood of Noah's time tells us anything, it is that humans are not responsible for global climatic events.[7] For others, the idea that human civilization could be altered irrevocably is somehow an affront to their understanding of divine sovereignty, as if climate change represents throwing the Earth off course from God's ultimate plan. Two topics,

4. For Christian examples of weighing the evidence, see Blanchard and O'Brien, *Christian Environmentalism*, 176n8 for Hayhoe and Farley, *Climate for Change* and McKibben, *Eaarth*; Intergovernmental Panel on Climate Change, "Fifth Assessment Report."

5. Steffen et al., "Anthropocene," 614–21.

6. Public Religion Research Institute and American Academy of Religion, "Believers, Sympathizers, and Skeptics," 14–15.

7. Goldenberg, "US Congressman." Texas congressman Barton said this in support of the Keystone XL pipeline project.

however, seem more critical to this issue than these just mentioned. First, human beings are very creative when it comes to deflecting responsibility for our actions. We are experts at this at both the personal and social level. If the garden of Eden narrative of Adam blaming Eve who in turn blames the serpent tells us nothing else, it makes this human capacity perfectly clear. Second, just as impressive is our implicit belief that God would not leave us to face the consequences of our actions. We find ourselves implicitly saying, "God would not possibly allow the Earth's ecosystems to crumble just because of our destructive behavior toward the world's poor and our nonhuman neighbors, would God?" If climate change is teaching us nothing else, it is firmly educating us about the interdependency and interconnectedness of life on this planet and that there are significant consequences for living the less-than-sustainable lifestyles that we do now.[8]

Part of the American Christian reticence for being convinced that the scientific data about climate change is accurate is due to the century-old debate about whether or not Christian theology and science are in competition. For many American Christians the perception that Christianity and science are in conflict with each other—because, for instance, they offer competing truth claims—is unfortunately alive and well.[9] This perception is, however, based on a host of problematic untruths.[10] As someone who is steeped in the history of the so-called "creation versus evolution" controversy, I strongly affirm that Christian theology and the findings of science are not in competition at all. Theologians and scientists can work together to tell a much more robust story about God's creation. In fact, they do and they have—for centuries. In our current predicament, we see the need for theologians and scientists working together like perhaps never before. When it comes to climate change, scientists may have laid out the case rationally for a change in behavior if we want to continue on as a species, but we still have not altered our consumer decisions or public policy in demonstrable manners that indicate we understand the severity of the threat. Theologians are in the business of thinking through behavior change, especially long-term behavior change, but we cannot pontificate effectively about a theological and moral response to climate change if we do not understand the science of the matter. Scientists often believe that behavioral transformation comes as a result of dispassionate, rational dialogue, but theologians know better than most that human beings rarely perform sacrificial acts, which will

8. See also Northcott, *Moral Climate*; McFague, *New Climate*.

9. Public Religion Research Institute and American Academy of Religion, "Believers," 26.

10. Barbour, *Religion and Science*.

be required, because of rational argumentation. On our best days, humans make decisions with our whole being, emotions and all, not with just our heads; on our worst days, which may be more often than not, we make decisions based upon lackluster thinking, if not blatant visceral emotion.

Another significant component to this, according to psychologists, is how humans process concern or worry about critical issues. Humans actually can be worried about only so many things at a time. This is referred to as a finite pool of worry.[11] This is especially important when considering climate change because when humans with limited capacities for worry increase the amount of worry in their lives, they tend to prioritize those concerns in such a way that alleviates mental strain. We often do this by paying closer attention to what we perceive to be near-term threats rather than long-term ones.[12] Another way to deal with critical issues is to deny their implications or literally deny their existence altogether. This human phenomenon can be seen no more clearly than in the denial of climate change. Whether it is literal denial, interpretive denial, or implicatory denial, citizens of the developed world engage in climate change denial in profound ways. We shall have to examine whether or not denial is a sinful behavior, especially as it relates to considering the evidence of the causes and effects of climate change.

Presupposition #2: Environmental Problems Are Moral and Theological Ones

We live in an American culture wherein environmental problems, like air pollution, soil erosion, or biodiversity loss, are often conceived of as either scientific, political, or economic in nature. For example, we might think of air pollution as a problem that can be fixed once researchers find the right type of scrubbers or sequestration systems to place on top of our countless smokestacks. Or we might hear some say that air pollution is the sort of problem that can only be alleviated when the federal government legislates acceptable air-quality standards and then formulates a regulatory scheme to enforce them. Or some might say that air pollution can only be cleaned up once we properly set a price on the value of clean air. Science (and the research that leads to technology), politics, and economics undoubtedly have crucial roles to play in solving environmental problems, but if we say that environmental problems are primarily scientific, political, or economic in nature, we shield ourselves from asking the fundamental question: Should there be anthropogenic air pollution at all? It is only after we ask this

11. Linville and Fischer, "Preferences," 5–23.

12. Weber, "Experience-Based and Description-Based Perceptions," 103–20.

question that we can legitimately ask questions like: Do all citizens benefit from and bear the burden of pollution evenly? Does pollution affect our ability to live healthy lives? Does pollution affect the ability of nonhuman creatures "to be fruitful and multiply"?

By claiming that environmental problems are primarily for scientists, politicians, and/or economists to address, many Americans tend to place the blame for environmentally destructive behavior on someone else. We say we want to drive environmentally friendly cars, but since scientists have not yet created ones that do not pollute, we have to drive these fossil fuel–burning ones. Or we hear, "I would really like to drive an environmentally friendly car, but until Congress makes everyone buy one how much good will it do if I am the only person to buy one?" Or, "I really want to buy an environmentally friendly car, but they are so expensive and I just cannot afford one." While at some level each of these concerns is legitimate, each fails to ask the fundamental question: How much, if at all, should I drive anyway?

In this book, I join the voices of a host of other Christian scholars who contend that environmental problems are not primarily scientific, political, or economic in nature; they are essentially moral and theological. For example, James Nash argues, "They are fundamentally moral issues, because they are human-created and soluble problems that adversely affect the good of humans and otherkind in our relationships. Ecological perspectives assume moral values, and they entail dispositions and actions that can be evaluated as morally right or wrong."[13] Ellen Davis maintains that environmental problems represent "a moral and even theological crisis because [they are] occasioned in large part by our adulation and arrogant use of scientific technology."[14] According to Sallie McFague, "The environmental crisis is a theological problem, a problem coming from views of God and ourselves that encourages or permits our destructive, unjust actions."[15] She goes on to assert, "The problem . . . is a 'spiritual' one, having to do with our *will* to change. We already know more than enough about the disaster ahead of us—having more knowledge (or technology) will not solve the problem. Only changing human wills can do so."[16] Even ardent critic Lynn White agrees with this. "More science and more technology are not going to get us out of the present ecological crisis until we find a new religion, or rethink our old one."[17] Seeing environmental problems as fundamentally

---

13. Nash, *Loving Nature*, 23.

14. Davis, *Scripture, Culture, and Agriculture*, 9.

15. McFague, *New Climate*, 31.

16. Ibid., 31; italics in original.

17. White, "Historic Roots," 1206.

moral and theological in nature represents a critical step in our thinking because an issue like air pollution exposes clearly what we believe to be good,
true, and beautiful about ourselves, our communities, and our ecosystems,
and subsequently how we conceive of God and our role in God's creation.
Whether or not toxic pollution affects disproportionately the poor of a
given society says much about the priorities and principles of that society
and much about our belief in God the Redeemer. Whether or not water pollution causes aquatic life to deteriorate or perhaps even go extinct suggests
amply what a given community thinks about the value of nonhuman life
and how we worship God the Creator.

Presupposition #3: Practically Speaking, What Kind of Problems Are We Dealing with Here?

Depicting environmental problems as moral and theological problems does
not change the fact that, practically speaking, many are essentially what
policymakers often call "wicked problems"[18] or "super wicked problems."[19]
Climate change is undoubtedly a wicked problem. Such a problem is defined as that which does not have a definitive comprehensive strategy to
solve it. Climate change is wicked because the parameters of the problem
will constantly shift as we attempt possible local, or even global, solutions,
due to the nearly infinite variables involved. For a myriad of reasons, our
ability to mitigate or adapt to climate change today will be far different than
it will be a decade or a century from now. We oftentimes cannot even agree
on what we mean when we use the term "climate change."[20] One group of
people hears it one way and thinks about one set of issues, while another
set of stakeholders hears it another way and ponders something else entirely. Climate change has been deemed a "super wicked" problem by some
because the time needed to solve the problem is running out (and quickly
so), those involved in solving the problem are also the primary cause of
it, the central authority to guide us toward a possible solution is weak or
non-existent, and suggested policy solutions tend to discount the future ir-
rationally. This is to say nothing of how we might begin to frame solutions
to this sort of problem. Sociologist Kari Marie Norgaard argues,

> [F]rom the standpoint of human social behavior and modern
> political theory, climate change is significant in two additional

18. Rittel and Webber, "Dilemmas," 155–69.
19. Levin et al., "Overcoming the Tragedy," 123–52.
20. Hulme, *Why We Disagree*.

important ways. The two citizen responses of skepticism and denial—that is, some know about climate change but manage to consider as no more than background noise the possibility that life as we know it will end, and some do not believe that science should be the basis for guiding public policy—are unique in modern history. No previous environmental problem generated either response with such force. Furthermore, in very different ways each type of response flies in the face of basic assumptions regarding human behavior that go back to the Enlightenment and the origins of modern society. Each of the these responses poses unique threats to democracy and unique challenges for social theorists and public commentators.[21]

Just articulating the sheer complexity of the intricacies of these sorts of problems can cause one to lose hope. And that is not to mention the specter of the trial and error (and likely failure) of possible solutions. Hopelessness saps the human spirit like few other forces we know. For instance, when we lose hope, we implicitly accept the reality of the status quo no matter how detrimental it might be because we lack the courage to imagine novel ideas or act on possible solutions. While the status quo of a warming planet will affect us all in some way or another, it is radically different for those living in the Maldives than for those living in the United States.

Whether brought about due to the consequences of wicked or super wicked problems, Christians should know how to speak about hopelessness. We affirm the events of Good Friday and Easter; the darkness of the crucifixion of Jesus that preceded the light of his resurrection. Yet, do we contemplate carefully enough the hopelessness that must have existentially crippled the disciples before the women shared the good news of the empty tomb? While Jesus had given hints about his resurrection to his closest followers, they did not seem to grasp the depth of what God had planned for that Easter Sunday. The disciples scattered because their hope in a leader who would bring about a new reign seemed dreadfully lost when Jesus was crucified on that Roman cross. God's utterly inconceivable act of conquering death in the resurrection is what it took to bring the disciples out of the darkness and into the light. God's novel act of grace in the resurrection of Jesus changed how the disciples thought, how they lived; it changed their very being. They went from being hopeless to having the courage to witness to God's work in the world even to the point of their own martyrdom; from the darkness of hopelessness to the light of the hope found through the resurrection of Jesus. This is precisely the message that Christians are called to proclaim as they seek to witness daily to the reality of the resurrection.

21. Norgaard, *Living in Denial*, 181–82.

We Are in Desperate Need of a Change

Philosopher Charles Taylor defines the primary ideas and practices that shape the ways in which contemporary societies function as our "social imaginaries." "By social imaginary . . . I am thinking, rather, of the ways people imagine their social existence, how they fit together with others, how things go on between them and their fellows, the expectations that are normally met, and the deeper normative notions and images that underlie these expectations." He goes on to say that "the social imaginary is that common understanding that makes possible common practices and a widely shared sense of legitimacy."[22] In this sense, genuine regard for issues like clean air and water, biodiversity loss, bleaching of coral reef systems, etc., is not part of the our social imaginary. Americans in particular and Western culture in general practice lifestyles that consume far more than they conserve and legitimate exploitation for blatantly anthropocentric concerns at every turn. The lack of environmental care inherent in our social imaginary applies as much to Christians as it does to anyone else. This is especially distressing since most Christians believe that environmental stewardship is a fundamental component of the Christian faith and witness. Tragically, we know that far too few Christians actually practice this aspect of their faith daily, if at all. It is not a part of our social imaginary.

While Lynn White famously critiqued Christianity for being the most anthropocentric of the world's religions and the reason for so much environmental degradation over the past 2,000 years of human civilization, the criticism of Christianity on this issue did not start in 1967.[23] During the nineteenth century, Ludwig Feuerbach wrote, "Nature, the world, has no value, no interest for Christians. The Christian thinks only of himself [sic] and the salvation of his soul."[24] It is hard to discount this charge. Calvin DeWitt notes that the charge is not merely from outside of Christendom; Christians themselves appear to care little for creation. He identifies five ideas that stand within churches today and seem to suggest that creation is far from being important to lives of Christians.[25] The first he calls the "utilitarian Earth" view and it is represented by the famous Secretary of the Interior and professing Christian James Watt, who claimed that the Earth was to be used by humans in profitable ways (meant both literally and metaphorically) on the way to heaven. The second is that the material world is

22. Taylor, *Modern Social Imaginaries*, 23.
23. White, "Historic Roots," 1203–7.
24. Feuerbach, *Essence of Christianity*, 287-89.
25. DeWitt and Nash, "Christians and the Environment."

unimportant, if not flatly evil. While this pseudo-Gnosticism flies in the face of the witness of the incarnation, it is implicitly a component of much of American Christian thought and practical living today. The third is that many Christians tend to associate Christians who care for creation with environmentalism, which they often correlate with pantheism, nature worship, New Age spiritualism, etc. The fourth he calls the "fear of Samaritans syndrome." By this DeWitt means that once Christians label someone an environmentalist because of pantheistic or New Age tendencies, that person is treated as unclean in a way that Christians no longer seek to dialogue with that person on any issue at any level. The fifth is the "no crisis/no stewardship philosophy." Those who exhibit this idea tend to deny climate change and thus any responsibility to review their behavior until better data comes along that determines conclusively that there is a crisis. Keith Dyer, in a slightly tongue-in-cheek manner, contends that some Christians live by six biblicist eschatological principles:

1. The principle of imminent cataclysm—Earth is headed for disaster (sooner rather than later).

2. The principle of disconnectedness—we humans don't have to share or feel responsible for Earth's fate (salvation is for humans, not Earth).

3. The principle of inevitability—there's nothing we (or Earth) can do about it.

4. The principle of transcendence—what really matters is the next world (or "heavenism" as [Norman] Habel describes it).

5. The principle of sovereignty—God is in ultimate (even direct) control of all this.

6. The principle of self-interest—God will rapture "believers" out of this mess in the nick of time.[26]

DeWitt's and Dyer's lists are obviously not representative of every strand of American Christianity, but they do speak to an unfortunate majority of the Christian theological witness in the United States today.

These sorts of ideas only reinforce the perception outside of Christendom that American Protestant Christianity, in particular, cares mostly about how to get souls to heaven and very little about what is happening currently on or to our planet. The radical dichotomies between body and soul or heaven and Earth or human and nonhuman have caused such deep schisms in our ways of thinking and living that it appears to many outside

26. Dyer, "When Is the End," 45. Dyer's list is a fundamentalist version of the six eco-justice principles promoted by the Earth Bible series.

of Christianity that Christians have forgotten the very nature and effect of Jesus' healing ministry on people. In a very real sense, many Protestant Christian traditions in the United States have become less "this-worldly" and more "other-worldly," and so when it comes to demonstrating sacrificial care for creation we are either explicitly antithetical to the idea or our behavior certainly implies as much. We must stop thinking of Christianity as other-worldly and remember how profoundly this-worldly Jesus' message really is. The idea of a this-worldly Christian faith should not disturb us as much as it does some. From his place in a Nazi prison, Dietrich Bonhoeffer asserted, "I don't mean the shallow and banal this-worldliness of the enlightened, the busy, the comfortable, or the lascivious, but the profound this-worldliness, characterized by discipline and the constant knowledge of death and resurrection."[27] At the beginning of the twentieth century, Walter Rauschenbusch wrote, "Ascetic Christianity called the world evil and left it. Humanity is waiting for a revolutionary Christianity which will call the world evil and change it."[28] I think that other-worldly Christianity acts similarly: it calls the world evil and leaves anything deemed to be worldly to its own devices. For many American Christians, issues like gay marriage or premarital sex are deemed important other-worldly concerns, while clean air, clean water, and wholesome food are considered this-worldly and thus worthy of little to no serious reflection about how they might impact the lives of those around us, whether Christian or not, or human or not. We are presently in desperate need of a Christianity that is disciplined and informed by the death and resurrection of Jesus and acts in ways that are radically inspired by them. Ultimately, we need to proclaim a Christian witness that boldly dares to exhibit Christian hope in the present. We have too often truncated the "already" parts of hope to be found in the Spirit's work and not challenged ourselves to manifest the "not yet" parts now. This, however, is the type of Christian faith the world needs in the age of climate change.

In the face of a social imaginary that represents such a poor witness of environmental care, we must ask: Is it possible to change a social imaginary? Thankfully, Taylor says yes.

> What exactly is involved when a theory penetrates and transforms the social imaginary? For the most part, people take up, improvise, or are inducted into new practices. These are made sense of by the new outlook, the one first articulated in the theory; this outlook is the context that gives sense to the practices. Hence the new understanding comes to be accessible to

27. Bonhoeffer, *Letters and Papers*, 369.
28. Quoted in Moltmann, *Ethics of Hope*, 39.

the participants in a way that it wasn't before. It begins to define
the contours of their world and can eventually come to count as
the taken-for-granted shape of things, too obvious to mention.[29]

Our society, indeed human civilization as we know it, is in need of new
"theories" quickly if we are to accomplish, in some form or another, the
monumental task of altering the present course of the planet in the Anthropocene Era.

   In order for Christians to change our social behavior, I believe that we
need to change our mindset. We are in need of a new theological imaginary,
if you will, that can inspire a new social imaginary. By theological imaginary
I mean those doctrines and theological concepts that Christians really take
seriously or at least believe we take seriously as we seek to exhibit our daily
Christian witness. These are the ideas that will help us demonstrate faithfully the mind of Christ.[30] I am not attempting here to be overly simplistic
and suggest that new thoughts or new theology will necessarily lead to new
behavior. For one thing, the hermeneutical loop between thought and deed
is not a one-way flow nor does good exegesis lead necessarily or directly to
long-term behavior change. One component of the construction of a new
theological imaginary is akin to the work of those who have sought to create "doctrinal keys"[31] or "hermeneutical lenses"[32] that might help us see the
Christian witness anew in light of climate change. The reading of Scripture
will include acts of recovery as there is much wisdom within Scripture that
might contribute meaningfully to a fresh understanding of our contemporary situation. It will also include acts of resistance since there are biblical
texts that at first glance do not seem to support a creation-care ethic and
will have to be interpreted as well; however, I believe it is possible to hold a
high view of biblical authority and still meet the ecological crises of our day.
If Christians cannot connect the practices of our daily lives with the most
fundamental concepts of our faith, then we are truly at a loss for transformation. Ultimately, a new theological imaginary that will lead to actual environmentally sensitive practices rather than destructive ones must be based
upon the very bedrock of the Christian faith. For me, that is the belief in the
resurrection of Jesus of Nazareth. Of course, I am not alone in thinking that
the resurrection is the linchpin of the Christian faith. The apostle Paul made

29. Ibid., 29.

30. 1 Cor 2:16; Rom 12:2.

31. Conradie, "What on Earth," 295–313. See also Conradie, "Ecological Hermeneutics," 123–35; Conradie, "Road Towards," 305–14.

32. Horrell et al., *Greening Paul*, 11–47.

this claim in his letter to the church in Corinth.[33] My concern is not that we no longer believe in the objectivity and historicity of Jesus' resurrection (that is a subject for another book), but rather that we do not live as if the resurrection matters to the daily expression of our Christian witness. If we believe that the resurrection really occurred, but do not reflect that reality in our daily lives, then, as the apostle Paul says, "we are of all people most to be pitied."[34] One of the goals of this book, then, is to create a reformed theological imaginary that might animate a Christian social imaginary that exhibits creation care and creation justice.

A reformed theological imaginary will be for naught if it does not inspire us to act differently. We must begin to behave differently if mitigation and adaptation to climate change are to become realities that affect more than just the wealthiest few. There are many both inside and outside of Christendom that are skeptical about the possibility of Christianity presenting itself as a "green" faith or inspiring its adherents to adopt more sustainable behaviors. For many Christians in the United States, it is not part of our social imaginary and it very well may not even be part of our theological imaginary. We are known by our fruits,[35] both currently and historically. So why should we believe that the Christian message can help us now when it seems to have been the source material for so much destruction in the past? This is a fair question and one that I will have to address throughout the course of the book, but until then I implore Christians to remember one central act of a Christian life: repentance. There are sins of commission, omission, and ignorance that demand our personal and collective repentance. For example, we have aided in countless events that have caused the extinction of thousands of species that were called by God to "be fruitful and multiply." Moreover, we have looked the other way and claimed that the behavior of one individual or a single family could not possibly make a difference environmentally, so we have maintained the status quo as the seas continue to rise around the Maldives. Unlike White and his many disciples, I do not believe that Christians bear special responsibility for the world's environmental woes because of an overly anthropocentric creation story. We are no guiltier than the civilizations of the Egyptians, Assyrians, Romans, Aztecs, or Mayans, to name a few. All of these civilizations caused significant environmental degradation to their local ecosystems and ultimately incurred momentous collapses. Environmental problems are caused by humans of all sorts, not only Christians. Christians, however, should not

33. 1 Cor 15.
34. 1 Cor 15:19.
35. Matt 7:17–20; Luke 6:43–4.

see this as a license for downplaying our responsibility for what has led us to this point. If we are ultimately to change our will and behave differently, then we must repent of our past and present environmental sins.

My argument in the following pages is simply this: In the face of the present environmental devastation we see around us and the knowledge that climate change will bring even further destruction to humans, nonhuman creatures, and the Earth alike, it is easy to become hopeless. Hopelessness should not appear plausible or even reasonable to Christians who believe in the resurrection of Jesus. The defeat of death in Jesus' resurrection should lead not only to an understanding of the inextricable link between God's work as Creator and God's work as Redeemer, but also to a manifestation of that unity in the daily lives of our Christian witness. And this witness can be seen no more clearly and explicitly than in how we live as hopeful creatures who care profoundly for creation—a created order that we are not only connected to and dependent upon, but fundamentally a part of. This plays out practically in our daily consumptive habits as economic agents and in the choices we make every single time we eat. We do these everyday things as witnesses to the hope of a resurrected life or as witnesses to a status quo that condemns so many humans and nonhumans to hopeless existences. It is our everyday routines that manifest a theological imaginary that is either centered upon the resurrection of Jesus or not.

After her time living in Norway conducting a lengthy study about why Norwegians think the way they do about climate change, Norgaard concludes, "What will make the public invest energy in these issues is not the conviction that the problems are real, but that we can do something about them."[36] Christians can legitimately do something about these problems by modeling a way of life that is centered upon the creativity and courage that comes from resurrection hope. Our civilization is desperately in need of a light that shines in the darkness and is not overcome by that darkness;[37] this is the witness of hope.

In many ways this book is in line with what Robert Jensen calls "apocalyptic invocation." I need "to tell as much of the truth as one can bear, and then all the rest of the truth, whether we can bear it or not."[38] The truth about anthropogenic climate change and its consequences to creation are profoundly grave, and they must be acknowledged for what they truly are before we can engage in the process of mitigation and adaptation. Perhaps we are in a similar situation to that of the earliest disciples, who for three days

36. Norgaard, *Living in Denial*, 191.
37. John 1:5.
38. Jensen, *Apocalyptic Now*, 65.

had to grapple with how Jesus' crucifixion affected their sense of identity, purpose, and faith before they became witnesses to the resurrection hope.

The use of appropriate language is crucial in the transmission of ideas, so allow me to make one quick note about my usage of the term "creation care" throughout this work. There are two primary reasons for my usage, one theological and the other practical. Theologically, I agree with Pope Francis, who puts it succinctly: "In the Judaeo-Christian tradition, the word 'creation' has a broader meaning than 'nature,' for it has to do with God's loving plan in which every creature has its own value and significance. Nature is usually seen as a system which can be studied, understood and controlled, whereas creation can only be understood as a gift from the outstretched hand of the Father of all, and as a reality illuminated by the love which calls us together into universal communion."[39] We could also substitute the word "environment" for "nature" and the statement would be equally accurate. Too much of Western society acts as if nature or the environment is only something to be controlled or mastered—Christians are often no different. Yet, Christians should be the first to dwell on the fact that creation is a gift and ultimately belongs to someone else. Our contemplation of that simple, yet decisive, affirmation should cause us to think much differently about how we treat nonhuman creatures and the rest of creation as an explicit daily witness of our faith. Practically, "creation care" is used so frequently in scholarly and popular Christian literature to describe something that should be seen as the virtuous practice of our faith that I am reluctant to introduce new terminology.

Overview of the Chapters

Far too many American Christians believe that God has little to no regard for nonhuman creatures and the rest of creation, or at least they live daily in such a way. The first chapter describes the picture painted by Scripture—a picture of a Creator God who loves nonhuman creatures, enters into covenants with them, and declares that all of creation is very good. I argue that the divine proclamation of goodness is radically and profoundly reaffirmed in the incarnation of Jesus, which then allows us to view the universe sacramentally.

Scripture also depicts God as Redeemer. This too has dramatic implications for an ecologically minded and sensitive theology. Chapter 2 examines the prophetic proclamation that there is a link between justice and righteousness as well as compassion for the widows, orphans, and aliens.

39. Pope Francis, *Laudato Si'*, 76.

The prophets also see a significant relationship between how Israel cares for the widows, orphans, and aliens and the treatment of the land. Both of these prophetic understandings have contemporary implications in light of recent concepts of environmental justice, food justice, and the status of climate refugees. The chapter closes with an exploration of the concept of redemption for nonhuman creatures and the rest of creation.

The biblical notions of God as Creator and Redeemer are radically re-affirmed in the resurrection of Jesus, which provides the basis of the Christian concept of hope and makes up the substance of the third chapter. While optimism and hope are often used interchangeably in our society, I contend that hope is fundamentally different from optimism. Optimism connotes a blind inevitability, while hope is a confident expectation of a good and novel outcome delivered by God. It is important to understand the phenomenon of hope and thus I investigate whether it is an emotion, disposition of the will, or something else entirely. I explore the reality of hopelessness in its forms of despair and presumption, and show how hope is a critical Christian answer to these forms of hopelessness, which are especially pernicious in the age of climate change. Finally, I contend that hope inspired by the resurrection is the foundation for why Christians should work hard to make creation care and creation justice a daily explicit witness of our faith.

In the fourth chapter I consider how to conceive of humanity in light of our relationship to the rest of creation. I first review the common idea of stewardship, its association with the Christian notion of the *imago Dei*, and how it often supports a decidedly anthropocentric view of creation. I assert that the typical Christian understanding of stewardship, and the an-thropocentrism it routinely encourages, is insufficient in the age of climate change, and a perverted truncation of how Scripture actually depicts human being and doing. As an alternative, I examine passages outside of Genesis 1 that describe more fully the biblical idea of humanity and then evaluate contemporary alternatives to stewardship.

I begin chapter 5 arguing that humility is the seminal virtue in un-derstanding what it means to be human and therefore to understand our place in creation correctly. I seek to situate humans as the creatures who hope in God and have considerable work to do in order to show that we do in fact love creation and exhibit that love through demonstrable activity. The chapter concludes by proposing a notion of ecological sin and calls for repentance.

It is imperative that a theological reflection of climate change consid-ers seriously the association between the Christian faith and the neoclassical economic structure that dominates the globe today. The sixth chapter begins by describing some of the critical presuppositions that hold up neoclassical economic thought and support the idol of economic growth. I then apply the critique of hope articulated in chapter 2 to show how our current economic system is stricken by the hopelessness of despair and presumption.

This leads to chapter 7 and a discussion of what the goal of an economy actually is, and whether or not the prevalent global practice of economics takes climate change as seriously as the world's scientists suggest we should. This does not lead me to advocate for a Christian economic order; instead I propose presuppositions for an economic worldview that might look more like a pale reflection of the kingdom of God. The final section contends that frugality is a subversive, yet hopeful and explicit, witness of Christian faith that can be practiced daily and has dramatic implications for one's relationship to the poor and dispossessed as well as the rest of creation.

The eighth chapter starts with an evaluation of the fundamental roots of the problems of the Western food system. I explore the theological roots of the problem—like the idols of control, efficiency, and convenience that dominate the way Americans eat—and I also discuss the significant issue of food wastefulness and the forgotten vice of gluttony. These latter two seem especially lost on American consumers in general and American Christians in particular. I conclude that this system is marked by hopelessness.

The answer to this is a form of hopeful eating based upon an understanding of how the Eucharist might apply to eating during the rest of the week; this is the topic of chapter 9. This includes not only how we treat people who grow, pick, and process our food, but also how the act of eating itself can draw us to a deeper faith in God. This chapter closes by analyzing the topic of eating meat within the larger notion of eating hopefully as a daily explicit witness of the Christian faith.

The book's final two chapters describe how the church should exist as a beacon of hope in a time of hopelessness brought on by climate change. After outlining what beacons are and how they play significant roles in society, I propose possible ways that the church might begin to act as a critical contemporary beacon. We need to broaden the discussion among American Christians about what political activity entails. We need to think more critically about what it means to seek justice in an age of climate change in light of the concept of "slow violence," which applies to notions of environmental justice, food justice, and seeing climate refugees as our neighbors. I also argue for the importance of Christians understanding and supporting the role that science plays in comprehending creation, labeling climate change denial for the sin it is, and thinking more carefully about how sacramental contemplation can help us see God's presence in creation more clearly. Finally, I look at the human relationship to technology and how it might be used in a manner that is hopeful and trusting of God rather than in a fashion that exacerbates inequality and leads to hubris.

1

God the Creator

There are two features of contemporary American Protestant Christianity that make thinking about creation care in general and climate change in particular exceptionally difficult at times. First, many American Protestants tend to believe that Christianity has very little to do with the matters of this world and instead are focused on preparing people for a life far away in heaven. We often preach an other-worldly faith in spite of the distinctly this-worldly emphases of the ministry of Jesus. Therefore, we tend to believe, or at least live as if we believe, that caring for creation is quite far down the list of Christian priorities, if it is a part of our witness at all. It is as if we are modern-day descendants of the Great Awakenings of the eighteenth and nineteenth centuries, attempting to save souls from the fiery pits of hell. While this may indeed be an important component of the Christian mission, it is not the entirety of the Christian gospel, by any stretch. Second, the Evangelical stress on individuals finding a personal relationship with our Lord and Savior Jesus Christ has also radically shaped the landscape of Protestant Christianity in the United States. Again, such a position may be defensible theologically, but it unduly shapes the character and concerns of many Protestant Christians. In particular, it dramatically reinforces a blatant sort of anthropocentrism that is famously critiqued by those outside of Christianity, and supposedly prevents Christians from dealing with environmental woes adequately. Perhaps these critics are onto something. If Christians believe that God is only interested in human affairs, then it is a short step to believing that we should not care about any creatures other than humans either. This view, however, is theologically indefensible; it finds no support in the biblical witness.

There are many ways that Scripture talks about God. God is our father; God is our rock; God is our shepherd; God is like a mother eagle who gathers her chicks; God is like a mother bear robbed of her cubs. Two dominant ways that the biblical witness and traditional Christian theology speak about God is as Creator and Redeemer. Both of these descriptions of

19

God are significant when it comes to understanding and addressing ecological crises. For example, we might ask: Does the Creator of the universe
really care about the myriad consequences climate change has on pandas,
penguins, and polar bears, not to mention palm trees, peppermint vines,
and pansies? If God does not, then maybe we should not either. But, if God
does, then what might our response be as creatures made in the very image of God? Or, we might ask: does the great Redeemer who brought the
slaves out of Egypt care that the effects of climate change are harming the
planet's poor and dispossessed disproportionately? Moreover, we might ask:
If God is solely worried about human affairs, then does God have a cosmic
redemptive plan or merely a plan to save humans?

God Cares for Nonhuman Creatures
and the Rest of Creation

It has become all too common among American Christians to believe that
God cares very little, if at all, for nonhuman creatures. Our anthropocentrism appears to know no bounds. Scripture, however, depicts something
very different from our self-centered view of the universe. God cares deeply
and intimately for nonhuman members of creation. God's omniscience is
not limited merely to human concerns. This care is demonstrated resolutely
in God's instructions to Noah in preparation for the flood. Noah was in-
structed to build an ark not merely to save his family, but to make suitable
room for the creatures that God would send to him to save as well.[1] While
there are obvious difficulties with claiming God cares for nonhuman creatures while reviewing a narrative that depicts God violently wiping out most
of creation, the inclusion of nonhuman creatures within the ark cannot be
undersold. In Leviticus, God instructs the Israelites to allow the land to lie
fallow every seven years so that it might rest and not be abused.[2] With current scientific knowledge explaining just how teeming with life healthy soil
is, the idea of a Sabbath for the land seems more pertinent than ever—even
microbiota can be overworked. One of the vastly underestimated components of the account of God sending Jonah to Nineveh is God's words in the
short book's final verse, which emphasizes the scope of God's concern. Jonah is furious that God decided not to destroy the people of Nineveh despite
their repentance. God responds thusly: "And should I not be concerned
about Nineveh, that great city, in which there are more than a hundred and
twenty thousand persons who do not know their right hand from their left,

1. Gen 6–7.
2. Lev 25:1–7.

and also many animals?"[3] God demonstrates how intimately God cares for creation by describing in explicit detail to Job in the whirlwind encounter the role God plays in the daily lives of its nonhuman members. God assists the lions and ravens with their search for prey. God knows when mountain goats and deer give birth.[4] "Pathos drives God's recitation of creation, beginning with the farthest reaches of the cosmos and concluding with the tightly knit scales of the sea-dragon, from the farthest to the smallest scale of perception, from cosmos to chaos."[5] Psalm 104 exhibits this sort of creation care as well. God makes sure the thirst of wild animals is quenched and causes the grass to grow for cattle. God listens for the lions' roars because they seek their food from God. God also created trees, mountains, and rocks for various creatures to make their homes secure from predators. The psalmist records God's care for inanimate members of creation and depicts God placing the mountains and waters in their proper places so that the foundations of the Earth might never be shaken. The psalmist also recognizes that without the divine presence the Earth would be devoid of life and all things would return to dust. The psalmist notes that creation is a source of joy for its inhabitants and its Creator.[6] God delights in the biodiversity of life that is present on the Earth. One could say that God displays biophilia. This is not limited to the Old Testament; Jesus reiterates this central theme by reminding his followers that God takes care of the needs of the ravens of the air and the lilies of the field.[7] God's love for the world or *cosmos* is the reason that Jesus came into the world.[8] In the longer ending of Mark, Jesus even commands his disciples to proclaim the gospel message to all of creation.[9] Indeed, God loves that which God has created.

God Enters into Covenants with Other Creatures

Scripture not only shows that God cares for creatures but depicts God explicitly entering into direct relationships with them. In the story of Jonah, God seeks the assistance of nonhuman creatures in teaching the prophet a lesson about humility and the inclusion of those outside of Israel in the

3. Jonah 4:11.
4. Job 38–9.
5. Brown, *Seven Pillars*, 125.
6. Ibid., 147.
7. Matt 6:26–30; Luke 12:24–28.
8. John 3:16–7.
9. Mark 16:15.

divine redemptive scheme. A fish, a plant, a worm, the wind, and the sun all assist God willingly in the attempt to reform Jonah. God not only sent a fish to swallow Jonah, but commanded the fish to vomit him up onto the land.[10] While the language might be rare, both passages indicate that God addressed the fish with speech and the fish obeyed the command. Later God "appoints" a plant to grow up and provide shade for Jonah, then a worm to kill the plant, and finally a wind arises and the sun beats down on Jonah's head.[11] "[F]rom the narrative's perspective, these nonhuman characters are understood as active, independent agents who obediently respond to the Lord."[12] We see in this story a topic that we shall explore in greater detail later: nonhuman creatures seem to recognize who God is and seek to obey God—the humans in the story are the ones who do not.

The biblical witness also depicts God entering into covenants with nonhuman creatures, not just humans. The first of these is recorded in Genesis after Noah and his family settle onto dry land following the flood. God's covenant has two parts. First, there is a reiteration of the command to be fruitful and multiply in order to fill the Earth, similar to the mandate in Genesis 1. Second, God promises not to destroy the Earth again using a flood, which is represented by a rainbow in the clouds. God says, "As for me, I am establishing my covenant with you and your descendants after you, and with every living creature that is with you, the birds, the domestic animals, and every animal of the earth with you, as many as came out of the ark."[13] The covenant between God, Noah, and all creatures is repeated four times (Gen 9:9–10, 12, 15, 17); while Noah is reminded of the animals being with him three times (Gen 9:10 [twice], 12). It is as if the Genesis writer is suggestively accentuating the point, "All flesh, all life on the earth, every living being in the millennia of the history of nature and of humanity is preserved in God's affirmation of [God's] creation."[14] This should serve to remind the audience not only of the profound interdependence and interconnectedness of all of creation described in Genesis 1, but of God's care for the richness of life, too. While one could easily counter that these words were addressed only to Noah and his sons and thus support an anthropocentric reading, such a reading would miss the thrust of the text: "the words that are spoken are unequivocally egalitarian."[15] While this covenant precedes the one that

10. Jonah 1:17; 2:11.
11. Jonah 4:6–8.
12. Person, "Nonhuman Characters," 87.
13. Gen 9:9–10.
14. Westermann, *Genesis 1–11*, 474. See also Arnold, *Genesis*, 110.
15. Olley, "Mixed Blessings," 137.

God enters into with Abraham and then with Israel on Sinai, there is no inherent reason to believe that it is superseded by these later covenants.[16] In other words, the Noahic covenant should still have meaning for Christians today.

Although this interpretation of Noah's covenant may be unfamiliar to Christians living in the United States, it was not unfamiliar to earlier Christian thinkers. For example, the famed fourth-century church father and archbishop of Constantinople John Chrysostom asserts, "Do you see the extent of the agreement? Do you see the unspeakable generosity of the promises? Notice how [God] once again extends [God's] generosity to the animals and wild beasts, and rightly so."[17] Hence, John Olley concludes, "The final focus of the flood narrative is not the reality of human violence to animals and to one another, but the promise of God given unilaterally to the 'earth' and all who live in it. Human readers of the text are encouraged to look beyond their own interests ('food') and to look at all creatures as partners in God's covenant. God is concerned for the well-being of animals and enters into covenant with them. It is God's intention to keep together the rich biodiversity of the earth."[18] This interpretation of the flood should inspire us to recognize that God's view of the universe is far more than an anthropocentric one.

The prophet Hosea also records God making a covenant with non-human creatures. God says, "I will make for you a covenant on that day with the wild animals, the birds of the air, and the creeping things of the ground."[19] This divine address is within the context of a larger prophetic critique of Israel's forsaking of God and their responsibilities as God's chosen people. Kris Hiuser and Matthew Barton assert, "Though this is a covenant which ultimately seems to have been entered into for the sake of humans, this does not detract from the fact that it is with animals that God once more enters into covenant."[20] And why should we not expect God to be in intimate relationship with that which God deemed "very good" in the Genesis 1 creation account? It should come as no surprise that God willingly chooses to participate in the lives of all of the creatures that God creates.

16. E.g., see McKenzie, *Covenant*, 48.

17. Krueger, *Cloud of Witnesses*, 127.

18. Olley, "Mixed Blessings," 139.

19. Hos 2:19. Steven McKenzie, however, argues that this has less to do with God's relationship to nonhuman creatures and more to do with what will happen when the Israelites once again live up to their covenantal responsibilities. McKenzie, *Covenant*, 22n21.

20. Hiuser and Barton, "Promise Is a Promise," 344.

All of this of course begs the question: What does it mean for God to make a covenant or enter into a covenantal relationship? In both the covenant with Abraham and the subsequent covenant with Israel, God enters into relationships with people wherein God commits to keeping certain promises and requires specific types of human obligation.[21] The human obligation is based upon both vertical and horizontal elements, if you will. Faithfulness to the conditions of the covenant and ultimately obedience to God is mandatory and thus makes up the vertical component. The horizontal piece includes how humans act toward each other, especially toward the orphans, widows, and resident aliens within their communities. Being just toward others is an explicit characteristic of God's covenant people. But what might this say about God, especially in the sense of God entering into a covenant relationship with nonhuman creatures? Scripture makes it evident that God's care and love go together with covenantal relationship. Hiuser and Barton conclude, "By God's self-chosen action, and dependent on God alone, God covenants with all of the creatures of the earth, and through doing so, makes explicit his value and care for his creatures. The implications of such an understanding lead very strongly to the idea of animals as loved by God, based on the fact that the Almighty chose to covenant with them."[22] God's action toward nonhuman creatures should affect how we understand our care of them as well, if that is part of what it means to exhibit the character of God as ones made in the divine image. We must be concerned not only about orphans, widows, and resident aliens, but nonhuman creatures, too.

This, however, may not be the only way that Scripture construes the notion of covenant.[23] Robert Murray provocatively, but persuasively, contends that the covenants alluded to in both Genesis 9 and Hosea 2 are references to a different sort of covenant that scriptural authors, especially the prophets, have knowledge of but do not name plainly. He calls this the "cosmic covenant" and argues that an understanding of this covenant pervades much of the ancient Israelite milieu.[24] By cosmic covenant Murray means a belief that ancient Israel shared with neighboring cultures that God wills a harmonious order that links the heavens and the Earth. According to the Israelite tradition, God bound the cosmic elements in such a way that prevented chaos from disrupting the justice, peace, and integrity of

---

21. McKenzie, *Covenant*, 140–42.

22. Hiuser and Barton, "Promise Is a Promise," 347.

23. For more on the use of "covenant" in Scripture, see Beckwith, "Unity and Diversity," 93–118.

24. Murray, *Cosmic Covenant*, xx–xxv.

creation that defined the divinely willed order. This tradition believed that this order could be threatened by forces hostile to God and humanity, but also that humans could participate in the work of God to maintain the order by practicing virtues like justice and mercy. It is this covenant that Murray argues is being thought about in not only Genesis 9 and Hosea 2, but also in Isaiah 56–66.[25] Through this cosmic covenant we see the origin of the link between creation care and justice for the oppressed. We shall examine this more closely later in this chapter.

Creation Is Good

The creation account in Genesis 1 contains many revolutionary theological statements. The God of Israel creates not by violence or sexual activity like the gods of neighboring cultures, but instead by speaking peacefully and allowing creaturely action to participate in the creative project. God is powerful and beholden to no other forces in the universe. All of nature obeys the divinely spoken command. There is also a certain orderliness to God's creative project: the skies are created and then filled with creatures; the seas are filled with water and then filled with creatures; the land is formed in between the skies and the seas and then filled with creatures. Everything seems to inhabit its proper place. Six times during the course of this creative task God calls what has been created "good."[26] God then deems the whole project "very good" at its completion.[27] Amidst ecological crises like drought, hurricanes, and ultimately climate change (not to mention the immeasurable amount of predation, suffering, and extinction that occurred before humans ever arrived on the scene[28]), it can be difficult at times to affirm the goodness that God sees in creation, but this is exactly the fundamental affirmation of the ancient Israelites. While at the risk of sounding like the person of "arrogant folly" whom John Chrysostom once chastised for daring to question God's declaration of goodness, I believe it is imperative for us to ask: What does God mean by "good"?[29]

William Brown notes, "In Genesis, 'good' is a many-splendored thing. God's approbation evokes a wide range of significance, from the aesthetic

25. Ibid., 27–37. For more on Isaiah, see Spencer et al., *Christianity, Climate Change,* 101–19.

26. Gen 1:4, 10, 12, 18, 21, 25.

27. Gen 1:31.

28. For an excellent introduction into the problem of evil from an evolutionary perspective, see Southgate, *Groaning of Creation.*

29. Chrysostom, *Homilies on Genesis 1–17,* 10.12 (136).

to the ethical."[30] In other words, "good" at least means lovely, pleasing, or beautiful.[31] God looks on creation and it pleases God or God finds its completed state to be beautiful. Even if we use "beautiful" to connote more fully the Hebrew *tov*, which we traditionally translate "good," we are still missing much of what the original term connotes. From the Western perspective, conceiving of the beautiful often conjures up the image of a particular being. We might think of a beautiful painting, sculpture, or even a person. The perspective of the ancient Israelites, however, is radically different because much art as we conceive of it today was forbidden for its potential idolatrous ramifications. For the ancient Israelites, the beautiful was found not solely in the beholding of something, but instead in the encounter with it. For example, when the Old Testament speaks about the beauty of the forests of Lebanon, "it is not merely the spectacle; it is saying something about the meaning of the forest for people and for the land. The Hebrew does not contemplate the sheer beauty of what exists prescinding from the function of what is contemplated."[32]

It is terribly important, according to Claus Westermann, for us not only to comprehend as best we can what the ancient Israelites meant by "good," but also who actually pronounces that creation is good. This is paramount because creation's goodness is not defined by humans and the scope of our experiences with the beauty of tigers and tulips, on the one hand, and the terribleness of tornados and tsunamis, on the other; creation is good because God declares it to be so. "'Good' in this context does not mean some sort of objective judgement, a judgement given according to already fixed and objective standards. It is rather this: it is good or suited for the purpose for which it is being prepared; it corresponds to its goal."[33] Brown puts it another way: "'Good' acknowledges creation's ordered integrity and its intrinsic value as beheld by God. 'Good,' moreover, affirms creation's self-sustainability, its proclivity for fecundity. Creation deemed good by God is creation set toward the furtherance of life."[34] God's recognition of a creature's goodness, in the sense of beauty or loveliness, is not an addendum after the fact; it is good because God created it to be such. God's valuation of creation is not only biocentric and cosmocentric in character and scope, but it also defies any sort of instrumentalism that often defines typical human valuation of nonhuman creatures. God calls creatures good not because they are

30. Brown, *Seven Pillars*, 45.

31. Brueggemann, *Genesis*, 37.

32. Westermann, *Genesis 1–11*, 167.

33. Ibid., 61.

34. Brown, *Seven Pillars*, 45.

instrumentally valuable to God, but because they perform their roles in the divine creative project; they are participating in the life-giving, fecund ways that God calls creatures to exhibit. It is this goodness that humans, through our climate-disrupting ways, seem to be trying to stamp out whether we realize it or not.

Furthermore, Westermann contends that because God's declaration of creation's goodness frees humans from the worry of passing judgment on what may or may not be good, we are therefore permitted to enjoy creation for what it is.[35] This gives us the permission to enjoy sharks, salamanders, snakes, and even the snails that daily seek to ravage my vegetable garden, along with sea otters, spider monkeys, sage, and strawberries. Our enjoyment of creation should engender a particular response: praise of the Creator for making creation very good. "It must also be realized that in Israel the peculiar, typical reaction to a confrontation with something beautiful was not contemplation nor beholding nor, least of all passing judgement; it was rather joy expressing itself in speech; and that is precisely what is meant by praise."[36] And so the witness of the psalmists and other Old Testament writers singing praises to the Creator after encountering the many creatures in creation is a vibrant and rich one.[37] This response is far too lacking in the mostly urban American churches of today.

The Incarnation Affirms Creation's Goodness

It is astounding that one of the fundamental assertions of the Christian faith is no longer understood to be as radical as it was in the first few centuries after Jesus. The belief that "the Word became flesh and dwelt among us"[38] is a bedrock of the Christian faith. While the radical nature and utter profundity of the incarnation oftentimes seems lost on many contemporary Christians, the idea that the Creator of the universe would take material form was veritable foolishness to Greco-Roman citizens of antiquity. The Christian affirmation that God actually became part of what God created is impossible to understate when thinking about our present ecological crisis because it points to how much God values what God creates. And yet, many Christians think that because God chose to be incarnated as a member of *Homo sapiens* the incarnation has very little to do with the others creatures in this "very good" creation.

35. Westermann, *Creation*, 62–63. See also Arnold, *Genesis*, 40.

36. Ibid., 63–64.

37. E.g., Pss 104, 148; Dan 3:56–82.

38. John 1:14.

The notion that Jesus of Nazareth came only to "save" humans from their sins is virtually ubiquitous to the way the story of salvation is told in American churches. However, David Clough argues that just as we have rightly deemphasized the particularity of God becoming flesh as a Jew rather than as a Gentile and as a male rather than as a female in order to understand the inclusivity of Jesus' mission for Gentiles and females alike, so too should we deemphasize Jesus' genus and species as the basis for the claim that Jesus only came to save humans.[39] Instead, we should focus more intently on the proposition that God became a member of creation—God became a creature. This is made evident by the Greek word *sarx*, which appears in the Gospel of John as well as other New Testament passages that speak about the incarnation.[40] *Sarx* has its roots in the Hebrew *basar*, which is frequently used in the Old Testament to refer to all living creatures, not just humans. Clough concludes, "The fundamental New Testament assertion concerning the incarnation, therefore, is not that God became a member of the species *Homo sapiens*, but that God took on flesh, the stuff of living creatures."[41] Additionally, he contends that the idea of a human-only-oriented mission denies other New Testament passages that portray Christ's cosmic significance (e.g., Col 1:15–20; Eph 1:9–10, 22; 1 Cor 8:6; John 1:3; Rev 3:14).[42]

If the incarnation is truly cosmic in scope, then what might that say about creation as a whole? We must not forget that the incarnation is a thorough reaffirmation of the divine proclamation in Genesis 1 that creation is "very good." The material nature of our reality is not wicked or of lesser importance, as many in antiquity assumed and many contemporary American Protestants imply. James Nash puts it thusly: "The Incarnation confers dignity not only on humankind, but on everything and everyone, past and present, with which humankind is united in interdependence—corporeality, materiality, indeed, the whole of the earthly and heavenly. It sanctifies the biophysical world, making all things and kinds meaningful and worthy and valuable in the divine scheme. It justifies 'biophilia,' the affiliation with and affection for the diversity of life forms."[43] The incarnation then is also a reaffirmation of Psalm 104. God loves the biodiverse members of creation and seeks to redeem them back to the divine self. The cosmic nature of the

---

39. Clough, *On Animals*, 84. See also Webb, *God and Dogs*, 170.

40. Eph 2:14; 1 Tim 3:16; 1 John 4:2.

41. Clough, *On Animals*, 85.

42. Ibid., 86–87.

43. Nash, *Loving Nature*, 109. For more on this point, particularly from a patristic point of view, see Watson, "In the Beginning," 127–39; and Santmire, *Travail of Nature*, 31–53.

incarnation also speaks to the cosmic scope of redemption, which we shall explore shortly.

The incarnation also severely refutes the other-worldly focus of much of contemporary American Christianity. "God is not anti-flesh or anti-world; in fact, just the opposite: the incarnation says that God is the one in whom we live and move and have our being *as* fleshy, earthly creatures. God does not despise the world; God loves the world and expects us to as well. We have been given permission to love the world by the incarnation of God in the world."[44]

As always, the theological and ethical are intertwined in Christian thought. For Christians, then, internal change should stem from the realization that God cares for more than just humans—God cares for every creature that has been declared good. Therefore, our belief in the incarnation demands that we treat creation in a particular manner. Unfortunately, too many American Christians do not see the implications of the incarnation for their daily participation in the world around them, and especially in their treatment of other creatures and landscapes.

The Universe as a Sacrament

For many Protestants the idea of a robust sacramental theology seems like a foreign, if not dubious, idea. If someone were twisting our arms hard enough we might admit that both baptism and the Eucharist are indeed sacraments, but we would likely be able to say very little about how they are explicitly sacramental in nature. We probably cannot define the term "sacrament" with any precision as our Roman Catholic or Orthodox sisters and brothers could, if we can articulate a definition at all. The idea that creation might be sacramental in nature, then, is likely an entirely alien concept to many Protestant American Christians. Seeking to comprehend creation as sacramental is not an attempt to rehash the age-old debate about general revelation and natural theology; instead, I want to contemplate this subtle question: Should we not expect something that is created by God, and thus imbued with divine grace, to "tell" us something, maybe even something about God? After all, the psalmist declares, "The heavens are telling the glory of God; and the firmament proclaims his handiwork."[45] The prophet Isaiah during one of his visions saw seraphs, "And one called to another and said: 'Holy, holy, holy is the Lord of hosts; the whole earth is full of his

44. McFague, *New Climate*, 34; italics in original.
45. Ps 19:1.

glory.'"[46] Is there not potential theological significance in the apostle Paul's pronouncement to the Ephesian church that God "is above all and through all and in all"?[47]

But first, what is a sacrament? A basic definition might be something like this: "A sacrament . . . means any object, person or event through which religious consciousness is awakened to the presence of sacred mystery."[48] In a more precise Christian sense of the term, "Sacraments are real, material things that connect Christian communities to our creator. Sacraments are also mysteries, demonstrating the limits of our ability to fully understand God and God's working in our world."[49] This should remind us of the oft-quoted definition offered by Augustine: a sacrament is a visible form of invisible grace. For Roman Catholics, in particular, the Eucharist is a prime example of this. The bread and the wine are tangible vehicles for divine grace, but the mystery of transubstantiation still holds powerful sway.

Can something be a sacrament that is not derived from human hands? In other words, can there be natural sacraments, in the sense of something in nature or created only by God? Could the wilderness or a coral reef 75 feet below the surface of the ocean be a sacrament of this sort? If a sacrament connects us to our Creator and to the divine presence in the world, then the answer is yes. It should be of no surprise how many biblical figures found themselves in the presence of God when they were in nature. For example, Hagar meets God in the wilderness after she is driven from the protection of Abraham's family;[50] Jacob wrestles with God until daybreak in the wilderness;[51] Moses encounters God in the wilderness through the burning bush.[52] While an encounter with God in nature does not reveal God's grace more fully than taking the Eucharistic elements or participating in baptism, there is something different about looking, listening, and/or waiting for God in a place that remains free from the definitive contours of human culture. Unfortunately, it is becoming more and more difficult on our planet to find a place that is completely untouched by human hands. One of the saddest lessons of anthropogenic climate change is that there is no portion of the Earth's atmosphere, surface, or oceans that is not impacted dramatically by human activity.

46. Isa 6:3.
47. Eph 4:6.
48. Haught, *Promise of Nature*, 76.
49. O'Brien, *Ethics of Biodiversity*, 59.
50. Gen 21:15–19.
51. Gen 32:23–32.
52. Exod 3.

The notion of a natural sacrament should not be limited to a particular bush or a specific mountaintop, but instead, if God "is over all and
through all and in all,"[53] as Paul affirms, then every bit of creation operates
as a possible site for an encounter with the Creator. This was clear for many
Christian theologians of the patristic period. For instance, Gregory of Nyssa
declares, "It is not in a part of human nature that the image of God is found,
but nature in its totality is the image of God."[54] Similarly, twentieth-century
Anglican bishop William Temple calls creation a "sacramental universe."[55]
Thinking about the entire creation as an active site of God's revealing, gracious presence allows Christians, especially Protestants, who often lack a
robust sacramental theology, to acknowledge the link between the incarnation of the Word and the working of the Spirit. In other words, recognizing
the sacramental reality of creation allows us to affirm more vigorously God's
daily creative presence in the life of creation. Whether we identify this sort of
contemplation as "sacramentality"[56] or as "sacramental consciousness,"[57] we
are attempting to practice what should be a fundamental Christian affirmation: if God is the Creator of our universe, then we should be able to see and
witness to signs of the Creator in creation. Sacramental awareness should
change the way Christians think and feel about creation. For Christians in
the United States this should be a potent reminder of the this-worldliness
of divine activity and thus our Christian faith as a whole. God's creation
of a sacramental universe allows us to encounter God in every moment of
every day instead of assuming that we are all waiting for some other-worldly
spiritual encounter when this universe wastes away.

Moreover, Kevin O'Brien argues compellingly that this sort of attitude
should build a specific virtue within us. "The moral call of sacramentality is to humility, to appreciate the fundamental mystery of this creation
and the God who created it, and to be cautious and careful because of that
humility."[58] Thus, while Moses's experience with the burning bush was a
seminal encounter with God for people of the Judeo-Christian tradition,
we should consider the whirlwind experience of Job as a similarly important natural sacramental experience for contemporary Christians. Through
this encounter, Job gains a new perspective on God and thus his role in

53. Eph 4:6.

54. St. Gregory of Nyssa, "Creation of Man." Quoted in Krueger, *Cloud of Witnesses*,
104.

55. Temple, *Nature, Man and God*, 473–95.

56. O'Brien, *Ethics of Biodiversity*, 59–61.

57. Hart, *Sacramental Commons*, xviii.

58. O'Brien, *Ethics of Biodiversity*, 73.

the created order. Job is profoundly humbled after seeing the vast scope and richness of a planet containing awesome creatures that he did not know even existed and consequently withdraws his charge against God. Additionally, John Hart contends that a natural sacrament is critical for two reasons: "It can be both a sign and a stimulus: a sign of a relational divine presence and ongoing divine creativity; a stimulus to explore more fully the intricacies of the universe, Earth, and living communities and to seek more in-depth relational bonds."[59] Perhaps the sacramental character of the universe, which allows us to encounter God, is reason enough for Christians to engage in conservation and preservation efforts of the planet's ever-dwindling wildernesses.

Are mountaintops and burning bushes the only sorts of things that can act as natural sacraments? How about nonhuman creatures themselves? Thomas Aquinas argues that the multitude and diversity of creatures that inhabit the universe (what today we call "biodiversity") are necessary to describe God's own goodness, even if inadequately. "For He [sic] brought things into being in order that His goodness might be communicated to creatures, and be represented by them; and because His goodness could not be adequately represented by one creature alone, He produced many and diverse creatures, that what was wanting to one in the representation of the divine goodness might be supplied by another."[60] At some level, this appears to be a theological explanation of what the psalmists wrote about in Psalms 104 and 148. According to O'Brien, the biodiversity of the planet is itself sacramental because it helps us understand something about God and hence serves to buttress our faith. Viewing biodiversity sacramentally "challenges us to consider why God made a world in which such diversity would evolve; it reminds us that God's presence and care for this world is not limited to human beings but extends to all creatures; and it reveals how much we do not know about both the creation and the creator."[61]

It is easy to imagine that viewing creatures or portions of creation as sites of sacramental witness might reinforce anthropocentrism and the subsequent idea that nonhuman creatures and creation are, in a sense, only of utilitarian value. In other words, they are only valuable inasmuch as they can help us humans see God more clearly. This unwittingly might deny these creatures' God-given worth. To combat this concern, Sallie McFague maintains that we need a "horizontal sacramentalism" that focuses more on nonhuman creatures or vistas in creation themselves rather than on their

59. Hart, *Sacramental Commons*, xiv.

60. Thomas Aquinas, *Summa Theologica*, 1.47.1.

61. O'Brien, *Ethics of Biodiversity*, 65.

potential divine message.[62] I remain unconvinced that a theocentric understanding of sacramental contemplation will devolve into merely utilitarian
thinking. Once again turning outside of the Protestant realm for help in
understanding what a sacramental life might entail, Elizabeth Theokritoff
contends, "The sacraments remind us that we relate to God as bodily creatures, so that the physical world surrounding and sustaining us is essential
to that relationship. The role of matter in sacramental life speaks to us both
of our dependence on material creation, and of our responsibility towards
it."[63] While the immediate context of Theokritoff's statement is about sacraments like the Eucharist and baptism, there is no compelling reason why
this contention could not be extended to the discussion about natural sacraments. Seeing God through other creatures, mountaintops, coral reefs,
etc., should remind us of not only the interdependent connectedness of
everything that God created, but also their goodness because they share a
grace-imbued existence just as we do. This sort of sacramental contemplation is a radical affirmation of the apostle Paul's claim that God "is over all
and through all and in all."[64] Moreover, it is a recognition of one of the key
notes in Genesis 1. God was working in creation and pronouncing creatures
and the universe to be good before humans ever arrived on the scene. It is
a powerful reminder that "[God] does not require our action in order to be
present in [God's] own creation."[65] This again reaffirms the call to humility
that sacramental contemplation can inspire and thereby ameliorate concerns about viewing creatures or creation only through a utilitarian frame.

One can easily imagine that some Protestant Christians might still be
concerned that sacramental contemplation may tempt us to exaggerate our
encounters with the Word in nature and sacrifice listening to God's Word
found in Scripture or possibly turn us into New Age spiritualists of some
sort. John Haught recognizes the temptation to allow a sacrament to become
an end in itself rather than remain a vehicle for experiencing the grace of
God. He argues that sacramental contemplation without an association with
mysticism, silence, and action can slide down a slippery slope to naturalism
and become idolatrous as we worship nature as the ultimate reality instead
of allowing nature to point beyond itself to its Creator.[66] By "mysticism,"
he means belief in the God who not only embraces creation but ultimately
transcends it, and that therefore all of creation yearns to be whole with its

62. McFague, *Super, Natural Christians*, 172–75.

63. Theokritoff, *Living in God's Creation*, 193.

64. Eph 4:6.

65. Ibid., 194.

66. Haught, *Promise of Nature*, 76–87.

Creator. Silence is needed because Christianity has an apophatic quality to it that confesses that the mystery of God cannot be captured or articulated by a single sacrament, which again is a reminder of the importance of biodiversity. Finally, if Christianity is to be this-worldly and matter to creaturely life at all, then it must be active. This reflects the mission of justice proclaimed by the prophets in their concern for the orphans, widows, and resident aliens, which was embodied especially in the ministry of Jesus of Nazareth. Therefore, Haught concludes that Christians should seek to balance these components carefully so that sacramental contemplation invites us to enjoy a grace-filled creation that causes us to be thankful, mysticism urges us to keep nature in its proper perspective as we await the consummation of the universe, silence guards against anthropocentrism and instrumental thinking by encouraging us to let nature be itself and demonstrate God's goodness, and action calls us to seek justice not only for humans, but for the nonhuman creatures of God's creation as well. These four components working well together help us to see the work of our Creator and honor it for the very good creation it is.

Thinking about God as our Creator—and not just the Creator of humanity, but the Creator of the entire universe and all that is within it—should give us pause to consider the magnitude of what it is we are a part of every single moment of the day. A Christian witness that does not reflect God's loving care for nonhuman creatures is severely limited and does not reflect the robustness of the portrayal of God as Creator in Scripture. One could say, in Chrysostom-like fashion, that only a Christian exhibiting arrogant folly might claim that God does not care deeply for the needs of all that God creates. But God not only created a universe, but a very good one, which is reaffirmed radically in the incarnation of Jesus. Additionally, the ability to contemplate the universe as a sacrament should lead us to a deeper engagement with God our Creator. All of this should help us significantly expand our theological imaginary. This, of course, is not all there is to say about God that should spark a new theological imaginary. We turn to God's work as Redeemer in the next chapter.

2

God the Redeemer

While the depiction of God as Creator appears first in the order of the books of the Bible, scholarly opinion puts the writing of Genesis long after the emancipation of the ancient Hebrew slaves from Egypt and their subsequent self-identification as Israelites. Yahweh God was known as Israel's Redeemer far before they conceived of God as Creator of the universe. God's declaration to Moses through the burning bush—"I have observed the misery of my people who are in Egypt; I have heard their cry on account of their taskmasters. Indeed, I know their sufferings"[1]—is the basis of our understanding of God's sense of justice and redemption. The idea of a just God is central to the scriptural portrayal of God's character. The prophet Isaiah says, "Therefore the Lord waits to be gracious to you; therefore he will rise up to show mercy to you. For the Lord is a God of justice; blessed are all those who wait for him."[2] Similarly, Jeremiah, speaking on behalf of God, declares, "I act with steadfast love, justice, and righteousness in the earth, for in these things I delight, says the Lord."[3] Perhaps more importantly, though, Scripture does not just depict God merely as one who executes justice or performs just acts, but also as one who loves justice. For example, the psalmist proclaims, "[God] loves righteousness and justice; the earth is full of the steadfast love of the Lord."[4]

God's love of justice is to be a distinguishing characteristic of God's people. This leads to very precise instructions in God's covenant with Israel to be just or do justice. For instance, during times of harvest the Israelites are directed to leave behind produce for the orphans, widows, and aliens living among them.[5] This is not merely the instantiation of the "love your neigh-

---

1. Exod 3:7.
2. Isa 30:18.
3. Jer 9:24.
4. Ps 33:5. See also Pss 11:7; 37:28; 99:4; Isa 60:18; 61:8.
5. Lev 19:9–10; 23:22; Deut 24:17–21.

bor as yourself" ethic that would come to permeate Jesus' ministry, but a definitive reminder to the Israelites that they were once slaves in Egypt and hence they should remember the plight of others who are oppressed.[6] This significant emphasis placed on justice, especially for the widows, orphans, and aliens, is a vital component of the message of the Israelite prophetic tradition. Isaiah declares to Israel, "Learn to do good; seek justice, rescue the oppressed, defend the orphan, plead for the widow."[7] Similarly, Zechariah exhorts his audience, "This is what the Lord Almighty said: 'Administer true justice; show mercy and compassion to one another. Do not oppress the widow or the fatherless, the foreigner or the poor.'"[8] Micah proclaims to Israel, "[God] has told you, O mortal, what is good; and what does the Lord require of you but to do justice, and to love kindness, and to walk humbly with your God?"[9] It is also a significant component of the wisdom literature tradition. "To do righteousness and justice is more acceptable to the Lord than sacrifice."[10] "When justice is done, it is a joy to the righteous, but dismay to evildoers."[11] "The righteous care about justice for the poor, but the wicked have no such concern."[12]

As noted in the passages above, justice and righteousness often go together in Scripture. They are even personified in such a way to describe the foundation of God's throne.[13] The link between the two generally connotes the way God calls us to behave toward one another in the social sphere.[14] We should recognize justice not as merely a leveling of the scales or administration of the judicial process with complete impartiality. Instead, the word pair suggests behavior that is similar to that of God, which includes kindness, goodness, and mercy toward those who are created and loved by God. This link between doing justice and loving kindness that we see in the famous passage from Micah quoted above is exactly what should be recognized as social justice, which is a worshipful act to God.[15] Moreover, this is why the prophets are so interested in kings, judges, and others in positions of power acting kindly and justly towards widows, orphans, and aliens. This

---

6. Deut 24:22.

7. Isa 1:17.

8. Zech 7:9–10, NIV.

9. Mic 6:8.

10. Prov 21:3.

11. Prov 21:19.

12. Prov 29:7, NIV.

13. Pss 89:14; 97:2.

14. Weinfeld, "Justice and Righteousness," 232.

15. Ibid., 238.

is exactly the concern of Zechariah in the passage listed above, too. This sort of behavior reflects the very way God loves the oppressed.[16] Justice, and its subsequent connection to righteousness, is not a static concept or a Platonic ideal, but instead a dynamic activity wherein God seeks to be kind and equitable to the oppressed who have little or no voice in society. We, as representatives of God, should see our vocation as nothing less than this same active pursuit and daily behavior if we are to heed the words of the prophets.

God's particular notion of justice and redemption is at the forefront of the ministry of Jesus, too. In the Gospel of Luke, Jesus' first public proclamation shows his distinct understanding of the divine mission: "The Spirit of the Lord is upon me, because he has anointed me to bring good news to the poor. He has sent me to proclaim release to the captives and recovery of sight to the blind, to let the oppressed go free, to proclaim the year of the Lord's favor."[17] In the Gospel of Matthew, Jesus addresses the crowds and tells them that in the final judgment care for the poor will define who is recognized by God and who is not. "Then he will answer them, 'Truly I tell you, just as you did not do it to one of the least of these, you did not do it to me.'"[18] Moreover, Jesus consistently demonstrates what it means to do justice and redeem those whom God identifies as children of God by associating openly with women, the outcast, children, and the otherwise disenfranchised and forgotten people of first-century Palestine. He treats them as human beings made in the image of God. Indeed, God has heard the cry of God's people.

While this is not the place for an exhaustive elucidation of the relationship between justice and love, let me propose a few basics of what it might look like, which I believe might be helpful to us in later chapters. First, while in much of Western culture we think of justice as the establishment, protection, and exercise of rights, especially if they are codified legally, God's notion of justice is something else entirely. Seeking justice or being just is an active behavior that does not wait for the correct politician to be in office or a more equitable law to be passed. A Christian can be just to widows, orphans, and aliens regardless of who occupies the oval office or whether civil rights are guaranteed by the law. Second, justice and love are obviously not the same terms nor do they necessarily connote the same behaviors in Scripture, but the relationship between them is quite fluid. Again, in much of Western culture justice can operate as the basic minimum that a person

16. Deut 10:17–8; Pss 103:6; 146:7.

17. Luke 4:18–9.

18. Matt 25:45.

is guaranteed by the codified laws of the land. While this notion of justice does not match up exactly with the prophetic call to seek justice for the widows, orphans, and aliens, it does give contemporary Christians something to consider seriously. Can we Christians say that we love our neighbors as ourselves if we are not acting justly toward them? James Nash states it well: "Whatever the correct relationship might be in detail, love demands more than justice, but it also demands no less than justice. Justice is a necessary condition for the existence of love; love incorporates justice."[19] This forces us to consider carefully whether or not Christians can legitimately claim to love their neighbors if they do not have access to basic necessities like clean air, clean drinking water, and nutritionally dense food. Third, according to the prophets, acting justly to the widows, orphans, and aliens affects the society in which the Israelites dwell. Justice often signifies a social or public element in ways that love does not. Whereas being just connotes knowledge of the minimum necessities of others, loving someone suggests knowing the intimate needs of the other. This can make justice seem more public and love seem more private, in the sense of knowing the general needs of someone versus knowing the specific needs of an immediate neighbor. (This is obviously not an unbreakable prescription, but a general guideline.) Moreover, justice may indeed require sacrifice, often by those who have either inherited power and privilege or those who illegitimately exercise them, but love is fundamentally decrepit without it. Finally, there is no inherent reason why God's call to be just to widows, orphans, and aliens and Jesus' call to care for "the least of these" should not be extended to nonhuman creatures and the rest of creation. While our ways of being just toward nonhuman creatures and the rest of creation will undoubtedly differ from how we are just to our human neighbors, we should not allow our lack of imagination to prevent us from exhibiting God's commitment to justice and our witness of God the Redeemer.

The Link between Justice for the Poor and Justice for the Land

American conservationist Aldo Leopold, who was very knowledgeable of the scriptural tradition even though he did not view himself as a Christian, once said, "Individual thinkers since the days of Ezekiel and Isaiah have asserted that the despoliation of land is not only inexpedient but wrong. Society, however, has not yet affirmed their belief."[20] Our society still does

19. Nash, *Loving Nature*, 166.

20. Leopold, *Sand County Almanac*, 203.

not affirm this belief; and sadly, most Christians in the United States do not explicitly affirm this belief either. Until recently, many biblical scholars did not even acknowledge that caring for the land was a topic of concern for Israel's prophets. Thankfully, as John Barton puts it, "Biblical study is gradually recovering from a kind of Barthianism that denied all continuities with the environing culture, and is instead coming to see the Old Testament as a very sophisticated version of much that was common in the ancient world."[21] As discussed above, there is a strong witness to a cosmic covenant of justice, peace, and the integrity of creation throughout the Old Testament texts, especially within the prophetic tradition. And contemporary Christians, based upon Murray's insight into this cosmic covenant, we must ask ourselves the following question: If God created this very universe, why should we not expect the universe in some way to reflect the God who created it?

Hilary Marlow proposes rather compellingly that both Hosea and Amos see a link between Israelite behaviors toward God and the oppressed, and their treatment of the land. The prophet Hosea maintains that by worshipping the gods of neighboring Canaan the Israelites have failed to adhere to the covenant with Yahweh, which is directly responsible for the land's lack of fecundity.[22] Whereas God honored the covenant by demonstrating righteousness, justice, kindness, and compassion, the Israelites did not and it became evident in their relationships with Yahweh and each other. Hosea, though, believes that the covenantal failure on the part of the Israelites has affected not only the land they use for farming, but the entire created order itself, as he paints the picture of a disruption of nature due to the collective unfaithfulness of Israel. This results in Hosea's proclamation that may seem, to some at least, radical today: "Hear the word of the Lord, O people of Israel; for the Lord has an indictment against the inhabitants of the land. There is no faithfulness or loyalty, and no knowledge of God in the land. Swearing, lying, and murder, and stealing and adultery break out; bloodshed follows bloodshed. Therefore the land mourns, and all who live in it languish; together with the wild animals and the birds of the air, even the fish of the sea are perishing."[23] This leads Melissa Tubbs Loya to assert, "In this prophetic oracle, creation is not simply the scenery in which the story of Israel's relationship with Yahweh plays out. Rather, creation actively mourns the subversion of the created order [by humans], and this results in the languishing and perishing of all who live on it: the

---

21. Barton, "Reading the Prophets," 52.

22. Marlow, *Biblical Prophets*, 158–94.

23. Hos 4:1–3.

animals of the field, the birds of the air, and the fish of the sea."[24] It is this sort of biblical analysis that should allow us to conclude that it is far too facile to conclude that all of Scripture promotes an anthropocentric worldview. Furthermore, Marlow contends that the rhetorical structure of Amos itself indicates a cosmic dialogue between the Creator and creation wherein the nonhuman members of creation are portrayed as responding to God's voice and cooperating with God not only to reveal the divine power, but also to participate in the judgment on human injustice.[25] "A wide range of natural elements act as YHWH's agents and are available to him [sic] to direct at those who have warranted his judgment. This agency sends a clear message that the world does not revolve around the anthropocentric concerns of its human inhabitants, but that they are at the mercy of the natural world and, ultimately, of its creator."[26] In the prophet's closing words, Amos provides his audience with a vision of hope that depicts the collaborative interaction of God, humans, and nonhumans. This should remind us once again of the interconnectedness and interdependence vividly portrayed in the two Genesis creation accounts.

Hosea and Amos are not the only two prophets who link care of the land with justice for the oppressed. Nick Spencer, Robert White, and Virginia Vroblesky argue that Isaiah 40–66, especially, describes a version of "the right order of things."[27] For them, Isaiah sees a close link between what we might call social and environmental sustainability, as the prophet depicts a world where environmental regeneration cannot be understood apart from social redemption, and neither can it be comprehended without a relationship to God. Isaiah reminds Israel that its hope should be found in God rather than in themselves or other social systems because God is the only one with the power to bring about redemption. Furthermore, living according to this right order of things is a moral issue, an issue of seeking justice for the oppressed and showing compassion to the widows, orphans, and aliens, rather than a search for the appropriate technology to solve environmental woes. Isaiah suggests that abiding by this right moral order brings one joy, as one recognizes that sacrifice for the sake of the other brings redemption to both humans and nonhumans alike.

Michael Northcott argues that Jeremiah is the first ecological prophet in literary and religious history. Jeremiah, according to Northcott, believes that justice is part of the very makeup of the universe that God created and

24. Loya, "Therefore the Earth Mourns," 62.

25. Marlow, Biblical Prophets, 120–57.

26. Ibid., 147.

27. Spencer et al., Christianity, Climate Change, 101–19.

therefore justice is a divine gift that reflects the character of a good God; justice is "ecologically situated and not just a human value."[28] In Jeremiah's time, the people of Israel and Judah were exiled from their ancestral lands because they neglected the covenant with God and polluted the land. "The devastation of the land is not only seen as the judgment of a wrathful God. It is also interpreted as the consequence of the human rebellion against the created order and wisdom of nature. Profligacy, waste, greed, injustice and idolatry are all sins which are contrary to the created order instituted by God, and so they undermine the goodness and harmony of that order."[29] In other words, by their failing to seek justice for the poor and oppressed, the land itself was despoiled. The environmental exile was to punish the rich and the powerful, who had taken so much land that the poor were left with nothing before the exile had even begun. Jeremiah's position is similar to that of other prophets who believed that Israelite worship of Yahweh was intimately tied to justice toward the oppressed and thus care of creation. Here we see theology and science in absolute agreement: human society is intricately bound to the ecosystems of this planet. Our neglectfulness of this theological and ecological fact is the reason for many of our significant contemporary environmental ills.

Environmental Justice

Unfortunately, the prophetic insight is as relevant today as it was in the time of ancient Israel. The treatment of the world's poor and oppressed is still linked to our care for creation.[30] In the United States, the treatment of the poor and oppressed is often linked to the color of one's skin. The landmark 1987 report *Toxic Wastes and Race in the United States*, produced by the United Church of Christ's Commission for Racial Justice, described in incredible detail what communities of color have known anecdotally for decades: race is the most potent variable in predicting where waste facilities are placed in America.[31] Race was found to be more potent than wealth, land value, home ownership, or even distance from schools and hospitals. In other words, if you know the racial makeup of a given city or county, you can predict with incredible precision where various waste facilities will be located. The 2007 follow-up report did not describe a better situation for

28. Northcott, *Moral Climate*, 161.

29. Ibid., 171.

30. For an introduction into a liberation-theological perspective on this link, see Boff, *Cry of the Earth*.

31. Commission for Racial Justice, *Toxic Wastes and Race*.

the relationship between race and waste in the United States.[32] The environmental justice movement in the United States arose out of the recognition of the unequal treatment of communities of color when it comes to issues like clean air, clean water, the placement of toxic release sites and waste facilities, as well as other policies that distribute environmental benefits and burdens. The United States Environmental Protection Agency (EPA) defines environmental justice thusly: "Environmental Justice is the fair treatment and meaningful involvement of all people regardless of race, color, national origin, or income with respect to the development, implementation, and enforcement of environmental laws, regulations, and policies. EPA has this goal for all communities and persons across this Nation. It will be achieved when everyone enjoys the same degree of protection from environmental and health hazards and equal access to the decision-making process to have a healthy environment in which to live, learn, and work."[33] Robert Bullard, the father of the environmental justice movement, argues that the legal definition and enforcement of environmental justice are critical, but the movement seeks to conceptualize and develop a much broader framework. The environmental justice framework addresses the ethical and political questions, "Who gets what, why, and how much?"[34]

Central to Bullard's research and work in the environmental justice movement is the notion of environmental racism. "*Environmental racism* refers to any policy, practice, or directive that differentially affects or disadvantages (whether intended or unintended) individuals, groups, or communities based on race or color. Environmental racism combines with public policies and industry practices to provide *benefits* for whites while shifting industry *costs* to people of color."[35] The scholars and activists in this field have been as diligent as they are meticulous in detailing the examples of environmental racism throughout the nation, and more recently throughout the rest of the globe.[36] Let us briefly examine two frequent types of environmental racism. First, while many white U.S. citizens have the opportunity to work in relatively clean and safe jobs, live in parts of towns that have relatively clean air, and drink relatively clean water, many persons of color in the

32. Bullard et al., "Toxic Wastes."

33. Environmental Protection Agency, "Environmental Justice."

34. Bullard, "Environmental Justice," 25.

35. Bullard, *Dumping in Dixie*, 98; italics in original.

36. For more on the environmental justice movement, see Bullard, *Quest for Environmental Justice*; Bryant, *Environmental Justice*; Nixon, *Slow Violence*; Sandler and Pezzullo, *Environmental Justice and Environmentalism*; Carmin and Agyeman, *Environmental Inequalities*. For a critique of the movement, see Pellow and Brulle, *Power, Justice, and the Environment*; Foreman, Jr., *Promise and Peril*.

U.S. do not live in communities with these benefits. When thinking about this, many white citizens often ask, "Why don't African Americans move out of their homes next to bus depots in order to breathe cleaner air?" Or, "Why don't Latino migrant workers choose other employment if they don't want to be exposed to carcinogen-laced pesticides when they are working in the fields picking our food?" After all, we often say, no one is forcing these folks to live somewhere or take a particular job. Luke Cole and Sheila Foster argue that this typical white American line of thinking is nothing more than perpetually blaming the victim for her/his participation in a specific lifestyle that lends itself to environmental injustice.[37] Two consequences are linked to this "blaming the victim" explanation. One, it allows the observer who is unaffected by an environmental burden to claim that disproportionate exposure to pollutants or chemicals is a decision that is made freely by the exposed person and could be presumably changed if the aggrieved party so desired. Moreover, this allows the observer to discount, if not completely ignore, the social and structural dynamics that might more readily explain why a person is disproportionately exposed in a particular job or part of a city. Two, by placing the burden of exposure on the individual, this sort of explanation assuages the observer of any guilt or responsibility for changing a situation that may be entirely unjust.

A second recurrent type of environmental racism often looks practically like this: A section of homes is situated next to a polluting industrial segment of town. The citizens begin to develop various respiratory ailments or cancer that may be related to pollutants being released from nearby companies, but no one can prove it scientifically because the local residents do not have the financial means required to perform the tests. An observer views this situation and asks, "Who came first—the companies or the citizens?" Suggesting that objective market forces are what drive land values and where people live and industries are built, and are thus the causative factor in why people live where they do and industries are zoned where they are, is again missing the mark. It separates the observer from asking what historical circumstances actually make some parts of town more valuable than others, because there is no such thing as a neutral, objective market, and it relieves the guilt of those who believe that if folks did not want to breathe polluted air, they would move to another side of town. Cole and Foster contend that the historical question might help us describe the various factors that led to the present tension in the community, but this sort of "chicken or egg" question misses the larger normative question: Should anyone, including persons of color, ever be subjected to living next to an

37. Cole and Foster, *From the Ground Up*, 58–60.

industrial center that pollutes the air, water, etc.?[38] Why are environmental benefits not shared and burdens not borne fairly in a given community? Are these not the sorts of concerns Christians should involve themselves with if we claim to care for the oppressed like God does?

Food Justice

Similar to how racial prejudice leads to environmental injustice, communities of color also are routinely exploited when it comes to the access to affordable healthy food. Communities of color, as well as low-income communities in general, not only regularly lack access to locally available, healthy, fresh food (e.g., fruits and vegetables), but what food is available is more expensive than similar food sold in wealthier, often white areas of town.[39] The lack of fresh food within a reasonable distance from one's home is referred to as a "food desert." Perhaps they are more accurately referred to as "food swamps." This latter term denotes the prevalence of fast-food restaurants and convenience stores that sell an overabundance of high-energy, low-nutrient foods rather than wholesome, nutritionally dense foods like fruits and vegetables. Communities of color are frequently situated in such places where these swamps are the densest, meaning that you are more likely to be in walking distance of a fast-food restaurant that sells cheap foods full of sugar and fat than a grocery store that sells affordable, healthy, fresh food. Whether termed a "food swamp" or "food desert," these communities experience fundamental differences in their access to food. Wholesome, nutritionally dense food is not only less available, but when it is available it frequently costs more than it does in other communities with traditional supermarkets. Many in these swamps also do not own automobiles, which dramatically affects their access to traditional supermarkets. While relying upon public transportation is not necessarily a bad thing, in the United States it tends to extend the hours one spends away from one's home and often dictates the choices of one's shopping experiences in food swamps or deserts. If one cannot get to a supermarket and return home in a reasonable amount of time, then one's food choices may be considerably constrained as well. Not to mention the difficulty and inconvenience of bringing one's groceries onto public transportation. It is out of this typical setting for many communities of color that the food justice movement arose. Similar to the environmental justice movement's emphasis on equal protection from environmental pollution and procedural justice, food justice advocates typi-

38. Ibid., 60–63.

39. Winne, *Closing the Food Gap*.

cally stress the importance of food access and food sovereignty.[40] By food access they mean the equal access to affordable, healthy, fresh food that most wealthy and white communities take for granted. By food sovereignty they mean the community's role in defining their own food and agricultural systems. In other words, do convenience stores and fast-food restaurants determine our food choices or do community members have a say in the matter? Food justice advocates then look to understand, critique, and transform "where, what, and how food is grown, produced, transported, accessed, and eaten."[41] It is easy to imagine that the Israelite prophets of the past might have much to say about this situation today. Are we really doing justice and loving kindness if we are not concerning ourselves with what our neighbors have the ability to eat?

Climate Change Refugees

If just the ice in Greenland melts, the global sea-level rise will be about 20 feet, which would then submerge as much as 80 percent of the world's cities. If the ice in Greenland melts and the ice in the West Antarctic ice sheet continues to melt and fall into the ocean, the sea-level rise would be even more dramatic, more quickly. Sea-level rise is a direct consequence of anthropogenic climate change and shows appreciably that climate change does not discriminate between developed and developing nations. Cities in the United States and United Kingdom will face the exact sorts of problems that cities in Bangladesh and the Maldives will. The difference of course is that the U.S. and U.K. have the ability to adapt to a rising sea level in remarkably different ways than Bangladesh and the Maldives. A rising global sea level, unfortunately, is not the only climate change–related consequence that will irrevocably change the way that human beings live in the coming centuries. Climate change–induced extreme weather events (e.g., tsunamis, hurricanes, tornadoes, etc.), which will occur more frequently along with drought and worldwide water insecurity, will force human migration to occur at unprecedented levels in the coming decades. Conservative estimates indicate that there will likely be 150 to 200 million "climate refugees" by 2050.[42] Moreover, women will be impacted disproportionately because of their lower levels of education, reliance on immediate natural resources for

40. Alkon and Agyeman, "Introduction," 8.

41. Gottlieb and Joshi, *Food Justice*, 5. For more on this, see Holt-Giménez, "Food Security," 309–30.

42. See Christian Aid, "Human Tide"; Brown, *Migration*; Stern, *Economics of Climate Change*; Friends of the Earth, "Citizen's Guide."

survival (e.g., they are the majority of the world's farmers), and caretaking of children while men move to cities for work,[43] even though they may hold the key to vital adaptation measures.[44] Climate refugees are undoubtedly the "widows, orphans, and aliens" of our time, but are not part of the explicit conversation about what American Christians should concern themselves with.

Cosmic Redemption or a Human-Only Heaven?

When most American Christians think about God's work of redemption, they are often thinking about the divine plan of salvation. It is God's business to save souls and take them to heaven. Many, if not most, Christians conceive of heaven as a place far away that is intended as our final home because "we are not of this world." Additionally, many of these same Christians believe that heaven is a place far, far away that is distinctly reserved for humans, as if the rest of God's creatures do not qualify. Some might argue that only those with souls go to heaven and thus humans are unique in this manner. Scripture, however, does not make such a simple distinction. All living creatures, human or otherwise, are *nephesh*, the Hebrew word commonly translated "soul," because Scripture does not seem to delineate so radically between human and nonhuman creatures as contemporary Christians are so fond of doing.[45]

Some Christians believe that because humans are the only creatures on the planet that sin, we are the only ones who need to be saved and therefore the only ones who deserve to be in heaven with God. This is a limited view of God's grace and the divine scheme of redemption on many levels, but for our present purposes let us look to why a human-only heaven is problematic. According to Christopher Southgate, this view is sincerely questionable for at least three reasons. First, this view does not reflect the more robust theological imaginary that one encounters in the biblical witness. There are a few "profoundly enigmatic" passages that strongly suggest that the extent of redemption may be far more cosmic in scope than the average American Christian would care to admit. Second, nowhere in Scripture are humans pictured apart from creation. We are members of creation just like everything that God graciously granted existence, and "it would be curious if this

43. Christian Aid, "Climate Justice for All"; United Nations, "Women, Gender Equality and Climate Change."

44. Figueres, "Women Are the Secret"; Robinson, "Why Women."

45. E.g., Gen 1:20–21, 24, 39; 2:7, 19.

were not carried forward into the realm in which relationships (presumably) are found at their richest and truest." Third, the issue of nonhuman suffering seems to demand an eschatological solution if divine goodness is to be affirmed seriously.[46]

One of those profoundly enigmatic passages is Colossians 1:15–20, the so-called Christ hymn. In this short passage, Paul, most likely using a preexistent Christian hymn, states that all things are created and reconciled through Christ. In other words, in Christ the work of creation and redemption are components of a singular divine plan, and in Christ creation and redemption are cosmic in scope. As James Dunn puts it, "The vision is vast. The claim is mind-blowing. It says much for the faith of these first Christians that they should see in Christ's death and resurrection quite literally the key to resolving the disharmonies of nature and inhumanities of humankind, that the character of God's creation and God's concern for the universe in its fullest expression could be so caught and encapsulated for them in the cross of Christ."[47] The usage of "all things" (*ta panta*) six times in relation to Christ's creating and redeeming work significantly points to this cosmic scope. This is also portrayed by Christ's relation to "all things" using the three prepositions "in" (*en*), "through" (*dia*), and "for/to" (*eis*). The use of the preposition *en* could mean that all things are created and exist in Christ's sphere of influence, or that all things are created and exist due to Christ's agency, or that all things are created and exist in relationship to Christ, or perhaps it presupposes a combination of the three. Ronald Cox contends, "This potential polysemy only serves to emphasize the intimate association between the Son and everything else. He cannot be divorced from the origin of things nor from their continued existence."[48] The use of *dia* signals again the relationship between God and Christ and Christ and the rest of creation. The use of *eis* indicates that the universe has a sense of direction; its goal is in fact Christ. Marianne Thompson concludes succinctly, "Indeed in three short prepositions the totality—*through* him, *in* him, and *for* him—capture in three short strokes the totality of God's work in creating and redeeming the world."[49] In other words, there is nothing that exists in this universe that is not created by Christ and thus nothing in this universe that Christ does not desire to be reconciled back to God through his redemptive work. Moreover, Richard Bauckham argues that Paul's inclusion of this hymn shows that the story of creation and the story of Jesus

46. Southgate, *Groaning of Creation*, 82.

47. Dunn, *Epistles*, 104.

48. Cox, "Why It All Matters," 137. For more on this, see Cox, *Same Word*, 163–93.

49. Thompson, *Colossians and Philemon*, 31; italics in original.

Christ are "intrinsically related . . . [as] the Gospel story—the story of the life, death and resurrection of Jesus—is focal and decisive for all creation."[50] Likewise, Dunn maintains that "the wholeness of God's interaction with the universe is summed up in Christ."[51] For those who might believe that only humans need to be redeemed back to God, this hymn reminds us powerfully that *all* things God created through Christ are meant to be redeemed back to their Creator. Anything less would not speak fully to the work of the cross and Christ's subsequent resurrection. Furthermore, it suggests that creation care and creation justice can and should be directly linked to one's belief in the sovereignty of Christ as Lord.

Another of those profoundly enigmatic passages is Romans 8:18–23. In the midst of a letter meant to comfort the Christians in Rome who were suffering for their belief in Jesus, the apostle Paul places their condition in the context of the broader groaning of creation. It is important to recognize that Paul's use of the word "creation" (*ktisis*) is most likely referring to the nonhuman components of creation, if not both humans and nonhumans who occupy God's universe.[52] While some, like Brendan Byrne, contend that creation's eager longing for the revealing of the daughters and sons of God is solely in the eschatological future,[53] Robert Jewett argues that the unveiling of the daughters and sons of God can be thought of more in the present tense because Paul is alluding to the advancing of God's glory, i.e., the furtherance of the gospel. "So what the creation awaits with eager longing is the emergence of this triumph of divine righteousness (cf. Rom 1:17), which will begin to restore a rightful balance to the creation once again, overcoming the Adamic legacy of corruption and disorder that fell as a calamitous curse upon the ground (Gen 3:17–19)."[54] Paul does not call for specific policies to be enacted in order to reverse the curse, but instead relies upon God's activity through the conversion of humans into the likeness of Christ, who will then discern appropriately how to repair the ecological distress found in a wounded creation. Jewett contends that Paul is explicitly referring to the abuse and despoliation of creation by Adam and his descendants in verse 20. "The basic idea is that the human refusal to accept limitations ruins the world. By acting out idolatrous desires to have unlimited dominion over the garden, the original purpose of creation—to express divine goodness

50. Bauckham, *Bible and Ecology*, 155.

51. Dunn, *Epistles*, 101.

52. Jewett, *Romans*, 511; Byrne, *Romans*, 256; Horrell et al., *Greening Paul*, 65.

53. Byrne, *Romans*, 257.

54. Jewett, *Romans*, 512

(Gen 1:31) and reflect divine glory (Ps 19:1–4)—was emptied."[55] In agreement, Byrne asserts strongly, "It is not fanciful to understand exploitative human pollution of the environment as part of that 'sin' story, along with other evils."[56]

Paul continues the letter telling the Roman Christians that a future hope awaits all of creation because God has not forsaken creation and has empowered humans once again to perform the vocation for which they were created. "Overcoming ecological disorder is depicted here as a divine gift enacted as a result of God's restoration of humanity to its position of rightful dominion, reflecting God's intended glory."[57] Paul is once again reflecting the message of Genesis 1: we are interdependently connected with the rest of God's created order. Again, it should make sense to us that Paul believes our sin causes creation to groan. Jewett notes that creation's misery is the consequence of Adam and Eve's sin depicted in Genesis 3:17–18 and the creation's groaning mentioned explicitly in passages like Isaiah 24:4–7 and Hosea 4:1–3. Richard Bauckham takes this one step further and argues that the prophetic understanding of the Earth's mourning is exactly what the apostle is relying upon as he writes this letter. "Crucially, what becomes clear is that Paul assumes the same kind of close relationship between human wrongdoing and the well-being of the nonhuman creation that the prophets do."[58] Moreover, the interdependent connectedness of creation is witnessed to again by Paul's understanding that all of creation groans with us and for the Spirit for the glory of God to be further advanced. "Creation's groaning is a co-groaning with Paul and other Christians and the Spirit, a shared travail that also represents a shared hope, though some aspects of that hope are distinctive to the 'sons [sic] of God,' who are here described as those who have 'the first fruits of the Spirit.' . . . The common vocabulary used to describe creation, humanity, and the Spirit indicates that somehow they are caught up in the same process, yearning for the same outcome, which the future dimensions of the story will go on to depict."[59] Creation eagerly anticipates us taking our rightful place as those who would do work that heals ecosystems rather than destroys them. While this does not mean that the tension between the "already" and the "not yet" is resolved, Paul places a genuinely heavy burden upon humans and the role of hopeful waiting and hopeful work that is required for those who call themselves Christians.

55. Ibid., 513.

56. Byrne, *Romans*, 259. This will be explored more fully in chapter 3.

57. Ibid., 515.

58. Bauckham, *Bible and Ecology*, 100.

59. Horrell et al., *Greening Paul*, 79.

Others throughout Christian history have also recognized the potential cosmic scope of God's redemptive plan. The second-century church father Irenaeus of Lyons definitely recognizes the possible cosmic scope of God's redemptive plan. Irenaeus disagrees with those who would interpret the nonhuman creatures gathering on God's holy mountain (Isaiah 60) to be symbols for different nations who had not yet been counted among the righteous of God. Instead, he maintains that the resurrection also applies to nonhuman creatures and thus they shall enjoy the redemption of all things as well. He concludes, "For God is rich in all things."[60] Basil of Caesarea, too, acknowledges the universal scope of God's redemptive plan in the following prayer:

> For those, O Lord, the humble beasts that bear with us the burden and heat of the day and offer their guileless lives for the well-being of humankind;
>
> And for the wild creatures, whom Thou hast made wise, strong, and beautiful,
>
> We supplicate for them Thy great tenderness of heart, for Thou hast promised to save both man [sic] and beast, and great is Thy loving kindness,
>
> O Master, Savior of the world.[61]

John Chrysostom not only emphasizes that humans should care for nonhuman creatures because they share the same origin we do,[62] but he argues that our futures are linked as well. "Just as the creature became corruptible when your [human] body became corruptible, so also when your body will be incorrupt, the creature will also follow after it and become corresponding to it."[63] Finally, Maximus the Confessor writes, "It is necessary that this world of things dies, just as a man [sic] dies, in order that it may rise again, young instead of old as it was before death. . . . And we who are man will also rise up, as part of the whole, as a small world within the big universe."[64]

Eighteenth-century Methodist leader John Wesley adds to this Christian insight by seeking to articulate why God might desire to redeem nonhuman creatures and what that redemption might entail. In his sermon entitled "The General Deliverance," Wesley states, "Nothing is more sure,"

60. Irenaeus, *Against Heresies*, bk. 5, ch. 33, 4.

61. Quoted in Linzey and Regan, *Compassion for Animals*, 86.

62. Krueger, *Cloud of Witnesses*, 121.

63. Ibid., 127.

64. Ibid., 168

than that God extends divine mercy to everything that God created.[65] He
goes on to note that it is difficult at times for members of creation, both
human and otherwise, to recognize God's mercy due to a "complication of
evils" that not only "oppress," but also "overwhelm" creation.[66] Wesley asserts that the language of Revelation 21, which affirms that God will make
all things new, wipe away tears, and eliminate pain, is not restricted merely
to human members of creation.[67] Although he is undoubtedly anthropo-
centrically hierarchical in his evaluation of the order of creation, he demonstrates an uncharacteristic theological imaginary both for his own time
period and for that of today in elucidating clearly God's care and sense of
justice for nonhuman creatures. "But though I doubt not that the Father
[sic] of All has a tender regard for even his lowest creatures, and that, in consequence of this, he will make them large amends for all they suffer while
under their present bondage."[68] Moreover, Wesley argues that God's sense
of justice is somehow thwarted if nonhuman creatures suffer now without
any hope of eschatological redemption. "May it not answer another end;
namely, furnish us with a full answer to a plausible objection against the
justice of God, in suffering numberless creatures that never had sinned to
be so severely punished. . . . But the objection vanishes away, if we consider
that something better remains after death for these poor creatures also; that
these, likewise, shall one day be delivered from this bondage of corruption,
and shall then receive an ample amends for all their present sufferings."[69]
Finally, and perhaps most exceptionally in relation to either his time period
or ours, he contends that God will not only redeem nonhuman creatures,
but make them "capable of knowing and loving and enjoying the Author of
their being."[70] Once again, while this statement is in the anthropocentric
context of humans being elevated in the consummation to the level of angels
and nonhuman creatures being raised to our previous unredeemed position, it shows incredible sensitivity toward nonhuman creatures and their
place in the eschaton. Wesley also says that there is an important ethical
payout to this theological affirmation: If God cares about nonhuman creatures this much, then should humans not demonstrate better care for them
as a result?[71]

65. Wesley, "General Deliverance," 1.
66. Ibid., 2.
67. Ibid., III.2.
68. Ibid., III.5.
69. Ibid., III.9.
70. Ibid., III.6.
71. Ibid., III.10.

Ultimately, if God's redemptive scheme is not cosmic, as many American Christians seem to think, then we run up against three significant problems. First, it seems to make no sense in light of the passages reviewed above. If the Word became flesh in order to redeem all things back to God, then that means all things. Second, the lack of a cosmic redemption makes little sense of God's declaration of creation's goodness recorded in Genesis, affirmed over and over again in the Psalms, and the supreme reaffirmation of that goodness in the incarnation event. Instead, we would view creation as merely instrumental to the salvation history of human beings, which leads to a final point. Third, God's morality or divine goodness is at stake if God does not redeem nonhuman creatures. In other words, the character of the God revealed to Abraham, Moses, and the rest of the Israelite people, along with the unique revelation through Jesus of Nazareth, suggests that God is a cosmic Redeemer. David Clough succinctly argues, "God must be understood to be the redeemer of all creatures, human and other-than-human, because God has determined to be gracious and faithful to them in this sphere, as well as in their creation and reconciliation, not because they would otherwise have a legitimate cause of complaint."[72] Anything less would mean that God is not the God of Jesus Christ we believe God to be.

Much more could be said about God our Redeemer, but this should inspire us to expand our theological imaginary significantly. A Christian witness that does not seek justice for the widows, orphans, and aliens, along with nonhuman creatures and the rest of creation, does not manifest the affirmation that God is our Redeemer, which was so critical to the history of Israel and the life of the early church. A Christian witness that does not take seriously the consummation of all things also does not fully consider the implications of God's work as Redeemer. While both the doctrines of God as Creator and Redeemer are fundamental on their own, they each receive new emphasis after the resurrection of Jesus.

72. Clough, *On Animals*, 148.

3

The Resurrection Hope as the Foundation for Creation Care

I was raised in and continue to associate myself with a denominational tradition that does little to celebrate Easter in the way that other Christian denominational traditions do. In fact, the leaders of the congregation of my youth often went to great lengths to remind us that Easter Sunday was just like any other Sunday; it was nothing special. If the tomb was really empty on Easter Sunday, though, and Jesus was really raised from the dead, then it is truly the most special of days to remember. While the Sundays of my youth might be uncommon in the greater landscape of American Christianity, discussion dedicated to the importance of Jesus' resurrection to our faith seems to occupy very little time in the lives of American Christians. Think about it: When was the last time outside of Easter Sunday that you heard a sermon about the resurrection? It appears fair to say that the resurrection does not play an active role in the practical articulation of our faith and the daily lives that we lead.

There is probably no singular reason for this. We live in a postmodern world wherein science allegedly no longer enjoys hegemonic control over truth claims, but some Christians at least still fear being ridiculed for holding onto a belief that cannot be proven scientifically. Objective interpretations of the resurrection affirming that the tomb was indeed empty and a transformed Jesus appeared to hundreds of witnesses can sound passé in a supposedly sophisticated culture like ours. While subjective interpretations of the resurrection may be more palatable for those who desire scientific verification for their truth claims, it has always been difficult for me to believe that persecuted Christians of the earliest centuries, especially the martyrs, affirmed anything less than a Jesus who was objectively raised from the dead by God. Why would someone be willingly tortured and killed for a belief that s/he did not believe was based upon an objective event? Perhaps American Christianity has failed to remember the centrality of the resurrection for the apostle Paul's witness and theology to the early church. In his letter to the Corinthian church, he reminds the Christians there that if Jesus is not raised from the dead, then their faith is in vain and they of all people should be pitied for hoping in a person and an event that did not actually occur.[1] Conceivably believing in the resurrection is an existential problem that affects us more than we would care to admit publicly. While the resurrection is a specific display of divine sovereignty (God really has power over death itself), maybe we really do not believe that "death has lost its sting,"[2] to borrow the apostle Paul's language, and we are ashamed that we live less than the magnanimous lives that God calls humans to live. Or is it possibly simpler than that? Whatever the answer, one thing is clear: American Christians have failed in relating the critical significance of the resurrection to our daily lives, even though it is the starting place for Christian ethics.[3] In particular, we have floundered in our duty to connect the relevance of the resurrection to the task of caring for creation, which has far more to do with our daily lives than we care to admit.

What Does It Mean that Jesus Was Resurrected?

N. T. Wright, perhaps the world's most articulate scholar on the importance of the resurrection to the Christian faith, argues that Jesus' resurrection indicates God's goodness as Creator and God's sense of justice as Redeemer.[4] It tells us much about the character of God and what God deems to be important. First of all, the resurrection of Jesus tells us that God's plan for us is not an escape from our bodies into some heavenly realm that exists above the clouds, but rather it signifies an ontological transformation. Jesus' body was literally transformed into something new, something that is no longer perishable, which becomes the symbol for the hope of our personal and collective future.[5] Just as the incarnation profoundly affirms the goodness of creation, so too does the resurrection of Jesus. The divine declaration of Genesis 1, that creation is very good, is not temporary, but rather eternal, as God's redemptive plan is to transform the material nature of creation, not reject it or destroy it. Moreover, the resurrection of Jesus does not signify that only humans will be transformed because humans are the only "good"

1. 1 Cor 15:19.
2. 1 Cor 15:55.
3. O'Donovan, *Resurrection*.
4. Wright, *Surprised by Hope*, 27.
5. 1 Cor 15:42–44

members of creation. As discussed earlier, early Christians had little difficulty believing in a truly cosmic redemption. "They believed that God was
going to do for the whole cosmos what he had done for Jesus at Easter."[6] By
raising Jesus from the dead, God demonstrates that God has power over the
one thing that seemed to be incapable of being defeated—death. And death
does not have the final say over what God proclaims to be good, whether it
be human or otherwise. God, not death, is the sole determiner of what has
value in both the present and the future, and God has decided not to aban-
don creation to the nothingness of death. The resurrection of Jesus shows us
that the story of the universe is far richer than we could ever have imagined.

The resurrection of Jesus also signifies the divine commitment to justice. This happens in two ways. First, one of the difficulties of our present
situation is that what we do in the present has no guarantee of existing in
or being carried into the future. Death constantly threatens to erase the efficacy of our charitable activities or the legacy of our righteous works. It
even threatens to steal away the knowledge and feelings of love that we
have for one another. Accepting this as just another aspect of the human
condition does little to negate the fact that it is unfair that our good deeds
and our love for each other are denied permanence by the specter of death.
The resurrection of Jesus signals that God recognizes this unfairness and
promises not to forget the significance of our lives. What we do actually
matters now and matters in the future, even when we are gone. Second,
in our overwhelming American Christian preoccupation with the idea that
the crucifixion of Jesus forgives us of our sins, we often fail to remember
and emphasize the fact that if Jesus really was who he said he was (i.e., he
was not looking to overthrow the Roman Empire militarily or politically),
then his death sentence was patently unjust. His crucifixion was a shameful
mockery of justice. In this sense, Jesus' resurrection shows that death does
not have the final say over what is just or unjust—God does. It would be
easy for someone outside of the Christian tradition to say that all the resurrection does is provide an eschatological "mulligan" that rights all of the
wrongs that cannot be corrected in our present situation. The resurrection,
though, should not be considered as an eschatological bandage that excuses
present or past injustices like slavery, war, or gender inequality, but instead
it gives us an insight into a way of living that God actually desires for us
and makes possible for us to live now. Through the resurrection of Jesus,
God is declaring that injustice is neither an intended part of God's good
creation nor a component of the divine redemptive scheme. The resurrection should propel us to a different sort of activity in our present situation as

6. Wright, *Surprised by Hope*, 93.

we are confronted directly with how the kingdom of God actually functions. Justice is of eternal significance, not injustice. Goodness is part of God's kingdom, not evil.

These two concepts, the resurrection's affirmation of God's identity as a good Creator and God's commitment to justice as our Redeemer, have radical implications for how Christians live on this planet today and how we interact with the rest of the nonhuman environment that surrounds us. But before we can turn to that, we must first deal with the stark reality that while Christians affirm living in a post-resurrection universe, we still live in a place that is marked by grief, pain, and injustice. We live hoping for the better future that the resurrection of Jesus signifies, knowing that God's kingdom is present in the simultaneous state of already and not yet. It is the idea of the resurrection as the basis for our hope that we must now explicate.

Christian Hope and Its Relationship to the Resurrection

What do you think of when you hear the word "hope" used or use it yourself? "I hope I get a new car for my birthday." "I hope it rains tonight because our garden really needs it." "I hope I make a good grade in Doran's class." The way we use "hope" in the American vernacular generally connotes a desire or wish for a specific outcome. While we would like to say that we have some sort of expectation for that outcome to occur, we do not often live according to that expectation. The connotation of "hope" in the three examples above, at some level, demonstrates a lack of certainty in a desired future outcome. While we might truly wish for a beneficial outcome, we may in fact be preparing ourselves for disappointment.

Others contend that hope is really just a synonym for optimism. Famed Australian public intellectual Clive Hamilton makes just this sort of contention. The ability of the mind to see some sort of benefit in the midst of tragedy could very well be an adaptive strategy that allows us to cope with pain and suffering without becoming debilitated. "Self-aggrandizing fictions help us maintain control over our situations. Feeling that we have control over events in our lives has been shown repeatedly to be essential to effective functioning."[7] But, like any other good adaptive strategy, optimism can get out of hand; it can become unrealistic. Within the phenomenon of unrealistic optimism lie illusion and delusion. "Illusions respond and adapt to reality as it forces itself on us, while delusions are held despite the

7. Hamilton, *Requiem for a Species*, 130.

evidence of the outside world."[8] Hamilton goes on to argue that the paradox is dramatic: while pessimism often leads people to "passivity and brooding," optimism, whether unrealistic or sensible, is more likely to lead people to significant action.[9] And yet, "Optimism sustained against the facts . . . risks turning hopes into fantasies."[10]

In the biblical witness, the concept of hope (based upon the Greek word *elpis*) has a connotation far different than mere desire or wishful thinking or unrealistic optimism. In the Old Testament, to expect something is not a neutral idea; one has a future expectation of a good event or a bad event.[11] To expect a good event is to be hopeful, whereas to expect a bad event is to be fearful. If one is hopeful and thus expecting a good event to occur, that expectation is often closely linked with trust. One of the central questions of Scripture is whether or not one can trust that a person, a deity, or a government has the ability to make that expectation a reality. There is also an element of yearning or patience involved in waiting for the expected outcome to happen. The early Christian concept of hope is based upon this Old Testament understanding. "If hope is fixed on God, it embraces at once the three elements of expectation of the future, trust, and the patience of waiting."[12] Each of these characteristics seems to be emphasized at different moments by New Testament writers. For instance, the apostle Paul notes that Abraham "hoped against hope" that he would become the father of many nations.[13] In this sense all three elements of being hopeful were on display: Abraham had a specific expectation of a good future outcome (he was to become the father of the Israelite people), he trusted in God to provide this outcome (God had delivered on promises in the past), and he waited patiently (in this case, past typical childbearing years). This situation details for us what Paul seems to believe is the paradox of hope: it is when we can no longer trust in what we can control and therefore trust solely in God's ability to deliver that we become hopeful.[14]

It is this sense of trust that bears a bit more exploration. We can put our trust in any sort of person or structure (economic, political, social, etc.), and in fact we do so regularly. But, does that person or structure actually have the capacity to perform consistently? Has that person or structure

8. Ibid., 131.

9. Ibid.

10. Ibid., 132.

11. Kittel, *Theological Dictionary*, 2:522.

12. Ibid., 2:531.

13. Rom 4:18.

14. Kittel, *Theological Dictionary*, 2:531.

really earned our trust because she, he, or it can deliver on promises? The witnesses of Abraham and countless other figures of Scripture attest to this very situation: we inevitably place our trust in someone or something, so where will we ultimately place it? The answer for Abraham and many others in Scripture is God.[15] This sense of trust will become more important later on when we investigate what other structures or systems we place our trust in, e.g., economic structures and food-production systems.

For the early church, the resurrection of Jesus clearly signaled a new understanding of God's interaction with creation and consequently the divine notion of hope. The resurrection of Jesus is God's ultimate answer to the question in whom should we place our hope. God made it clear through the resurrection that we can confidently expect God to make good on any and all divine promises. The resurrection of Jesus becomes the Christian basis for hope because, against all odds, God defeated death and demonstrated soundly that God's power and future plans will not be thwarted even by the most significant of enemies. The link between the resurrection and hope, according to Jürgen Moltmann, could not be more clear. "Christian hope is resurrection hope, and it proves its truth in the contradiction of the future prospects thereby offered and guaranteed for righteousness as opposed to sin, life as opposed to death, glory as opposed to suffering, peace as opposed to dissension."[16] The resurrection is God's definitive answer to suffering, evil, and death, which for Christians is the basis for being hopeful. Moreover, it is a "living" or "lively" hope[17] because God is impacting our lives presently, bringing good news to us now while we are in desperate need. In light of this investigation, and for the purposes of the rest of this study, I shall employ the following definition: Christian hope is a confident expectation of a good and novel outcome delivered by God. While this definition may not be exhaustive, I believe it does well to honor the three components (expectation, trust, and patience) of the biblical notion. Specifically, it recognizes God's ability to deliver an outcome rather than the human capacity, whether individual or structural (economic, political, social, etc.), to do such. It bears reiterating that this is fundamentally why the link between the resurrection and hope is so critical for Christians. The resurrection is a clear demonstration that God has the capacity to deliver a

15. For example, see Pss 31:24; 39:7; 42:5; 62:5; 130:5; Isa 40:30–1; Jer 14:22; 29:11; Lam 3:24.

16. Moltmann, *Theology of Hope*, 4. For more on the Christian notion of hope see Bloch, *Principle of Hope*; Rahner, *Theological Investigations*, 242–59; Thomas Aquinas, *Summa Theologica*, II.II, qq17–22.

17. 1 Pet 1:3. For more on "living" or "lively" hope, see Ramsey, *1 Peter*, 19; Elliott, *1 Peter*, 334.

good and novel outcome, something that is unprecedented, out of even the direst of circumstances.

The Christian understanding of hope then is not merely a synonym for optimism. Optimism often connotes a blind inevitability that all will be well, regardless of the evidence that might say otherwise. Being optimistic is based upon a trust in our capacity to achieve something out of nothing or in some cosmic notion of fate. Christian hope, however, is different. It is reasonably skeptical of the human capacity to bring good out of the deepest tragedy because humans lack the power to do so. It also rejects the concept of fate because fate has no power over death and no power to redeem injustice. Things do not just get better because fate makes it so. Instead, Christian hope trusts in the sovereignty of God and patiently anticipates the novel, unprecedented possibilities that divine grace inspires for the future. Christian hope acknowledges that God is actively working in the world. Whereas unrealistic optimism can lead to illusions and delusions, Christian hope is a living hope essentially connected to the present as it critiques the injustices that plague both the human and nonhuman "least of these." Unrealistic optimism that leads to illusion and delusion does not demand that humans seek solidarity with and act on behalf of the oppressed, as it relies on the inevitability of goodness to overcome; consequently, it supports the unjust status quo, even if only unwittingly. Christian hope, on the other hand, fosters solidarity with the least of these and demands action from those who believe in the resurrection. Christian hope is intrinsically active, as it requires one "to do justice and to love kindness";[18] it does not merely sit passively and wait for God to clean up the mess.

What Does It Mean to Hope?

Is hope a disposition of the will? Is it an emotional commitment? Or perhaps something else entirely? According to Thomistic philosopher Josef Pieper, hoping for something is a volitional act, which is based upon a specific notion of what type of creatures human beings are. We find ourselves in the *status viatoris*; we are in "the condition or state of being on the way."[19] As creatures who even in our dying breath find ourselves on the way, we experience simultaneously the absence of fulfillment as well as an orientation toward fulfillment; we constantly live in the state of not yet. "The virtue of hope is preeminently the virtue of the *status viatoris*; it is the proper virtue of

18. Mic 6:8, ESV.
19. Pieper, *Faith, Hope, Love*, 91.

the 'not yet.'"[20] He goes on to assert that if we conceive of hope as a "natural" virtue, then hope leans toward magnanimity, in the classical sense of greatness of mind or heart, with humility protecting us against vice. The problem is that natural hope can be directed toward good as well as toward evil, since it can be oriented toward a good end or be a false hope that one eventually finds unfulfilling, if not destructive. Because of this Pieper contends that hope is a theological virtue because hope must be oriented toward God if it is to find its true fulfillment—happiness in God.[21] Christ, then, is both the foundation and fulfillment of our hope. "This inherent linking of our hope to Christ is so crucial that one who is not in Christ has no hope (1 Th 4:13)."[22] Ultimately, Pieper does not reject the idea that hope is an attitude, but simultaneously affirms that a human being chooses one's attitude, and consequentially one's conduct, according to a decision of the will.[23] In other words, one chooses whether to accept Christ as the foundation and fulfillment of one's hope, and that decision makes one a hopeful person or not in both attitude and deed. In short, one chooses to be hopeful.

For theologian and philosopher John Macquarrie, hope is something more than merely an act of the will; it has emotional, volitional, and intellectual aspects to its character, none of which can be completely separated from the other. He calls hope an attitude. "By this I mean it is a set or disposition of the whole person, a stance or posture which one takes up toward experience or sectors of experience, and from which one relates to such experience."[24] Attitude, according to Macquarrie, connotes two important features. First, an attitude can be a well-founded belief that a person has about the world; there is a cognitive aspect to it. Second, an attitude is not entirely based upon cognitive reflection on past experience; it also involves a certain amount of "feel" for the world. "Such attitudes also promote some kinds of behavior rather than others, and encourage a measure of consistency in behavior."[25] The emotional aspect of hope deals with the positive mood we might have when we exhibit a hopeful attitude.[26] Such elements of this mood might be trust and expectancy, and thus, perhaps, an openness to one's environment as one waits for the future to become the present. The

20. Ibid., 98.

21. Ibid., 100.

22. Ibid., 106.

23. Ibid., 114.

24. Macquarrie, *Christian Hope*, 5.

25. Ibid.

26. Ibid., 6–7.

antithesis of a positive hopeful mood would be the emotional doldrums brought on by fear.

Macquarrie agrees with Pieper that there is a volitional aspect to the character of hope. "Hope can only begin to have its definite influence on action and to produce policies of action when it has been made more specific and raised to the level of a settled disposition."[27] Three features are fundamental to his understanding of the volitional aspect of hope. The first of these is hope's relation to freedom. If the world is completely deterministic, then there is no possibility for hope. "Hope implies that there is, so to speak, an empty space before us that affords us room for action; or, to put it in a slightly different way, an open road along which we can choose to move."[28] The second he refers to is hope as the dynamic of action. Humans only choose to act if they believe they can reach the goals of their actions. Both extreme optimism as well as extreme pessimism can lead one to hopelessness because of the distinct possibility of not reaching an achievable goal. Hope strives for a good that might be terribly difficult to attain, but it is definitely possible to achieve. And the third feature is hope serving as a moral and social critique. If hope is truly seeking to actualize a good future, then hope undoubtedly criticizes the present situation for its injustice, violence, cruelty, etc. "This close connection between hope and judgment cannot be too strongly stressed. . . . This note of judgment is nothing different from the vision of hope. It is simply the other side of the single reality. To cherish a hope is not to escape into dream and fantasy. It is, as we have seen, to embrace that which is difficult but possible to attain—possible because there is a righteous God at work in the world."[29]

While Pieper's insistence on hope being purely an activity of the will is helpful, it seems to me that Macquarrie is onto something when he says that hope relies on cognitive as well as emotional aspects of human nature. In particular, I argue that the biblical concept of hope suggests more than a volitional act. The conditions of expectation, trust, and patience connoted by hope demand more than just cognition and an activity of the will. One wagers one's entire existence on whether or not God raised Jesus from the dead; it is not solely an act of the will. The depth of this existential wager is further witnessed to by Jesus' own articulation of the first commandment, "Love the Lord your God with all your heart and with all your soul and with all your strength and with all your mind."[30] Therefore, for a Christian to

27. Ibid., 8.
28. Ibid.
29. Ibid., 37.
30. Luke 10:27.

believe in and live according to a hope that is a confident expectation of a good and novel outcome delivered by God is to place one's entire existence (heart, soul, strength, and mind) humbly at the feet of the God who raised Jesus from the dead. To hope in God, then, is to spur one into a type of activity that not only critiques the present, but also simultaneously strives toward accomplishing that which does not seem possible. It is not a passive waiting game wherein we do nothing until Jesus returns.

The Opposite of Hope

Pieper argues that there are two types of hopelessness: despair and presumption. Both despair and presumption have their roots in the same problem; they both anticipate faulty expectations of fulfillment. "Against all reality, they transform the 'not yet' of hope into either the 'not' or the 'already' of fulfillment."[31] Despair is "a perverse anticipation of the nonfulfillment of hope," a decision of the will that hope will not be fulfilled. In other words, it is a decision to give up on God's promises too early and then to adopt the disposition that God has not acted and will not act on the matter in the future. Pieper maintains that despair is a particularly pernicious sin because "it threatens man's [sic] moral existence, for man's self-realization is linked to hope."[32] Macquarrie also sees despair as dangerous, but from a slightly different vantage point. "In despair, a person surrenders the possibility of action, for all courses of action seem equally futile. [One's] mind is prey to apathy and indifference, and the result is inaction."[33] Pieper's identification of the source of despair is also elucidative. "[T]he beginning and the root of despair is *acedia*, sloth."[34] Sloth is not merely the lack of activity or a debilitating form of laziness. These are only secondary consequences of a primary cause. The primary cause of sloth is sorrow toward the good or a sadness about living the good life to which God calls humanity. Eventually, sloth is especially destructive because one lacks the capacity to care about the fact that one no longer cares about living the good life God intends. In an American Protestant Christian landscape, which does not often take the classical list of the seven deadly sins seriously, we might suppose that the opposite of sloth is merely industry, employment, or diligence, but it is not. Pieper asserts that the opposite of sloth is magnanimity, which is not merely the virtue of doing great things, but the great things that God desires for

31. Pieper, *Faith, Hope, Love*, 113.

32. Ibid., 116.

33. Macquarrie, *Christian Hope*, 10.

34. Pieper, *Faith, Hope, Love*, 117; italics in original.

humans actually to accomplish, whom God created to do great things. "One who is trapped in *acedia* has neither the courage nor the will to be as great as he [*sic*] really is. He would prefer to be less great in order thus to avoid the obligation of greatness. *Acedia* is a perverted humility."[35] This is the sort of perverted humility that Moses demonstrated when he told Yahweh that he was too ineloquent to serve as God's emissary to the Pharaoh.[36]

Presumption, on the other hand, has to do with the "already" aspect of fulfillment; it is "a perverse anticipation of the fulfillment of hope."[37] Presumption is hope's "fraudulent imitation" because it assumes that God's plan has already reached its fulfillment by denying the "not yet" part of reality.[38] Pieper's identification of the root of presumption is again illuminating. He contends, "For the essential nature of presumption is, as Saint Augustine says, a 'perversa securitas', a self-deceptive reliance on a security that has no existence in reality."[39] The source is a false sense of self-esteem continually affirmed by the individual's own will and derived from a lack of humility, "a denial of one's actual creatureliness and an unnatural claim to being like God."[40] This sort of hopelessness is likely manifested when we place our trust in ourselves or other structures rather than in God.

The Resurrection Is the Answer to Presumption and Despair

Far too many American Christians live under the impression that the resurrection has everything to do with living with God eternally and little, if anything, to do with how we live on Earth now. This, however, is not the Christian message of hope that inspired the early church to care for widows, orphans, and aliens, to break down social norms that separated males from females, and ultimately to be executed for their faith. The contemporary interpretation is one of despair or presumption. As a message of despair, we live as if the resurrection has no impact at all on our present reality, as if God does not work currently to bring sight to the blind and good news to the poor.[41] Perhaps we are legitimately overwhelmed by the injustice we see daily in the world and have become convinced that there is nothing

35. Ibid., 119.
36. Exod 6:30.
37. Pieper, *Faith, Hope, Love*, 113.
38. Ibid., 124.
39. Ibid., 125.
40. Ibid., 127.
41. Luke 4:18–9.

we can really do to affect it; so we become apathetic or indifferent, which leads to inaction and supports the status quo. Either way, by acting as if God's kingdom has no impact on today's world, we become slothful, which leads to despair. It is confounding to imagine ourselves as slothful because Americans are very busy people, but as we fail to live the magnanimous lives that God created us to live and that resurrection hope should inspire us to live, we become deeply filled with despair.

American Christians can also both implicitly and explicitly preach a message of presumption—a message that claims aspects of God's kingdom are completely manifest in the present. Market-based capitalism must be the divinely inspired form of economy because it has brought so much prosperity to so many people; representative democracy must be the divinely preferred form of political government because all are created equal by nature's God; and the United States must be God's new Israel because we have prospered so greatly and wielded power so benevolently. This presumptive attitude prevents us from seeing injustice as it is. While capitalism has indeed created a vast amount of wealth, it tends to place that wealth into the pockets of fewer and fewer people as the chasm between the wealthy and poor becomes even more gaping. While, perhaps, white men who owned land in the eighteenth century were created equal by nature's God, persons of color and women have found themselves poorly represented politically throughout many, if not most, parts of American history. And while generations of Americans have believed and continue to affirm that America is particularly prized in God's providential plan, this seems rather disconnected from the general New Testament notion that the church is the new Israel. Like despair, presumption can also create a spirit of apathy and indifference, which ultimately leads to inaction. What injustice is there actually to address if we are living in the "already" of God's plan for us?

Both despair and presumption radically neglect the hope of the resurrection and its impact on our present situation. The Christian belief in the resurrection should inspire us to live hopefully because it compels us to live a different life in the present, precisely because Jesus was resurrected. Wright puts it this way: "Precisely because the resurrection has happened as an event *within our own world*, its implications and effects are to be felt within our own world, here and now."[42] The resurrection means that the good works we do are meaningful now and are carried into the future by God because death no longer has the power to wipe them out of existence. "What you do in the present—by painting, preaching, singing, sewing, praying, teaching, building hospitals, digging wells, campaigning for justice,

42. Wright, *Surprised by Hope*, 191; italics in original.

writing poems, caring for the needy, loving your neighbor as yourself—will last into God's future. These activities are not simply ways of making the present life a little less beastly, a little more bearable, until the day when we leave it behind altogether. They are part of what we may call building for God's kingdom."[43] Living now in the post-resurrection age of the Spirit, God emboldens us to help transform as much of the "not yet" of the future kingdom into the "already." One could even say that God dares us to do so. This is the daring divine proposition that we have been given in light of the hope of the resurrection, which calls humans anew to the great task to which we are commissioned: act as if we were created in the image of God.

As discussed already, hope offers a critique or judgment on the present situation because it stands in stark contrast to God's vision for the future. Moltmann asserts, "Hope finds in Christ not only a consolation *in* suffering, but also the protest of the divine promise *against* suffering. . . . Those who hope in Christ can no longer put up with reality as it is, but begin to suffer under it, to contradict it."[44] But despair mutes this critique while presumption renders the judgment meaningless, as each form of hopelessness disposes one to apathy and indifference, and consequently inaction. Apathy and indifference are especially deleterious for American Christians because in our apathy- and indifference-induced inaction, we implicitly and explicitly support the status quo of injustice, violence, and suffering, which allows us, for instance, to continue upholding our standard of living rather comfortably, but disengages us from the critical reflection that hope demands. Ellen Davis maintains that prophetic speech, the combination of judgment and a vision of hope, "is the antidote to the illness from which we are not eager to recover, namely, apathy—the inability to feel shock, horror, and remorse for our actions."[45] Furthermore, the resurrection hope should cause us to live a new life, a life characterized by the hopefulness that God offers. And yet, we must not be discouraged because we are not the source of the future or the novel possibilities that God's future holds. For this future, according to the prophets, is "qualitatively new, wholly unprecedented."[46] Moltmann contends, "The believing hope will itself provide inexhaustible resources for the creative, inventive imagination of love. It constantly provokes and produces thinking of an anticipatory kind in love to man [*sic*] and the world, in order to give shape to the newly dawning possibilities in the light of the promised future, in order as far as possible to create here the

43. Ibid., 193.

44. Moltmann, *Theology of Hope*, 7; italics in original.

45. Davis, *Scripture, Culture, and Agriculture*, 14.

46. Bauckham and Hart, *Hope against Hope*, 78–80.

best that is possible, because what is promised is within the bounds of the possibility."[47] We can really ask whether capitalism is a just kind of economy, particularly if we take seriously the vantage point of the preferential option for the poor.[48] We can really ask whether there is environmental justice for all communities or just the ones that happen to have a particular skin color and deep pocketbooks. Hope then opens up these possibilities because, as Bauckham and Hart argue, "Hope is . . . an activity of imaginative faith."[49]

The hope we find through the resurrection of Jesus is not just the source of novel possibilities; it is also the source of our courage to transform those possibilities into reality. Jesus' resurrection proves that God has the power over death, which for Christians should be the foundation for our inspiration to live truly magnanimous lives. This affirmation should provide Christians with an immense source of courage in the face of the threat of physical pain, violence, or even death itself. While the "principalities and powers,"[50] governments in particular, attempt to make us fearful and thus hopeless through the threat of death, we must bear witness that this threat was rendered ineffectual by the empty tomb. While I acknowledge that this is easier said than done, we must reflect frequently on the fact that the scattered disciples returned courageously to preach on Pentecost and were imprisoned shortly thereafter due to their witness. These courageous acts are part of a long history of Christian martyrdom, witnessed by the earliest Christians, that should remind us that death holds no power over the life that God calls us to live.[51] We need courage not just in the face of physical harm, but we need courage in the face of popular opposition, shame, and severe discouragement. If hope inspires us to criticize unjust ways of living for what they are and suggest novel solutions to injustice, then we must stand courageously in the face of diligent opposition from our neighbors, governments, transnational corporations, and the rest of the "principalities and powers." In this sense, courage does not incite us to be aggressive, but rather to stand firm and endure that which challenges us to relent.[52] The resurrection hope should compel us to lead magnanimous lives precisely because God is the wellspring of the courage it takes to live this way. I am

47. Moltmann, *Theology of Hope*, 19.

48. See Gutiérrez, *Theology of Liberation*.

49. Bauckham and Hart, *Hope against Hope*, 53. See also Macquarrie, *Christian Hope*, 13–14; and Moltmann, *Ethics of Hope*, 40.

50. See Eph 3:10; 6:12; Col 1:16; 2:15.

51. For more on this, see Ferguson, *Early Christians Speak*, 197–225; Arnold, *Early Christians in Their Own Words*, 59–98.

52. For more on courage as the ability to endure, see Thomas Aquinas, *Summa Theologica* II.II, q123, a6.

skeptical about the ability of optimism, whether realistic or not, to inspire the necessary courage to face severe opposition or the specter of death. The disciples who built the early church were not optimistic that things would work out in the end, but confidently expected that God would provide because God had done so over and over in the past. Moreover, optimism does not have the capacity to help us stand and endure injustice because it is relies solely upon the reservoirs of strength that the human potential can provide and that the principalities and powers are keen to extinguish. The resurrection, however, shows that the God of Jesus Christ is able to endure and rise victorious despite the best efforts of the principalities and powers.

In the end, as John Cobb puts it so eloquently, "We know that we are not masters of history, but neither are we mere victims."[53] It appears that God expects much from us, as we are to be magnanimous rather than slothful. At the same time, we must remember our place in the universe: we are creatures and so we must remain humble. Magnanimity and humility are two critical elements to living hopefully.[54] This again differentiates Christian hope from mere optimism. Optimism does not exhort us to be great nor does it remind us of our creatureliness. It has no underlying anthropology that reminds us of who we are and who we are called to be. It merely wishes for the best outcome possible, but it cannot compel us to great feats. God invites us to work alongside of God in the construction of new and enduring things that will mark the "already" portion of God's kingdom. Hope also challenges us to ask whether "not yet" aspects of kingdom living can be made part of our present reality. While we do not have the ability to eliminate tears and sorrow completely, we do have the capacity to imagine novel possibilities to deal with injustice and violence by listening for God's whispers of grace. For example, can we imagine an economic order that has justice and ecological integrity as its goal? Can we imagine a food system that not only feeds people nutritionally dense food, but also does not denude the rest of the natural landscape in the process? According to Bauckham and Hart, "To be a Christian might be defined as living in the light cast by the resurrection; living, that is to say, as those who insist on interpreting this world in terms of its (surprising and unexpected) future as made known to us in the resurrection of Jesus by his Father and in the power of the Holy Spirit."[55] This is the vocation of the Christian and it connects us to an ethic of creation care.

53. Cobb, *Sustainability*, 11.
54. Pieper, *Faith, Hope, Love*, 127.
55. Bauckham and Hart, *Hope against Hope*, 70.

The Foundation of Creation Care

There is no doubt that the challenges are vast, and viable solutions to the wicked problems of climate change seem nearly impossible to imagine— hundreds of millions of climate refugees in the coming decades due to climate-disrupted famine, drought, and disease, on one hand; the human-induced extinction of a radical amount of the biodiversity God created, on another; from greenhouse gases changing the physical composition of our oceans to the point where marine creatures can no longer create shells to live within; to unpredictable weather events that alter agricultural patterns that human civilizations have relied upon for millennia. Moreover, the effects of any tenable solutions (if that is even the correct word) of mitigation or adaptation may take generations for us to see and evaluate their potency, which can cause shortsighted creatures like us to become even more hopeless and thus concentrate more heavily on our own situation here in the immediate present.

Additionally, far too many American Christians do not affirm creation care as a part of their faith, as evidenced by its lack of explicit witness in our daily lives. We tend to exist in lives of hopelessness, mired in both despair and presumption, especially if we consider the countless intentional and unintentional decisions we make that affect creation and therefore us. Being presumptive and full of despair robs us of our ability to engage in the critique of the present that hope demands, while at the same time preventing us from listening to the novel possibilities that God offers that can actually transform the "not yet" into the "already" of hope. Sloth-induced inaction by Christians, which also permeates much of our culture, only further encourages people to believe that the principalities and powers have truly won. We have declined the obligation of greatness that God has bestowed upon us and instead we implicitly and explicitly embrace the status quo since, in many ways, it seems to benefit Christians in the United States greatly every day. Hope in the age of climate change seems harder than ever to come by.

I cannot help thinking that our circumstances are in some manner analogous to what the first disciples encountered when they scattered after the crucifixion of Jesus. They had followed a man for years who ended up in the same way that anyone else who took on Rome did. Hope was lost. It appeared as if God had deserted them. In the light of the empty tomb, though, God's activity was manifest and the work that Jesus' followers needed to do became clear. It was through the witness of the resurrection that the earliest Christians demonstrated that hope is truly an activity of an imaginative and courageous faith. We must remember that we stand on this side of the resurrection. We stand in the light of unprecedented divine possibility. We are dared by God to be witnesses of a lively hope; we must not allow the darkness of the present situation, the dimness of what a future might look like, or the lack of sufficient political will about climate change to dictate our Christian response. This resurrection hope makes it possible to do novel transformative work in and for creation. It should give us the imagination and courage to confront the principalities and powers and witness to God's work as Creator and Redeemer. We must respond by thinking and living hopefully every day. The reality of the resurrection demands this sort of call to action. We have magnanimous and courageous work to do as Christians; we have creation-care work to do now.

4

Are We Really Stewards?

C hristians in the United States often demonstrate just what sort of inter-
esting creatures human beings are when it comes to discussing the relationship between science and theology. For instance, many claim that they
do not "believe" in evolution. While it is difficult to understand precisely
what this means and why it is that many hold this view,[1] I think much of it
has to do with the resistance of many Christians to the component of evolutionary theory called "common descent." If humans descended from apes,
then the idea of human uniqueness is seemingly lost, which means, to some
at least, that we must relinquish the idea of being made in the image of God.
This is in itself a problematic statement because it misrepresents a critical
understanding of evolutionary biology: humans did not descend from apes,
but humans and apes descended from a common ape-like ancestor. While
this misunderstanding may or may not alter the question of human uniqueness, it signals the stakes for so many Christians: we believe that humans are
the most unique and special of God's creatures.

At the same time, many of these same Christians do not "believe" in
climate change because they remain unconvinced that humans could possibly cause a global disaster on the scale that many scientists say is currently
occurring and will only worsen in the future, because this suggests that humans are somehow encroaching upon the sovereignty of God by causing a
premature end to human civilization as we know it. Implicitly, and perhaps
explicitly, these Christians believe that humans are just not special enough
or powerful enough to thwart God's plans for creation, especially those God
has for humans. But how can so many hold these two views at the same
time? How is it that American Christians can simultaneously believe that
we are the most unique creatures of God's creation, made in the very image
of God, but not actually special enough to cause the extinction of countless species and radically change the way of life for trillions of creatures,

1. I, for one, am firmly convinced that evolution is the correct scientific theory that
explains the rise of biological complexity on our planet.

both human and nonhuman? Our ability to revel in the affirmation that we are made in God's image and simultaneously deny that we have the capacity to irrevocably change the course of biological life on this planet as we know it demonstrates how utterly intriguing, and possibly self-delusional, we human creatures really are. On the one hand, we have become hubristic in our attempt to claim a uniqueness that separates us entirely from the rest of creation; while on the other hand, we simultaneously proclaim to be humble, which may in fact be a charade. When it comes to understanding what role we play in God's creation, and especially as we examine the possible causes of and solutions to environmental disaster, we must analyze the dominant themes that shape our theological and social imaginaries about what it means to be human.

What Is Our Role?

The idea of humans playing the role of stewards of creation appears to be the "default position" of most Christians.[2] Unfortunately, many, if not most, Christians cannot articulate successfully what it means to be a steward nor do we tend to live by any reasonable measure as good stewards of creation in our daily lives. Perhaps Bill McKibben states it best: "No one stands up and declares that we should be bad stewards of the land. But this of course is [the problem]—the idea of "stewardship" is so lacking in content as to give us very little guidance about how to behave in any given situation. (In fact, many of the worst stewards of the earth are the most vociferous in talking about stewardship.)"[3] If we really did know how to act as stewards, then we would not be in the ecological mess that we are in. If pressed, I think the average Christian in the United States believes that being a steward of creation involves the following: First and foremost, a good steward exercises the divine mandate in Genesis 1:28, "Be fruitful and multiply, and fill the earth and subdue it; and have dominion over the fish of the sea and over the birds of the air and over every living thing that moves upon the earth." For many, the mandate to subdue and have dominion is a significant, if only implicitly stated, component of exercising stewardship. We must "whip" nature into shape if we are to fulfill this divine commandment given solely to us. This may be the only divine commandment that we carry out so willingly. But herein lies the crux of the matter: most Christians think little about stewarding creation past this particular mandate, at least if we measure it by the way we live daily. Our lives reflect a complete lack of thought about

2. Southgate, "Stewardship," 185.
3. McKibben, *Comforting Whirlwind*, 51.

whether our ability to be fruitful and multiply should be restrained in order to let other creatures have the same opportunity, which was mandated by God's covenant with Noah and the rest of creation after the flood.

If pressed further, we might say stewardship means taking care of someone else's property or responsibly managing the resources given to us by another party. We might remember as well something about the parable of the talents told by Jesus in the Gospels of Matthew and Luke. The American Christian interpretation of that parable often has a direct financial connotation to it, i.e., we are to steward the financial resources that God gives us. For others, who focus more on the English translation of "talent," there is a connotation that God has given us talents or gifts that God expects us to use wisely or multiply so that we might maximize our human potential. Strangely enough, we do not actually entertain the very real task of assessing our stewardship record, which is something that Jesus' parable makes abundantly explicit.[4] We merely assume that we are quite good stewards. Yet, we reflect very little upon whether our stewardship practices are building Christlike character within us. We fail to have serious conversations about how we would justify our stewardship behavior to the one who actually "owns" creation.

The charge to be stewards is undoubtedly a difficult one. "Stewards are charged with a seemingly contradictory obligation: they are to promote the good of the Landowner through conservation and through change. On the one hand, stewards are to preserve what is valuable and essential; on the other they are to profit the owner through risking the estate, by making changes in what is entrusted to their care. How can they do both—preserve and change; conserve and risk?"[5] Our collective laissez-faire attitude toward this supposedly bedrock Christian idea unfortunately seems to justify any sort of behavior that satisfies the "subdue" and "dominion" aspects of the command, no matter how vulgar and unChristlike that behavior might be. Anthropogenic climate change and a human-induced extinction event that rivals anything the Earth has witnessed in millions of years are just some of the legacies of Christian nonchalance toward actual stewardship of creation. It is no wonder that Lynn White's oft-repeated critique of Christianity for its failure to promote an ecologically minded theological imaginary continues to resonate for so many outside of the faith.[6]

4. Matt 25:14–31.

5. Reichenbach and Anderson, "Tensions," 113. These two go on to list five "important and difficult" questions that Christians spend very little time discussing: What are we to change? Is change permissible or obligatory? For what purpose are we to change? What are the limits of the change? What are the risks of change?

6. White, "Historic Roots," 1203–7.

While some believe that the idea of a human stewardship of creation should no longer be seriously considered for an ecologically minded theological imaginary, there are still those that defend it confidently. Douglas John Hall offers the most theologically sophisticated version of stewardship, but starts with the following frank confession: "At this point we must try to be quite honest with ourselves. It is true that stewardship has been retained in our New World Christianity; but it is equally true that it has been retained in a form that scarcely lends itself to the larger meaning and usage we need today. What we have by way of stewardship in our churches is in fact a drastically reduced version of the biblical concept."[7] In framing the relationship of humankind to "otherkind," Hall considers three formulations.[8] The first is the traditional witness of Christians: humanity above nature. Humans believe that being made in the divine image means we are endowed with gifts (e.g., the capacity to think rationally) that make us so distinct that we are vastly superior to the rest of creation. This formulation has tremendous difficulties, though, since human priorities historically always seem to win out over those of other creatures. The second he designates humanity in nature." The characterization of this relationship seeks to correct the idea that humans are so radically different from other creatures that we are not a part of creation by placing humans alongside other creatures in value and purpose to God. Ultimately, this position is problematic because it does not take into account the differences that humans actually do exhibit in contrast to the rest of creation. Finally, Hall's theology of stewardship relies on a third depiction: humanity with nature. With this position Hall seeks to balance the creatureliness of humanity that makes us similar to the rest of the creation with the differences that allow us to be called by God to a particular vocation. "On the one hand, the steward is singled out for special responsibility. The steward is different. Unlike the other servants, the steward is truly answerable for what happens in the household. All the same, the steward is one of the others, by no means superior to them, having no absolute rights over them, but liable to judgment because of his [sic] treatment of them. The steward is different, but the steward is also the same. Like all the others, the steward is recipient of that which can never be his or hers to own."[9] Hall provides one critical caveat to this description of the relationship of humans to the rest of creation: that of gratitude. In order to exercise dominion correctly, he maintains that gratitude must "wholly and unambiguously [permeate] our being"; we must be especially thankful to

7. Hall, *Steward*, 12. See also Hall, *Imaging God*.
8. Hall, *Steward*, 191–215.
9. Ibid., 213.

all of our fellow creatures and the roles they play in creation.[10] While Hall's optimism regarding this concept is laudable, it taxes the imagination in this age of climate change to see how any minimal level of thankfulness is being practically expressed toward other creatures or the owner for whom we steward this place.

One of the harshest critics of the biblical stewardship model is Clare Palmer. She argues that the term "steward" is never used in Scripture in direct association with nature and it in fact has far more to do with the steward's (often a slave) management of financial resources than it does anything else. This understanding of stewardship suggests that God has handed over Earth to humanity and we are to find successful investments for its natural resources in order to show God that we have been wise with the resources when God demands an account of our activity. She asserts, "The primary emphasis is on the steward and the use of the resources, rather than on the relationship between the master and the steward,"[11] which she believes leads reasonably to a deistic conception of God and the resulting type of divine interaction with the world. Furthermore, she contends that Scripture uses "steward" so differently in multiple contexts that it is difficult to delineate exactly what it means in a way that makes it consistent with all of its uses. "Claiming a biblical pedigree for the idea is at best to oversimplify, and may be largely mistaken. It raises the question of why stewardship of nature is so popular among Christian writers, given the lack of actual biblical support for it."[12]

It would be easy to dismiss Palmer's critique in way similar to how many dismissed Lynn White's: as an oversimplistic critique of an established Christian concept. While in some manner that may be the case, I believe there is merit to components of her contention. First, while I do not think the stewardship model per se leads one to a deistic version of God, its explicit and primary biblical connection to the management of financial resources is pertinent. The use of "steward" as our primary, if not only, description of our association with nature is especially troubling in a culture wherein most American Christians, if not most Westerners, view creation as a repository of natural resources that must be transformed into something that can be bought and sold in the market rather than as something that has value merely because God declared that it is good. It perpetuates a particular relationship with creation that sees it solely in economic terms rather than as a site of moral, aesthetic, and theological consideration. This is further

10. Ibid., 211.

11. Palmer, "Stewardship," 68.

12. Ibid., 66.

exacerbated by our contemporary cultural context that seeks earnestly to transform everything from aesthetic sensibilities to our leisure time into commoditized units that can be expressed economically.

The lack of explanatory precision for the term "steward" in Scripture is also not a problem on its own, as many biblical notions lack the analytical exactness that philosophers are accustomed to using; however, Palmer is again onto something important. Scripture's explicit lack of using "steward" in relation to creation is more telling than we care to admit. The historical usage of this term is an important addendum to this story. The association of stewardship with creation is not as old as Christianity, as many Christians might guess, but goes back only to the seventeenth century when Sir Matthew Hale appears to be the first to apply it directly to our relationship with the natural world.[13] Peter Harrison asserts that from the earliest Christian centuries through the Middle Ages Genesis 1 was regularly interpreted allegorically and thus the mandate to exercise dominion was viewed as a struggle to control humanity's inner beastly nature. In similar ways to how other allegorical interpretations were cast aside for more literal ones, many Protestant Reformers chose to literalize the concept of dominion as well. In the early modern period, scriptural exegetes considered the work of dominion to be that of restoring nature to its prelapsarian condition rather than exploiting it. For these exegetes, human dominion is meant to undo the curse of Eden's original human inhabitants and the effects their sin wrought upon the rest of creation.[14] Unfortunately, none of this seems to inform the theological and social imaginaries that contemporary Christians operate within today. Finally, while Palmer's contention that the relationship between master and steward is the primary emphasis when Scripture uses the term may once again be a bit oversimplified, it points in a thoughtful direction nevertheless. Instead we should ask: Does the stewardship metaphor assist us in conceiving of creation as a gift of divine grace? Or does conceiving of ourselves as stewards help us model Christian humility? It is difficult to imagine that the answer to either of these questions is yes, as centuries of Christian behavior suggest otherwise.

Ruth Page argues, "No steward worthy of the name would allow exploitation of the creatures under her/his care, nor the exhaustion of vital resources."[15] Anthropogenic climate change should force us to ask candidly: What sort of God are we portraying as creatures supposedly made in the divine image? William Brown notes, "As God is no divine warrior who slays

13. Attfield, "Environmental Sensitivity," 81.

14. Harrison, "Having Dominion," 17–31.

15. Page, *Web of Creation*, 159.

the forces of chaos to construct a viable domain for life, so human beings are not ruthless tyrants, wreaking violence upon the land that is their home."[16] James Nash asserts that any sense of dominion that includes the extinction of species or the wanton despoliation of habitats is highly problematic. "It is a playing God in hubris. It is a distortion of the image and a perversion of dominion."[17] Additionally, in our rush to be stewards who invest wisely lest the master return and find that we have done nothing with our charge, we have demonstrated a profound lack of humility when it comes to long-term planning and usage of natural resources. We implicitly presume "that there is some state or character of the non-human creation, knowable to humans, that we are in a position to steward."[18] How we practice stewardship often suggests that we believe that we know enough to make wise investments, when time and time again history shows far more ambiguous results concerning our long-term vision.

The prominence of the stewardship metaphor in the minds of so many Christians is likely linked to its association with our self-understanding of human uniqueness, which is tied to being made in the image of God. The Christian preoccupation with the *imago Dei* is confounding. While the description of being made in God's image takes up very little space in Scripture, it has for centuries grasped the minds of many of Christianity's most prominent thinkers. Like stewardship, the *imago Dei* is one of those Christian ideas that we believe we can explicate thoughtfully until we are put on the spot. Christian history is replete with differing definitions about what the writer means in Genesis 1. Three dominant modes of *imago Dei* interpretation have evolved since the earliest days of Christian reflection.[19] The most common view, from the patristic period through the Middle Ages and into the present, is the substantive interpretation. Thinkers as varied as Augustine, Aquinas, Martin Luther, John Calvin, and Reinhold Niebuhr argue that some property or capacity that is intrinsic to human nature allows us to identify ourselves as *imago Dei*. This substance has also historically been viewed as what essentially separates humans from the rest of God's creatures. Typically, this classic interpretation affirms that the human capacity for rational thought is this very substance. Our intellect or reason is

16. Brown, *Ethos of the Cosmos*, 45.

17. Nash, *Loving Nature*, 104.

18. Southgate, "Stewardship," 189. This critique comes from outside of Christianity as well: "The arrogance of stewardship consists in the idea of superiority which underlies the thought that we exist to watch over nature like a highly respected middleman between the Creator and the Creation. We know too little about what happens in nature to take up the task." Naess, *Ecology, Community and Lifestyle*, 187.

19. E.g., see Herzfeld, *In Our Image*, 10–32.

what defines us as *imago Dei* and hence defines us as humans. Throughout much of Christian history, unfortunately, most thinkers held that reason was only associated with the male members of our species and so the *imago Dei* became an unwitting expression of misogyny. If we use reason as the defining line between what is made in God's image, and hence human, and what is not, then a host of humans who are born with mental disabilities or become mentally diminished over the course of their lives would somehow be less than human. In more recent years, it has become clear through a host of ethological studies of a multitude of species that rational thought is not as peculiar to the *Homo* genus as previously thought. Those thinkers holding onto a version of the substantive interpretation must be very careful to show how the *imago Dei* is an inclusive, rather than exclusive, characterization of what we demarcate as human.

Another is often referred to as the relational interpretation. An especially influential proponent of this position is Karl Barth.[20] According to Barth, human beings are social creatures who reflect the very social arrangement that exists within the Trinity. The *imago Dei* is not the capacity for relationship per se, but the relationship with God. In other words, being made in the divine image indicates that God is in relationship with you. While this interpretation has the distinct advantage of placing the burden of how the image functions upon God, and so it cannot be stripped away from humans due to mental defect or injury, it still begs the question: What other than God allows us to form a relationship with God? Is it reason, intellect, or some other God-given trait entirely that allows us to comprehend the relationship that we are in? Or are we merely automatons who lack the ability to respond to God freely? This interpretation's largest difficulty, however, is its lack of direct biblical exegetical support. There is very little in the Genesis text itself that suggests the writer's theological imaginary endorses this as a legitimate option.

The final prominent interpretation arose as a result of a great deal of biblical exegetical scholarship during the twentieth century. The functional interpretation of the *imago Dei* is most famously articulated by Gerhard von Rad. Taking into account the historical and social contexts of the ancient Near East that would have influenced the Genesis 1 writer, von Rad maintains, "Just as powerful earthly kings, to indicate their claim to dominion, erect an image of themselves in the provinces of their empire where they do not personally appear, so man [*sic*] is placed upon earth in God's image as God's sovereign emblem. He is really only God's representative, summoned to maintain and enforce God's claim to dominion over the

20. Barth, *Church Dogmatics* III.1, 183–91.

earth."[21] He goes on to contend that nonhuman creatures participate in a new relationship with God through humanity because God hands over to humans the obligation to exercise dominion over the Earth.[22] Moreover, the idea of humans as God's vice-regents on Earth makes the most sense of other biblical statements related to this concept, e.g., the penalty for taking human life in Genesis 9:5–6.[23] Additionally, Richard Bauckham asserts, "Factually humans do have unique power to affect most of the rest of creation on this planet. . . . What the Genesis mandate does is to recognize this power and to situate it within a framework of God's creative intention, so that humans exercise it responsibly."[24] Feminist and ecological critiques notwithstanding, the functional interpretation is the most compelling if one holds a high view of biblical exegesis. If we extend this idea to include basic insights from modern science, then the functional interpretation becomes even more persuasive. James Nash states it well: "Applied ecologically, the image concept recognizes a basic biological fact: humans alone have evolved the peculiar rational, moral, and therefore, creative capacities that enable us alone to serve as responsible representatives of God's interests and values, to function as protectors of the ecosphere and self-constrained consumers of the world's goods."[25]

Our deliberation over the possible connotations for the *imago Dei* is incomplete if we do not connect Genesis 1 with how New Testament writers develop the concept even further. The Gospel of John tells us that God became flesh in the person of Jesus of Nazareth; therefore, God has been made known to us and we have seen the very glory of God.[26] Paul tells the Colossian church that Jesus is "the image of the invisible God."[27] In a letter to the church at Corinth, Paul proclaims that Christ is "the image of God."[28] The Hebrews writer states powerfully, "[Jesus] is the reflection of God's glory and the exact imprint of God's very being."[29] The New Testament witness is clear: the *imago Dei* is perfectly exhibited in Jesus.[30] How might this inform

21. Rad, *Genesis*, 58.

22. Ibid.

23. Wenham, *Genesis 1–15*, 32.

24. Bauckham, *Crisis of Freedom*, 173.

25. Nash, *Loving Nature*, 105.

26. See John 1:14–18.

27. Col 1:15.

28. 2 Cor 4:4.

29. Heb 1:3.

30. For more on this, see Clough, *On Animals*, 100–102.

a more ecologically minded theological imaginary? We shall return to this question at the end of the chapter.

The historical Christian infatuation with the *imago Dei* concept is one of many factors that have led critics to claim that Christianity is an anthropocentric religion. This critique seemed unassailable after Lynn White's claim, "Especially in its Western form, Christianity is the most anthropocentric religion the world has seen."[31] This charge rings like a dissonant bunch of clanging cymbals in the hearts and minds of the many Christians who believe that our faith can be a measure of hope in the age of climate change. So what does White mean by this exactly? He specifically rebukes Western Christianity for thinking that humans are separate from nature, similarly to how God transcends creation, and that God wills for humans to exploit nature to meet their own ends. If this is the sort of anthropocentrism that is implied or, worse yet, explicitly proclaimed by the biblical witness, then Christians find themselves in a poor place indeed to advocate for the needs of nonhuman creatures and the rest of creation. After laying out a broader theological imaginary, however, I conclude that White's notion of Christian anthropocentrism is a caricature, but unfortunately one that far too many Christians implicitly and explicitly manifest in their daily lives.

Especially in light of White's charge, there has been an effort among theologians, biblical scholars, and other Christian eco-thinkers to delineate more carefully the contours of the term "anthropocentrism." There are at least two types of anthropocentrism to assess. First, there is an anthropocentrism that is epistemological in nature. "Anthropocentrism is inescapable for humans: since we are neither angels nor earthworms, our primary perspective on the world is a human one, bounded and shaped by the determinants of specifically human existence."[32] It is highly likely that just as humans see reality from our perspective, dolphins, ants, and lizards "see" reality from their unique vantage points as well. The idea of other creatures somehow seeing reality from their own perspectives should come as no surprise to Christians who believe that all of creation seeks to praise God and thus is a robust reflection of God's glory. Second, there is a theological or ethical anthropocentrism. A host of scholars identify this as anthropomonism, which is the exclusive role for and emphasis on humanity in God's plan of redemption that isolates humans from the rest of creation and hence tends to manifest itself in ways that assert human needs and wants take ultimate priority over the rest of the created order.[33] This

31. White, "Historical Roots," 1205.

32. Watson, "In the Beginning," 129.

33. E.g., Bartholomew I, *Cosmic Grace, Humble Prayer*; Vischer, "Listening to

is the sort of Christian attitude that White labels as anthropocentric in his famous critique. David Clough delineates the issue further between what he calls "inclusive teleological anthropocentrism" and "exclusive teleological anthropocentrism."[34] Clough defines inclusive teleological anthropocentrism as the affirmation that both humans and nonhumans have a place in God's plan of redemption, but that humans take center stage in God's plan. This position not only witnesses to the practical reality of the human effect, technologically or otherwise, on the planet, but also to the theological claims about the roles of the sons and daughters of God in the redemptive scheme made by the apostle Paul in Romans 8.[35] The latter position, exclusive teleological anthropocentrism, is synonymous with anthropomonism. While the advantages of inclusive teleological anthropocentrism are significant, such as a possibly correct theological rendering of the incredibly difficult Romans 8 passage, and also the ethical mandate it places upon humans, Clough argues that "Christianity should be distinguished by its theocentrism, rather than anthropocentrism."[36] Therefore, according to Clough, humanity's central role in God's plan for creation is overblown and detracts from the prominence of God in bringing creation to its consummation.

While the nuancing of the language of anthropocentrism may seem tedious at times, it is entirely appropriate as we attempt to witness daily to the reality of the resurrection in our lives. Ultimately, though, I maintain that Clough has struck an important chord in representing the biblical witness. The bible narrates a story that may be anthropocentric because we can only tell the story from our human perspective; but it is fundamentally theocentric in character, it is about God and the divine plan of redemption and the roles of all that God created within it. It may be true that we play a more prominent role than other creatures because practically we can affect creation more than other creatures, but, lest we forget the lesson of Psalm 104, we are the only creatures whose sin mars the Earth as the rest of creation praises its Creator. The call to focus on the distinct theocentric emphasis of the biblical witness will not only help us tell the story of God more accurately, but also help us in our never-ending struggle to remain humble and accept our place in creation and God's plan of redemption.

Creation Groaning"; Watson, "In the Beginning."

    34. Clough, *On Animals*, xvi–xx.

    35. E.g., Horrell et al., *Greening Paul*, 121–26; Southgate, *Groaning of Creation*, 92–115; Byrne, "Creation Groaning," 193–203.

    36. Clough, *On Animals*, xx.

Are There Other Options?

If we allow ourselves to become fixated upon the divine mandate in the last part of Genesis 1, we fail to realize that Scripture speaks about the human vocation in far more subtle ways elsewhere. We often act as if the whole of the human vocation is summed up in the command to be fruitful and multiply so that we might subdue the Earth and have dominion over it. But what of the rest of Scripture, or the rest of Genesis 1 for that matter? In the Genesis 1 creation account, God creates the vast majority of creation before humans ever arrive on the scene. God creates light, water, land, and then plants, and creatures to fill the water and skies of this place merely by God speaking them into existence. On the last day, God brings forth creatures to occupy the land. It is on this day that God creates beings who are in the very image and likeness of the divine. The account ends thusly: "God saw everything that God had made, and indeed, it was very good."[37] The human fixation with the specialness of our position within creation as the only creatures created in the divine image belies three significant theological points Genesis 1 actually makes. First, regardless of the specialness of our station, humans are created on the same day as other creatures who are also meant to fill the Earth. We were not created on a separate day as many seem implicitly to believe. Moreover, this theological fact, if you will, is reflected in our very mandate to be fruitful and multiply. Richard Bauckham maintains, "When humans obey the command to be fruitful and multiply, to fill the Earth and to subdue it, they are not imitating God in a unique way but behaving like other species. All species use their environment and, though agriculture is unique to humans, it can be seen as a peculiarly human extension of the right of all animals to use their environment to live and to flourish."[38] In other words, we are far more like other creatures than we would like to believe, and the command to fill and subdue the Earth is just one more example of our common creatureliness. Second, everything in this narrative shares a similar characteristic: it is spoken into existence by divine fiat. Theologically, if not existentially, we should recognize that this creation account proclaims that everything depends radically upon God for its existence. This seemingly simple point denotes a profound sense of interdependence among things that God creates. Once again, humans should realize that we are dramatically similar to everything else in creation. Third, God does not deem creation to be "very good" merely because humans were created. God pronounces creation to be "very good" after viewing the total-

37. Gen 1:31.
38. Bauckham, *Bible and Ecology*, 19.

ity of the divine work. "What is lacking . . . is any sense of building towards a culmination. Humans, the last creatures to be created, have a unique role within creation, but they do not come last because they are the climax of an ascending scale."[39] From this creation account alone, it is reasonable to conclude that humans are a part of this creative project, but not the reason for the divine declaration about its goodness.

Stopping at Genesis 1 truncates the very theological imaginary that we require to understand the human vocation. While the creation story of Genesis 1 appears rather majestic in its portrayal of the scope of God's creative enterprise, the narrative in Genesis 2 is far more intimate. God does not speak things into existence; instead, the scene is mostly set. The Earth and the heavens have already been created and are waiting for the water that will cause things to grow. The land is waiting for someone to till it. It is at this point that God forms the first human out of the Earth's soil. The Hebrew wordplay in Genesis 2:7 is striking: the human (*adam*) is fashioned out of the fertile soil (*adama*). Ellen Davis explains that the Hebrew words used here are actually indicative of the resemblance of the color of the Earth with the color of skin. "Both words are related to adom, 'ruddy'; in the Levant, brownish red is the skin tone of both the people and the earth. Terra rossa, 'red earth,' is the geological term for the thin but rich loam covering the hill country where the early Israelites settled. Thus adam from adama is localized language; it evokes the specific relationship between a people and their particular place."[40] In English we might say that the human is made out of the humus or "we share common ground with the Earth because we are *common ground.*"[41] Our very identity as human creatures cannot be understood without acknowledging our connection to the soil from which we came.[42] Once again, the text highlights the theological fact that interconnectedness is part of the very fabric of God's created order. A second critical component of this creation account is that the human placed in the garden is meant to do something with the soil. The human, Adam, is meant to till it. The relationship between Adam and the soil is intrinsically reciprocal and mutually beneficial: the soil needs Adam's toil and Adam needs the produce that the soil can provide.[43] Any mistreatment of the soil has deleterious effects on Adam as well. While we are the only creatures in charge of tilling

---

39. Ibid., 14.

40. Davis, *Scripture, Culture, and Agriculture*, 29.

41. Newsom, "Common Ground," 62; italics in original.

42. Wirzba, *Paradise of God*, 29.

43. Bauckham, *Bible and Ecology*, 19.

the garden, the Genesis 2 author suggests we are far more interdependent with the rest of creation than we care to admit.

Some Christians point to Psalm 8 to demonstrate the uniqueness of humanity, especially in comparison to the rest of creation. After all, the psalmist notes that God made humans just a bit lower than the divine and all things were placed under their feet. In the race to remind each other of how special we are in the eyes of God, we have missed the broader message of this particular text. First of all, this psalm has less to do with extolling humanity and far more to do with exalting the awesomeness of God. The repeated first and last verses of this psalm exhort us to remember that God alone is majestic. God is sovereign; God alone decides who is given dominion over creation. There is nothing intrinsic to humanity that should allow us to believe that we deserve somehow to be placed in a leadership position. God, and God alone, has bestowed this role upon us. The juxtaposition between divine power and human power is stark: one is sovereign and one is conferred. Our place in the universe may be a little lower than God, but it is a place determined by God and not us. If we become transfixed upon the idea that we are just below God, we miss one of the psalmist's key declarations. Staring up into the starry night the psalmist is reminded of the majesty of the God who created the universe. Upon being awestruck by this gaze into the vast sky, the psalmist wonders why God is mindful of human beings at all. The expanse of the universe leads the psalmist to this rhetorical question, not the supposed specialness of humanity. This insight by the psalmist cannot be overstated.

Psalm 104 may not seem like an important text when constructing an anthropology because on the surface it mentions very little about us. This psalm depicts God as the creator and sustainer of all life on our planet. Using wisdom God not only made all of the creatures of the Earth, but God cares deeply for each of the creatures that call Earth home as God attends to their daily biological needs, like rain for the plants and food for the young lions. It is within this scene that humans are briefly mentioned. The psalmist says that God brings forth plants for humans to cultivate and bread to strengthen our hearts. Similar to how lions go out in search of food, humans go out to work from dawn till the evening. Taking into account the context of the entire psalm, the psalmist is portraying a familiar theme: humans are part of the fellowship of God's creation, we are not distinct from it. All creatures depend upon the breath of God for life; without it, all creatures return to the dust. The distinction between contemporary Christianity and the psalmist could not be more striking. In our theological and social imaginaries we relish the discussion about human uniqueness; the psalmist, however, recognizes the profound dependence that all members of creation have upon God, humanity's place within creation, and the praises sung to the Creator. At the same time, in the very last verse, the psalmist does note one feature that may radically define human uniqueness more than we care to admit: "Humans are the creatures who spoil the otherwise rosy picture of the world . . . This human despoiling of creation is in fact the psalm's strongest indication of human exceptionality."[44] This is reminiscent of the reason given for the flood: human wickedness.[45] William Brown goes a step further and argues that God's delight in creation, which is made manifest by the psalmist, requires a response from humans. "God's active delight in creation only heightens human agency in behalf of creation, for it all comes down to this: to feed the flame of biophilia, both God's and ours, we must preserve and sustain creation's biodiversity . . . If creation's wondrous variety is diminished, then the psalmist's worst fear is realized: creation left to wither away. It is incumbent upon God's most powerful creatures to ensure that divine delight is sustained so that the world be sustained."[46] This puts a rather unique theological spin on the idea of biodiversity conservation and hence a rather significant responsibility upon Christians.

These biblical texts are unequivocal that we are members of a universe that was created by God and declared to be "very good." We depend upon God for each breath of our existence and are interdependently linked with the rest of creation. Creation is indeed a gift from the Creator. According to the psalmist, this should be reason enough for us to rejoice in the majesty of God as the creator and sustainer of the universe. While we are undoubtedly similar to much of creation, we are decidedly different in many ways from our sisters and brothers on Earth as well. For one, we seem to be the only species on the planet that spends time oft contemplating in excruciating detail how unique we really are. While valiant attempts to reform the concept of stewardship are admirable, I fear that the reformation of a concept that is practiced so poorly by so many and built upon such truncated and faulty interpretations of Scripture is an effort in futility. Our theological imaginary must take into account far more scriptural insight than the concept of stewardship historically has done. Only a more robust theological imaginary can lead to a better witness of our faith. Let us turn to some possible alternatives.

Some Orthodox theologians have turned to the notion of priesthood to elucidate humanity's relationship with the rest of creation.[47] John Ziziou-

---

44. Ibid., 70.

45. Gen 6:5.

46. Brown, *Seven Pillars*, 159.

47. This view is not limited to the Orthodox. See also Linzey, *Animal Theology*, 45–61.

las, for example, argues that humans are the very priests of creation. Built upon the Orthodox idea that every member of creation is part of a cosmic liturgy that awaits transfiguration in Christ, humans function as the priests of creation by joining the wordless praise of creation with the conscious reflections of humans and offering it to the Creator. The Orthodox understanding of the Eucharist is one such instance of this kind of priestly activity. Nature produces wheat and grapes that humans then transform into bread and wine in order to offer them to God. As such, humans play an exceptional role in the cosmic liturgy. According to Elizabeth Theokritoff, "the responsibility that goes with our dominant position is not primarily administrative, but *doxological*. Our 'power' is directly related to our responsibility to refer all creation to God, to offer conscious praise on its behalf."[48] Zizioulas goes on to maintain that humans are "the only possible link between God and creation, a link that can either bring nature in communion with God and thus sanctify it; or condemn it to the state of a 'thing', the meaning and purpose of which are exhausted with the satisfaction of man [*sic*]."[49] He concludes that this notion of priesthood "involves an *ethos* that the world needs badly in our time. Not an ethic, but an *ethos*. Not a program, but an attitude and a mentality. Not a legislation, but a culture."[50]

This Orthodox notion is not without its critics. Some contend that this view is anthropocentric in a way that only exacerbates ecological problems already caused by teleological exclusive anthropocentrism or anthropomonism.[51] Integral to this charge is the downplaying of the capacity of nonhuman creatures to praise their Creator. Richard Bauckham contends that human mediation on behalf of other creatures to God is not needed. "The psalmists and we ourselves can put creation's wordless praise into human words, but we cannot suppose that God needs us to do this before he [*sic*] can hear and appreciate other creatures' praise."[52] Ruth Page goes one step further: "The presumption involved in believing that there is no connection between God and the natural world unless human beings make it seems to me totally unwarranted and extremely dangerous. If God does not care directly, without mediation, about what happens to the rain forests, polluted rivers, habitats in drought and habitats in flood, then there is nothing

---

48. Theokritoff, *Living in God's Creation*, 79; italics in original.

49. Zizioulas, "Priest of Creation," 290.

50. Ibid., 289; italics in original.

51. E.g., see Northcott, *Environment and Christian Ethics*, 133–34; Bauckham, *Bible and Ecology*, 83–86.

52. Bauckham, *Bible and Ecology*, 84.

distinctively Christian to bring to the ecological crisis."[53] While proponents
of the Orthodox position would point out vociferously that the priestly position is theocentric rather than anthropocentric in character,[54] the idea that
humans are needed to mediate the praises of nonhuman creation is outside
the immediate theological imaginary of the biblical witness and appears to
downplay the Genesis 1 affirmation that creation was good before humans
ever arrived on the scene. Additionally, it places humans at the apex of creation, which is problematic not only from an evolutionary perspective, but
from a theological one as well.

There is no reason, however, to dismiss this Orthodox insight outright. The notion of humans as the priests of creation reminds us of one
critical component that we find attested throughout Scripture: humans are
different from the rest of the created order. Theokritoff, relying on Gregory
of Nyssa, contends, "Man's [sic] 'oversight' of creation is not just practical
management or 'stewardship'; it is inextricably bound up with being aware
of the mystery of creation, discerning God's wisdom in the depths of created
things."[55] She goes further, stating, "The language of 'priesthood' underlines
the Godwardness of creation as a whole: it leads us to see our habitat as
an 'immense cathedral' and our daily life as a Eucharist."[56] This insight is
not unique to Orthodox theologians. Christopher Southgate argues that we
must remember human uniqueness even amidst a common evolutionary
ancestry. "This specialness enables us to see the created world whole, and
to offer it up in praise. The creation of humans in the image and likeness
of God (Gen. 1:26), and to praise and glorify God for ever, must lie behind
every description of our calling in relation to the rest of creation."[57] Our
capacity to see the creation as a whole, however limited that vision might be,
and to be aware of creation's mysterious depth that points to the existence
of a creator should not be underestimated, even if we seem to spend very
little time as Protestant Christians in the United States contemplating this.

Psalm 104 portrays a created order wherein creatures are truly companions who depend utterly on the "generous extravagance" of God's grace.[58]
Ruth Page argues that companionship is fundamental to God's creation and
is especially critical as we consider our response to present ecological cri-

53. Page, *Web of Creation*, 163.

54. E.g., see Theokritoff, "Creation and Priesthood," 345–50.

55. Theokritoff, *Living in God's Creation*, 68.

56. Ibid., 215.

57. Southgate, "Stewardship," 192. See also Southgate, *Groaning of Creation*,
111–13.

58. Brueggemann, *Theology of the Old Testament*, 156.

ses. "The first and most important relation, the one on which all others are based and from which they take their character, is that of companion. If human beings cannot see themselves as sharing this planet (as companions, literally, share bread) with the rest of creation, then all the features of the ecological crisis, from overpopulation to pollution, will simply spiral on to catastrophe—catastrophe for human beings, among others."[59] She further contends that companionship is foundational to Jesus' command to love our neighbors as ourselves, joining the chorus of Christian thinkers who believe that our nonhuman creatures can be conceived of as our neighbors. Additionally, if we view our nonhuman neighbors as companions, then we are bound to act in a certain manner. "If all sense of companionship has to be abandoned for a particular course of action to take place, then that action should not be undertaken."[60] She specifically applies this to our current practice of industrial farming and slaughterhouses. While Page is highly skeptical of stewardship as the primary model of defining the human relationship to creation, she maintains that if companionship is seen as a guiding presupposition to stewardship, then we might avert further troubles that brought us to the present situation.[61]

Lutheran theologian Paul Santmire sees the need to move past a theology of stewardship and adopt what he calls a theology of partnership. According to him, Genesis 1 affirms an account of creation wherein God has a purpose for all creatures, not just the human ones. He notes that the air, the waters, and the Earth are all participants in the divine creative project, as God blesses them and calls upon them to "multiply," "bring forth," and "fill" the Earth. This is significant: "All creatures are, in this sense, some explicitly, others by implication, partners with God's creativity, not merely objects of His [sic] creative will posited for the sake of His relationship with humans."[62] For Santmire, then, there are three "fundamental expressions or emphases" of this partnership: creative intervention in nature, sensitive care for nature, and awestruck contemplation of nature.[63] The Genesis 1 narrative is clear that humans are to fill the Earth, i.e., establish human communities. This calls for a partnership with God and nature that requires creative intervention in nature, which will be guided by divinely inspired notions of justice and peace.[64] Noah is the paragon of this sort of partnership, as he blends the

59. Page, *Web of Creation*, 154.
60. Ibid., 156.
61. Ibid., 158.
62. Santmire, "Partnership," 392.
63. Ibid., 385.
64. Ibid., 401.

needs of his human family with the divine vocation that he is called to perform. His respect for his human community as well as for other members of creation shows that creative intervention is not anthropocentric. "Human intervention in nature is thus envisioned by the priestly writers as within *limits*, both theocentric and cosmocentric."[65] The Genesis 2 narrative and its portrayal of a particular association of humanity with the soil emphasizes a different sort of partnership. Adam and Eve are required to care sensitively for nature in order to partner with God in the effort to sustain the fecundity and biodiversity of creation. In particular, the divine charge to till and keep the soil means *"identifying and responding to needs of the land itself and protecting the land from abuse or destruction."*[66] This painstaking work is also a feature of what it means to be a partner. Finally, the story of Job stresses a type of partnership that respects the wildness and the otherness of nature by esteeming it appropriately. "Partnership with God in the midst of nature and partnership with nature now means stepping back from nature, *letting nature be and seeing it for what it is for God and in itself, apart from the interventions and the caring of humans."*[67] By the end of the whirlwind theophany, Job has a new understanding of his place in the universe; he is *"coram Deo*, as one among many creatures, all of whom are God's children, all of whom have been nurtured and set free by God."[68] Job is the archetype of a new awareness of partnership.

Instead of stewards, priests, companions, or partners, some opt for the model of servants of creation. For Ellen Davis the notion of serving creation is integral to the Yahwist account in Genesis 2. In fact, the language used here might suggest that the mandate to have dominion is oversimplified, if not completely inappropriate.[69] The language used in Genesis 2:15 is strikingly suggestive of the unique relationship humans have with the soil that we are to "till" and "keep." The Hebrew verb translated "till" could also be translated "work," as in the common expression "to work the soil." But, as Davis asserts, there is more to this passage: "[T]he wider usage of the verb suggests that it is legitimate also to view the human task as *working for* the garden soil, serving its needs."[70] In a very real sense, humans are meant to serve the needs of the soil. Norman Wirzba adds that "service does not connote oppression or humiliation, but rather the necessary and ennobling

65. Ibid., 396; italics in original.

66. Ibid., 402; italics in original.

67. Ibid., 407–8; italics in original.

68. Ibid., 410.

69. See also Habel, "Wild Ox," 183.

70. Davis, *Scripture, Culture, and Agriculture*, 29; italics in original.

work that promotes growth and health. To serve is to be attentive to and to work with the natural orders that ensure survival and well-being."[71] This has profound ethical implications. "According to the Yahwist, the human voca-tion is not to manage the ecosystem of which humans are a part, but rather to align its activity to meet the demands and observe the limits imposed by this system upon all of its members. Humans must measure their activity by the health of the larger biotic community which they share."[72] The Hebrew word very often translated "keep" has two frequently used connotations. On the one hand, it can connote the idea of keeping a flock or a household; on the other hand, it can also connote "observe," as in observing the workings of the world or observing the Lord's commands or Sabbath. Davis concludes, "So it may be that the human is charged to 'keep' the garden and at the same time to 'observe' it, to learn from it and respect the limits that pertain to it."[73] For Wirzba this sort of service to the soil develops gratitude as well as humility. We become more grateful by recognizing that the blessings of God found in creation are far more abundant than we deserve and could pos-sibly fathom. We become more humble by acknowledging this abundance. This development of virtue is not purely contemplative and hence possibly passive, it is to be expressed actively in the service of creation by preserv-ing it and caring for it.[74] In a culture where people often take more delight in being served rather than serving others, Wirzba reminds us that we are participating in the very work of God, who models self-giving through ser-vanthood in the very act of creation and in the ministry of Christ.[75] Finally, we must not think that our service to the soil and to the rest of creation should demand little of us. "To think of our service to creation as patterned on a fundamental divine hospitality is to recognize that service must finally know no bounds. It does not stop at the limit of personal comfort or social convention."[76] Noah is the model of this sort of servanthood.[77] He takes on the needs of others, both human and nonhuman. He is attentive to the individual needs of the animals on the ark and is rigorous in his preparation

71. Wirzba, *Paradise of God*, 31.

72. Hiebert, "Human Vocation," 150–51.

73. Davis, *Scripture, Culture and Agriculture*, 30. See also Bauckham and Hart, *Hope against Hope*, 148. This notion of tilling as service takes on a particularly different light if Newsom is correct that the word we translate "garden" actually connotes something more like a forest and Adam's work is conceived of as more like permaculture. Newsom, "Common Ground," 64–65.

74. Wirzba, *Paradise of God*, 137–38.

75. Ibid., 136–37.

76. Ibid., 143.

77. Ibid., 141–43.

for meeting the demands of those sharing it with him. For these reasons and more God deems him righteous.

The standard historical notion of human beings as God's stewards of creation is tougher than ever to maintain. Contemporary scholarship has helped to show just how troublesome this notion is and how it is rather new in the history of ideas even though many believe it goes back to the earliest days of Scripture. Moreover, while so many American Protestant Christians believe they are being God's good stewards, too many do not exhibit any substantial behavior on a daily basis that would convince anyone inside or outside of the Christian tradition that we are worthy of the title. Yet, even after all of the surveyed options of possible replacements for "steward," I ultimately remain unconvinced that they will stand as viable substitutes. Let us now turn to an examination of a single virtue that may help us be Christians who better witness to the creation-care work the resurrection inspires us to perform.

5

Humans: The Humble Creatures
Who Hope in God

It is clear from the witnesses of Genesis 1 and 2 and Psalms 104, as well as many other portions of Scripture, that creation is a gift of grace from God. The response for such a gift should be gratitude in the form of praise toward our Creator. The biblical witness is unambiguous: the nonhuman portion of creation does just this. Nonhuman creatures praise God by performing their roles in the created order. Humans, however, are exceptional in that we seem to be the only members of creation who do not live as grateful recipients of divine grace. Instead of performing our role in the divine scheme, we intentionally and unintentionally seek ways to thumb our nose at the divine gift in an attempt to take a place in creation that is not ours to have—that of God.[1] Our lack of gratitude toward God's gift of grace causes us to be prideful, which is ultimately caused by a lack of humility.

Being Humble

Humility is an oft-forgotten or misremembered virtue that is paramount if we are to act responsibly in the age of climate change. Being humble often connotes thinking lowly of oneself or devaluing one's own intrinsic worth or self-esteem in order to fit appropriately into a hierarchical structure. This attitude goes all the way back to Aristotle, who viewed it as the vice of pusillanimity. Friedrich Nietzsche places it within the values of slave morality. It has been widely derided by those who think that humility prevents humans from excelling intellectually or downplays our creative ingenuity. In a contemporary cultural milieu that is known more for crafting sophisticated branding campaigns that promote image, humility seems rather passé. One of the classic definitions of humility comes from the twelfth-century

---

1. Ps 104:35.

Christian monk Bernard of Clairvaux, who relies on Augustine: "Humility is the virtue by which a man [sic] recognizes his own unworthiness because he really knows himself."[2] This definition does nothing to deter those who believe humility is about low self-esteem or demeaning oneself. For Bernard as well as other Christian theologians, though, humility is viewed as the virtue in direct juxtaposition to the vice of pride. Pride is not about a healthy sense of self-worth, but rather a delusional sense of the self. Pride is the rejection of our creatureliness and an exaltation of ourselves to the place of God. We view ourselves as God rather than accept our place in God's creation. To live a life of humility is not to devalue one's dignity, but rather is to understand one's proper place in creation. It is not to think of ourselves too highly, but not too lowly either. To know ourselves and our unworthiness is not degrading; it is a fundamental acknowledgment that humans are indeed creatures and not God. "Humility trains us in the art of being creatures."[3]

The story of Job illustrates this remarkably well. In response to Job's demand for answers concerning his unjust treatment, God takes Job into the whirlwind and gives him a tour of creation. God questions Job about the intricate details of the establishment of the universe and shows Job glimpses of magnificent creatures, like Behemoth and Leviathan, that he had no idea even existed. At the very end of the theophany, Job answers God with one of the more enigmatic statements in all of Scripture:

> I know that you can do all things,
> and that no purpose of yours can be thwarted.
> "Who is this that hides counsel without knowledge?"
> Therefore I have uttered what I did not understand,
> things too wonderful for me, which I did not know.
> "Hear, and I will speak;
> I will question you, and you declare to me."
> I had heard of you by the hearing of the ear,
> but now my eye sees you;
> therefore I despise myself,
> and repent in dust and ashes.[4]

To the audience this appears to be a rather unsatisfying ending to Job's demand for an explanation about his tragic suffering. Instead, Job recognizes something similar to what the psalmist declared when he stared up into the starry night: God is indeed the Creator of the universe and Job is merely one

2. Bernard of Clairvaux, "On the Steps," 103.

3. Wirzba, "Touch of Humility," 241.

4. Job 42:2–6.

single creature within that universe. There is a qualitative difference between Creator and creature. For all of our insight into how the universe functions, creatures like Job and us cannot know everything there is to know about creation nor can we see the universe from the divine viewpoint. This should not dissuade us from searching for answers; it certainly did not discourage Job, but in the end we must realize that the difference between Creator and creature is fundamental and thus our only response is that of humility. We, like Job, are challenged to accept our proper place in the universe. We are called to be humble. Gustavo Gutiérrez asserts that Job's final pronounce-ment is a sign that he had a "joyous encounter with the Lord," as he realizes that God is sovereign and that reality is far more profound and rich than he believed possible.[5] Job's final repentance indicates to the audience that Job now "surrenders to Yahweh with renewed trust."[6]

God's whirlwind message to Job also dismantles any sense of anthro-pocentrism that he or the sages of the Israelite wisdom tradition might have previously embodied. At the end of God's first speech in the theophany, Job proclaims, "See, I am of small account; what shall I answer you? I lay my hand on my mouth."[7] According to Gutiérrez, "Acknowledgement of his littleness may thus be an important step toward the abandonment of his anthropocentrism."[8] Job's place in the universe is neither at the apex of creation nor separate from the wildness of creation he marveled at from the vantage point of the whirlwind. Instead, a newly humble Job understands himself to be a part of creation, intimately known and cared for by God. "Job discovers himself to be created *of* the world, inextricably linked to all life, including the wild. This paradigmatic human exists alongside, beside, in tandem with all the creatures of the wild."[9] This is another echo of a bio-centric vision contained in Scripture. James Crenshaw goes one step further, arguing that the divine speeches shatter "every human illusion of occupying a special place in God's sight,"[10] and are "an equally radical criticism of the anthropocentric presupposition of the ancient sages. Human hubris bursts before this rapturous celebration of a universe in which women and men play no role other than that of awestruck witness to grandeur and terror."[11] Recognition of one's creatureliness is subsequently recognition of one's

---

5. Gutiérrez, *On Job*, 83.

6. Ibid., 87.

7. Job 40:4.

8. Gutiérrez, *On Job*, 76.

9. Brown, *Seven Pillars*, 130; italics in original.

10. Crenshaw, "Form and Content," 70.

11. Ibid., 80.

interconnectedness with and interdependence upon the rest of creation. Brown argues that Job is supposed to learn something from nonhuman creatures in his whirlwind experience. "[Job] is to find in himself something of Behemoth's strength and Leviathan's fearlessness when confronting human presumption, theological distortion, and rampant injustice. But he is also to see himself among the brood of ravens that 'cry out to God' for food (38:41). The frail and the fierce are both his kin. Job discovers himself to be a child of the wild."[12] This witness from the wild becomes a fascinating touchstone for a theological imaginary that exhibits a life of hope inspired by the resurrection. This is the sort of courage we need to prevent the extinction of species that have no voice and seek environmental justice for the poor and disenfranchised. Furthermore, Job's revelation suggests that nature might teach us not only something about the majesty of God and the richness of creation, but about ourselves too. In light of God questioning Job about whether he understands the establishment of the universe and whether he has the power to control any of it, the idea of having dominion over the Earth seems, practically speaking, rather suspect. "No longer are conquering and controlling nature part of the equation for discerning human dignity . . . With all these creatures, human dominion has no place, but human dignity does."[13] Job's dignity is affirmed, his place in creation is assured, even if he no longer is meant to have dominion over it as he believed before. In other words, God's whirlwind revelation calls an oversimplistic understanding of the divine mandate in Genesis 1 into considerable question. In our present century, climate change serves as another reminder that human dominion, in the anthropocentric ways we typically conceive of it, should hold no significant place in our theological and social imaginaries.

The call to be humble is exemplified by none other than Jesus of Nazareth. In the Gospel of Luke, Jesus tells a parable about a Pharisee and a tax collector who go up to the temple to pray. While the crowd might have expected the Pharisee to model exactly what God desires, Jesus exalts the tax collector, who stands far away from the temple and will not even look to the sky when he prays. He begs God for forgiveness rather than counting his worthy accomplishments. Ultimately Jesus says, "for all who exalt themselves will be humbled, but all who humble themselves will be exalted."[14] Jesus' call to be humble is not merely in word alone. In the Gospel of John, the writer records Jesus washing his disciples' feet even at the initial protest of Peter. After washing their feet, Jesus says, "Do you know what I have

12. Brown, *Seven Pillars*, 131.

13. Ibid., 375–76.

14. Luke 18:14.

done to you? You call me Teacher and Lord—and you are right, for that is
what I am. So if I, your Lord and Teacher, have washed your feet, you also
ought to wash one another's feet. For I have set you an example, that you
also should do as I have done to you. Very truly, I tell you, servants are not
greater than their master, nor are messengers greater than the one who sent
them."[15] Jesus knows his place in God's redemptive plan, and that is to serve
others, even to the point of death on a cross.

This is exactly the point the apostle Paul makes in his letter to the early
church in Philippi:

> Let the same mind be in you that was in Christ Jesus,
> who, though he was in the form of God,
> did not regard equality with God
> as something to be exploited,
> but emptied himself,
> taking the form of a slave,
> being born in human likeness.
> And being found in human form, he humbled himself
> and became obedient to the point of death—
> even death on a cross.[16]

By being humble Paul says that God exalted Jesus highly. Humility, then, is
not the diminution of self-worth, but recognition of one's proper place in
God's plan for the universe. To accept our place is an opportunity to allow
God to celebrate our participation in the redemptive scheme for creation,
just as God did with Jesus. This celebration is a witness of the hope to be
found in the resurrection of Jesus.

In the example of Jesus we also see that love flows from humility. Jesus'
love for women, the outcast, little children, the sick, his disciples, and many
others is demonstrated uniquely by his sacrifice. Noah exhibits this sort of
love as well when he attends to the various needs of his family and the nonhuman creatures under his care, as he prepares for the flood by building
the ark and gathering provisions for the stay within it. Both Jesus and Noah
model the depths of sacrifice God is willing to endure in order for love to be
shown. In fact, it is difficult to imagine love without some form of sacrifice,
whether minimal or maximal. The Christian claim to follow a savior whose
sacrifice included being crucified on a Roman cross has led some to imply
that the Christian notion of sacrifice is inherently masochistic. While sacrifice merely for the sake of sacrifice would be decidedly so, this is not what

15. John 13:12–16.
16. Phil 2:5–8.

the Christian notion of sacrifice is about. Jesus did not sacrifice himself on the cross merely for the sake of sacrifice, but instead to fulfill his role in the divine plan to redeem creation back to God. Jesus' sacrifice was a means to an end, not an end itself. The same could be said for Noah. In light of this delineation, the sacrifice of one's possessions, time, or even one's own life does not happen without a greater good in sight, e.g., extending compassion, being merciful, or healing a broken relationship. For Christians, sacrifice as a means to an end gives purpose to sacrifice and ultimately demonstrates hope that God conquered death in the resurrection of Jesus and that our actions now can endure past our own lifetime. It is difficult to imagine that our care for creation will not include sacrifice if we are to bear a true witness to the life of Christ. While it may be easier to imagine how we might sacrifice for those suffering from environmental injustice or those doomed to be climate refugees, we must be equally creative when it comes to sacrificing for our nonhuman sisters and brothers and the rest of creation. This is the sort of love that a faithful witness to Jesus demands.

What Are We to Be as Humans?

Ultimately, I am skeptical of a single symbol like steward, priest, partner, or servant representing the human relationship with, to, or in the rest of creation. Our theological and social imaginaries become too restrictive by dogmatic adherence to one such symbol. Instead, we need to listen to the broad theological imaginary of Scripture and describe what attributes are associated with being properly human, especially in a time of ecological crisis. First, humans must remember that creation is a gift of divine grace. As such, we should be grateful for that gift explicitly in the daily witness of our faith; grateful to God for creating, sustaining, and directing creation; and grateful to our fellow creatures for sustaining us in our place in the food chain, if nothing else. However, both the theological and social imaginaries that promote stewardship as a Christian practice fail miserably to remind us of this quintessential reality. Our unsustainable use of most of the planet's natural resources suggests strongly that we do not perceive them as gifts from God. That is to say nothing of our treatment of the planet's wildernesses, oceans, and biodiversity. We need daily to exhibit gratitude for the grace of God's good creation if we are adequately to address the consequences of climate change. As we shall see in the following chapters, this theological starting point should have a pronounced effect on how we conceive of our economic decisions and our choices about food as well.

Second, if we are appropriately grateful, then we can easily acknowledge the etymological link between humans, humus, and humility. Creation is a gift of grace from God and our place within it is given to us as well. We do not have the power to call ourselves into existence nor to dictate how creation functions. The witness of Scripture is clear: humans are part of a vast interconnected and interdependent created order. A social imaginary that embraces stewardship and priesthood tends to act far too easily as if humans are the pinnacle of creation and not one of many creatures within it. Our acknowledgment of this theological and biological fact should prompt us to appreciate and care for the web of creation in which we find ourselves.[17] This is not merely part of a new theological imaginary; it has roots in the patristic period. John Chrysostom argues, "Surely we ought to show [nonhuman creatures] great kindness and gentleness for many reasons, but above all, because they are of the same origin as ourselves."[18] William Brown argues that Job becomes more empathetic as a result of his time in the whirlwind. "Empathy becomes the heuristic tool for new discoveries, transforming objects, whether of pity, disdain, or fear, into subjects of intrinsic worth."[19] It is hard to imagine being appropriately empathetic without being grateful and humble. The relationship between humility and gratitude is obvious, but perhaps understated in Christian circles. Humility reinforces a grateful spirit and gratitude reminds one of one's place in the universe. And as we saw with Job, humility can renew one's trust in God and is a reason for joy. Even in the vastness of the cosmos, God remembers us little humans, and that too should cause us to give thanks.

Third, even though we are from the same soil and interdependently connected, we are different than other creatures. As noted above, we seem to be the only creatures who can see the "whole" of creation. To our knowledge no other creature possesses this insight. We have the ability to see the depth of creation that points to the mystery of its Creator. Moreover, we have the capacity to recognize the cosmic covenant that undergirds the universe and allows the creation to flourish when it is honored. However, we cannot truly see the whole without being humble since the whole points us toward God and not ourselves. The universe is theocentric, not anthropocentric, in character. We must humbly acknowledge that our ability to see the whole is limited by our creatureliness. As brilliant as we may be at times, we are neither omniscient nor omnipotent. Climate change reveals this truth more directly than perhaps any other. Also, as tillers of the soil we are different

17. McFague, *New Climate*, 53.

18. Quoted in Krueger, *Cloud of Witnesses*, 121.

19. Brown, *Ethos of the Cosmos*, 365.

in our vocation. No other creature has the task of "working" the soil. Just as Jesus washed the feet of his disciples and Noah built the ark, we are able to serve the needs of creation. No other creature may be able to watch the soil carefully and "keep" to the limits that allow creation to function beneficially for both human and nonhuman creatures. No other creature can willingly sacrifice its needs for the sake of others in love the way that we can. We must humbly resist the urge to allow our vocational mandate to make us believe that we are the zenith of creation and therefore become prideful. Job's whirlwind experience effectively demolishes anthropocentrism and replaces it with theocentrism. Again, we must think carefully about the exhortation of the psalmist: human exceptionalism is defined more by our wickedness than our righteousness. This, after all, is the very reason for the flood.

Fourth, our infatuation with being made in the image of God and our contrived notion of dominion have undoubtedly led to the historical despoliation of ecosystems and even the extinction of species as our behavior has reflected a God who is more tyrannical than loving, dictatorial than servant-like. If we are to revel in the notion that we are made in the image of God, then we must accept the vast responsibilities that come with this theological fact. Humans are made to act as God's representatives here on Earth. What we do directly reflects who we believe God to be. Therefore, we must learn to value what God values and how God shows it. By declaring that all of creation is very good, God exhibits a cosmocentric, rather than anthropocentric, focus. Through the whirlwind encounter with Job, God shows a biophilic streak that includes caring for the needs of all creatures, not just those of humans who do not know their proper place in the universe. We are to act justly by showing mercy and compassion to the widows, orphans, and aliens as God does. We are to acknowledge and proclaim a gospel message that includes the redemption of all creatures that God has created because God desires to be face-to-face with all good things at the consummation of the universe. In order to be *imago Dei* properly, we must heed the advice of the New Testament writers who connected the image of God with the image of Christ. If God became incarnate in the person of Jesus, then Jesus truly models the *imago Dei*. When we take this link seriously we come to a new understanding of dominion. "Thus when interpreted in the context of Christ, the realization of the image and the proper expression of dominion are not manifestations of exploitation, but rather *representations of nurturing and serving love*."[20] Moreover, Jesus' ministry to the widows, orphans, and aliens shows us how the love of God knows no boundaries. Hence, there is no compelling reason why this facet of God's

20. Nash, *Loving Nature*, 105; italics in original.

character should not be extended to those with no voice, like the vast multitude of nonhuman creatures around the planet. Consequently, the concept of dominion is far more limited than many Christians would like to believe. "[Dominion] is primarily the protection of the planet and its inhabitants *by* humans *against* human exploitation."[21]

Finally, it may be the case that humans are the only creatures who have the ability to have hope or place their hope in God, consciously at least. A lack of humility prevents us from trusting God fully and hence prevents us from being hopeful and manifesting hopeful behavior. The lack of humility caused by sloth eventually leads to despair and inhibits us from displaying the courage that hopeful followers of Jesus demonstrate knowing that death has been conquered. The perverse security that leads to presumption hampers us from acknowledging our proper place in the universe and therefore we place hope in ourselves and our technology rather than in God. This behavior prevents us from seeing the whole of creation clearly, and especially our ability to make mistakes and to sin. Hope, though, is built upon humility, which, as Job shows, leads to a renewed trust in God for grace and unprecedented possibilities. It is also symbolized by the resurrection of Jesus because in that event we are reminded of Job's seminal whirlwind insight: God is the Creator and we are creatures. As creatures, we cannot sustain our own existence nor conquer our greatest enemy—death; however, God can and that was exhibited radically in Jesus' resurrection. Therefore, recognition of creatureliness is not devaluing; it is the first step toward humility. The humility found in accepting our creatureliness allows us to be confidently expectant that we have a place in the final consummation of the universe as well as work to do presently, both of which should be reasons for joy. A person who hopes in God displays courage in the face of adversity, even death, because our trust is in God rather than in ourselves. We see this in the lives of martyrdom led by the earliest Christians as well as by Noah in the story of the flood. A person of hope also knows that sacrifice is not always rewarded in the present or immediate future, but that radical patience is often required. This is nowhere more evident than in the lives of those on the ark, who did not know when the rain would subside, or in the lives of the earliest Christians, who did not see the immediate return of Christ as they believed that they would. This lesson is just as pertinent today in the age of climate change as our sacrifices now will not be rewarded in the near future since we are unlikely to see climate stabilization in our lifetimes or the lifetimes of those even in the distant future. In spite of that we can be

21. Ibid., 106; italics in original.

confident that those sacrifices will form us more into the likeness of Christ and will not be forgotten by God.

In the end, it is difficult to comprehend how the common, but essentially vacuous, idea of stewardship helps Christians engage in theological and social imaginaries that meet the needs of our present time. Christians are in no significant way more grateful because we consider ourselves to be stewards of creation. Christians are in no demonstrable manner more humble because we see ourselves as stewards who are supposed to manage the rest of the created order. While we believe that sacrifice is necessary for disciples to model the love of Jesus, Christian stewardship seems to require no consequential amount of sacrifice in our care for creation. There is no reason to believe that the notion of stewardship makes us more hopeful Christians; instead, it appears to lead us toward hopelessness. Our practice of the stewardship of creation demonstrates a level of presumption as we rely on a security that has no basis in reality. We trust in our own vision of the future and our capacity to execute it rather than in God. This reinforces our prideful attempt to be God as we deny our creatureliness and our place within creation. And thus, we are at a loss to consider meaningful mitigation and adaptation strategies to climate change because we cannot come to grips with the basic truth of our present situation: our very vision of the good life is indeed what is causing the problem and must be changed drastically. We believe that we are living in the "already" aspect of hope's fulfillment, which prevents us from recognizing our lack of humility for what it is. In a lesser way, our practice of stewardship might also lead us toward despair. If the stewardship of creation does not demand that we sacrifice as we model the life of Christ, then we may subtly give ourselves over to sloth. The witnesses of Noah and Jesus both demonstrate that it is impossible to be magnanimous according to the call of God if one is not willing to sacrifice.[22]

Ecological Sin

If the above attributes and behaviors are the basis of what it means to be properly human, then ecological sin, or eco-sin, is caused by the painful and tragic lack of these same attributes and behaviors. If sin is the alienation of humans from God, our neighbors (both human and nonhuman), creation, and ultimately ourselves, then eco-sin may be defined as the rejection of creation as a gift from God, which is indicated by a lack of gratitude. Eco-sin is characterized by a lack of humility that comes from believing that we are the culmination of creation rather than interconnected and interdependent

22. Matt 10:39.

members that witness to the glory of God, like nonhuman members of creation do everyday. At the same time, it is the failure of recognizing that joy comes from accepting our creatureliness. It is also the failure to see the whole of creation as it points to the mysterious depth of God, and the rejection of the idea that creation has limits that we are supposed to be mindful of and keep as tillers of the soil. Eco-sin is the rejection of sacrifice as a component of love and of justice as a way of living, not merely awaiting the changing of law; both rejections are derived from the failure to think that our human behavior (e.g., progress, technological achievement, economic development, etc.) should be constrained as we seek to serve others, whether human or nonhuman. Eco-sin occurs when our perverted sense of humility does not acknowledge our creatureliness or our magnanimity, but instead is "a smokescreen to disguise willful ignorance and abrogation of responsibility,"[23] which leads to sloth and to the hopelessness of despair. Eco-sin can also be caused by the *perversa securitas* that makes us believe that we can rely on ourselves and our technology rather than on God. This can turn into an escape from the reality of the situation before us and the hopelessness of presumption.

Are eco-sins sins of commission or sins of omission? The short answer is that they can be both. It is easy to imagine us consciously and overtly exhibiting behaviors that demonstrate our ungratefulness toward God for creation's many gifts, e.g., our willingness to participate in activities that show we believe that we are the apex of evolution and thus are under no moral obligation to constrain our behavior and sacrifice for others. These are sins of commission. At the same time, ecologically sinful behaviors could also be sins of omission: we know the good we are to do but we choose to avoid doing it.[24] It is hard to believe that most world leaders want the planet's poor and dispossessed to suffer more intensely due to drought-induced famine brought on by climate change, but the lack of genuine action to mitigate these risks suggests a critical sort of omission. In the same way, it is difficult to imagine that most Christians desire for countless species around the world to continue to go extinct, but the lack of action that might actually save dwindling numbers of thousands of species of creatures suggests collective sins of omission, too.

There is, however, another category that we must consider: unintentional sins or sins of ignorance. This is not outside the theological imaginary of Scripture even if we spend little time discussing it.[25] Many eco-sins, whether

23. Moo and White, *Let Creation Rejoice*, 166.

24. Rom 7:19; Jas 4:17.

25. Lev 4; Num 15:22–28.

they are sins of the individual or social structural ones, fall into this category, especially for American Christians. For instance, we simply think very little about the ecological ramifications of our food choices at the grocery store or consumer decisions about the clothes we buy or the vacations we take with our family. Yet, everything we do has ecological consequences, some of which are better than others, but all of which happen regardless of whether we are cognizant of them or not. Whether we understand the particular details or not, industrially farmed meat has significant ecological consequences on the land, water, and air that surround the "farm" as well as the regions down-stream from the facility. (This does not even take into account the common unjust behavior exhibited toward the mostly migrant laborers who process the meat.) Whether we know it or not, when we buy cotton-based clothing made from non-organic cotton we are buying materials that have been covered with some of the most hazardous and destructive pesticides ever created, which not only affect consumers, but definitely degrade ecosystems surrounding and downstream from these farms. (This does not factor in the likely possibil-ity that the cotton was picked and the clothing manufactured by child labor.) Remember, in either of these scenarios or the countless other ones that we encounter everyday as average citizens in a developed nation like the United States, we are participating in activities that either form us more into the like-ness of Christ or not. Our lack of explicit recognition of the consequences of our actions does not take away from the fact that we either exist as Christians who witness to the hope of the resurrection in every aspect of our lives or as people who are succumbing to despair and presumption.

Is this sort of ignorance the individual fault of someone who calls her-self a Christian? Well, yes and no. Whether you went to a public school in a particular state or a private school with certain convictions can greatly influence the basics of your ecological education. Whether you were raised in a family of strong political leanings to the left or to the right can say much about how you understand the delicate balance between creation care and economic development. Corporations, lobbyists, political action groups, and numerous other "principalities and powers" have spent countless dol-lars in the past decades in order to shape the way that we see environmental issues around us as well. It is all too clear now that fossil-fuel companies and their vast network of think tanks, marketers, and other unscrupulous subsidiaries have spent hundreds of millions of dollars in the past half-century obfuscating the truth about the critical link between fossil fuels and anthropogenic climate change, much in the same way that the American tobacco industry deceived its customers for decades about the association between smoking and various forms of cancer even though the industry knew the science was absolutely credible.[26] Those engaged in deceiving the American public about the fossil-fuel industry's participation in anthropogenic climate change have undoubtedly committed intentional sins of commission, and they continue to do so. The results of these sins are not only anthropogenic climate disruption, the extinction of thousands of species, and millions of climate refugees needing new places to live, but the deceitful shaping of a generation of Americans into believing that climate science was not settled or that climate scientists had a hidden liberal agenda that could not be trusted or that the governments of the world were really using climate change as one component of a larger agenda to dismantle personal freedoms. Unfortunately, far too many American Christians have allowed themselves to be duped by these sophisticated and well-funded campaigns of chicanery. Part of this is due to the American Protestant Christian culture that demonstrates an incredibly limited theological imaginary, as we seem to believe that only a small range of behaviors constitute sins worthy of contemplation or perhaps are actually sins at all. Our contemporary focus on issues like abortion, gay marriage, and premarital sex prevents us from asking significant questions about the authenticity of claims made by those who deny the reality of climate change or the other examples listed in the paragraph above. Additionally, we seem content with being deceived because, for the most part, we benefit greatly from the status quo these principalities and powers peddle since most American Christians have not been directly affected by climate change in explicitly perceivable ways. We have not been forced to migrate from our homes. Food prices have not yet dramatically risen. Biodiversity loss does not factor into meeting the demands of a monthly budget. By allowing ourselves to be deceived and failing to ask critical questions about the vision being cast by the principalities and powers, we exhibit an intellectual laziness that only serves to promote injustice against humans, nonhuman creatures, and the rest of creation.[27] This prevents us from engaging in the critique of injustice that hope demands and modeling the hopeful lives that Christians are invited to live.

Should Christians feel guilty about eco-sin, whether they are intentional or unintentional? The short answer is yes. We feel guilty when we know that our behavior is in some manner or another wrong. Guilt demonstrates that we have a moral compass, of some sort at least, that recognizes the difference between right and wrong. So is it possible to have ecological guilt or eco-guilt? Psychologist Robyn Mallett argues that it is. She defines it thusly: "Eco-guilt is guilt that arises when people think about times they

---

26. Cf. Orestes and Conway, *Merchants of Doubt.*

27. I am thankful to Gabriella Palmeri for assisting me with this idea.

have not met personal or societal standards for environmental behavior."[28] This might manifest itself as guilt for using too many natural resources, for using them inappropriately, for not protecting the environment, or for not being environmentally responsible. The guilt that may arise as a consequence of these sorts of behaviors comes from complex relationships of cultural conditioning, personal decision-making, and societal enforcement of norms, whether that is through legal or other means. She contends that eco-guilt can motivate one to engage in eco-friendly behavior because "Repairing harm is uniquely motivated by feelings of guilt."[29] There is, though, a twofold problem. First, what if someone does not have the cultural conditioning or social imaginary that might cause a person to have the sort of moral compass that would lead one to feel eco-guilt? Theologically speaking, what if a Christian's theological imaginary does not include a notion of eco-sin, or something like it, that gets one to feel guilty about ecological wrongdoing? This is obviously a significant problem. It is hard for us to feel guilty about destroying God's good Earth if we believe that we as stewards are morally obligated to subdue it as we see fit and we are convinced that we are doing a pretty good job at being stewards, whatever that might actually mean.

Second, we must ask: Does eco-guilt have the capacity to change our social imaginary and thus influence behavior? Does it effect short-term or long-term behavior change? Theologically speaking, we might ask: Does guilt really cause us to have a change of heart leading to long-term behavior change? I remain unconvinced that guilt alone causes a change of heart. Instead, guilt alerts an individual that something might be wrong, possibly even dreadfully wrong, but guilt alone does not spur us into a new way of living. It does not make us hopeful. For Christians, though, guilt should stimulate us in an important way. It should stir us toward repentance. Augustine's profound insights into linking the sins of his youth with the grace of God are illustrative here. "I intend to remind myself of my past foulnesses and carnal corruptions, not because I love them but so that I may love you, my God. . . . The recalling of my wicked ways is bitter in my memory, but I do it so that you may be sweet to me, a sweetness touched by no deception, a sweetness seen and content."[30] By the constant recounting of his sin, Augustine remembered his need for God's grace and subsequently the sweetness and nearness of divine love. Analogously, we need to feel eco-guilt by reminding ourselves of our eco-sin in order that we might remember that we are creatures and God is the Creator; that we are to be humble and grateful instead of domineering

28. Mallett, "Eco-Guilt," 223.

29. Ibid., 229.

30. Augustine, *Confessions*, 24.

and excessive; that our ability to see the whole of creation should cause us to care for it rather than despoil and destroy it. Much like Augustine, we need to repent of our past sins, especially our eco-sins. Eco-guilt should move us to repentance, and through repentance we can be open to the unprecedented possibilities offered by hope.

The Greek verb *metanoew* which is translated "repent" carries with it four distinct emphases. Repent could connote the emotional regret of feeling sorry for one's actions; it could imply existential movement, in the sense of changing one's mind; it could signify the need for expiatory contrition on the part of the offender; and it could suggest a radical change in the relationship between God and humanity—a conversion.[31] In light of the specter of our historical eco-sins as well as the severe consequences of human-induced climate change, Christians need to repent in all four senses of this word. We need to feel guilty for the sins of commission, omission, and ignorance that we have perpetrated against God's creation and against so many of its nonhuman inhabitants. We need the guilt of our past and present eco-sins to stir our very existence in order that we might change our minds. We must take seriously the idea that sacrifice will be required to obtain any sort of absolution for our destructive ways. Finally, we must recognize that we are in need of a significant conversion—a conversion from truncated notions of God, creation, and humanity that have led us to this crisis. Our repentance needs to start with a prayer of confession that might lead us toward repentance. I submit the following from the fourth-century theologian Saint Basil to serve as that prayer.

The earth is the Lord's and the fullness thereof.

O God, enlarge within us the sense of fellowship with all living things, even our brothers [and sisters], the animals, to whom Thou gavest the earth as their home in common with us.

We remember with shame that in the past we have exercised the high dominion of man [sic] with ruthless cruelty so that the voice of the earth, which should have gone up to thee in song, has been a groan of pain.

May we realize that they live, not for us alone, but for themselves and for Thee and that they love the sweetness of life.[32]

31. Kittel, *Theological Dictionary*, 4:975–1008.
32. Basil of Caesarea, "Liturgy of Basil," quoted in Krueger, *Cloud of Witnesses*, 83.

6

The Idol of Economic Growth

I t is amazing what an impressive trait human intuition is. Our initial
gut reaction to an event has often been known to keep humans out of
trouble; it has even been known to save lives. The growl of a bear heard
in the distance can trigger one's flight response immediately. This intuition
has also been known to help students on examinations, as failing to trust it
by second-guessing often leads to wrong answers. When I get to the economics portion of a course that I teach on Christianity and sustainability,
I draw two figures on the board.[1] The first figure is a large circle with a
square inside of it. The circle is labeled "Earth" and the square is labeled
"Economy." The second figure is a large square with a circle within it. The
labels for the circle and square in the first figure remain the same. These
rather simple figures are meant to represent the fundamental assertions of
two different ways of looking at how we understand the relationship of the
planet to the economy. Is the economy dependent on the Earth's resources
or is the Earth merely a subset of the larger economy? The first figure, the
one with the economy constrained by the Earth, is a crude representation of
the fundamental presupposition of what is often referred to as the "ecological economic model,"[2] while the second figure is a portrayal of the essential
starting point of what is often called the "neoclassical economic model."
I then turn to my class and ask, "Intuitively, which relationship between
the Earth and the economy makes sense?" Inevitably, my classes choose the
first figure; the economy is dependent upon what the Earth actually has to
give us. Next I ask, "Does technology change this equation at all?" In other
words, does technology somehow allow us to overlook the finite nature of
Earth's resources? Undoubtedly, a good student or two will chime in and re-

1. Adapted from Clapp and Dauvergne, *Paths to a Green World*, 107; adapted
from Daly, *Beyond Growth*, 29.
2. For an introduction to ecological economics, see Eriksson and Andersson,
Elements of Ecological Economics; Common and Stagl, *Ecological Economics*; Daly and
Farley, *Ecological Economics*.

mind the class that technology might allow us to use natural resources more efficiently, but it does not somehow transform nonrenewable resources into renewable ones. Once all of the oil is used, it is gone regardless of how clean-burning our cars might be. I then ask my class one more question: "Which one of these figures symbolizes the way the United States operates?" To date, each class has answered that the United States operates as if the Earth is a subset of the economy. We intuitively know that the Earth's finite amount of resources should set the limits of our economy, regardless of technological achievement, but we live according to an economic worldview that functions as if the world's resources are infinite or technology will at least allow us to live as if they are. Sadly enough, many Christians (among many others within the developed and developing world) have been duped into thinking that our intuition is in fact wrong.

The Idol and Its Priesthood

The United States, most of the rest of the developed-world nations, and an increasing portion of the developing world operate according to some version of neoclassical economic principles. The World Bank, the World Trade Organization (WTO), the World Business Council for Sustainable Development, the G-8, the G-20, and treaties like GATT and NAFTA are just some of the economic and political entities that typify the ubiquity of the neoclassical economic worldview. Central to this worldview is a belief in the concept of economic growth—and not just a belief in economic growth per se, but a belief that the more unfettered the economic growth, the better. And yet, economic growth is not merely a concept within a broader vision of economic theory; it is has become "the secular religion of the advancing industrial societies."[3] To borrow Paul Tillich's language, economic growth has taken on the character of "ultimate concern," as it seems that is all that our society is fixated upon.[4] From a Christian point of view, economic growth is not merely Western culture's new religion, but perhaps its chief idol. If we make the appropriate sacrifices, then consider what economic growth is supposed to give us: a higher standard of living, more participatory democracies, significant alleviation of world poverty, and more leisure time are among its principal promises. Economic growth can allegedly foster moral progress[5] and help us to determine the difference

3. Bell, *Cultural Contradictions*, 30.
4. Tillich, *Dynamics of Faith*.
5. Friedman, *Moral Consequences*.

between right and wrong.[6] What reasonable person would not sacrifice the
appropriate offerings to this idol? Indeed, the sacrifices in some measure or
another in much of the world have been severe: the dignity of human labor,
health of employees, sovereign political democracies, and ecosystem vigor
and stability, to name a few. While the sacrifices have been abundant and
offered consistently since the middle of the twentieth century, the promised
gifts have only been delivered to a very select few in the developed world.[7]
The priests of economic growth (the World Bank, the WTO, the leaders of
many developed-world nations, many of the world's leading transnational
corporations, etc.) insist that if the blessings of economic growth have not
been procured, then the sacrifices have not been substantial enough. And
so there are calls for more deregulation, less-stringent environmental laws,
less concern about national infrastructure development, less protection in
the workplace for laborers, etc. These priests do all that they can to prevent
us from asking this critical question: Does this idol actually have the power
to deliver on its rather lofty promises? This question marks the beginning of
the critique that hope demands of Christians in the age of climate change.

Before we get to that question, we must determine what economic
growth precisely is. Economic growth refers to the increase in the market
value of the goods and services produced by a given economy over time.
Economic growth is often measured by Gross Domestic Product (GDP),
which accounts for all of the goods and services that are exchanged for
monetary value in a given economy. When economists talk about GDP
per capita, they are discussing a common indicator of the standard of living produced by a given economy. Simply put, when economic growth is
steep our ability to consume goods and services expands; when economic
growth is stagnant or declining our capacity to consume decreases. While
consumption itself can be vilified from time to time, like many things, it
can be either a good thing or a bad thing. Human beings are biological
creatures who must consume other organisms in order to stay alive since
we lack the ability to transform sunlight into energy as our fellow creatures
with chloroplasts can. But, we know that the consumption of too much food
can in fact be a very bad thing because it can make us obese. Yet we find
ourselves asking the question, "If an apple a day keeps the doctor away, then
why not eat 10 apples a day?" For most of human history there has been an

6. Robert Nelson argues that economists' sense of "efficient" and "inefficient" has
replaced "right" and "wrong" in the American sense of civic morality. Nelson, "Theology of Economics," 92–94.

7. For a view of the economic system from the perspective of the Global South,
see Anderson, *Views from the South*; Shiva, *Earth Democracy*; Shiva, *Soil Not Oil*; Bello,
Deglobalization.

intrinsic link between more and better.[8] Moreover, there is an inextricable connection between consumption and happiness. For most of us, eating a piece of chocolate every once in a while can make us happy. So we are often tempted to ask ourselves, "If a small piece of chocolate after dinner makes us happy, then won't a large piece of chocolate after each meal make us very happy?" At this point, we must weigh our immediate sense of gratification from eating an exquisite piece of stone-ground chocolate against the likelihood of becoming obese due to eating chocolate excessively. Consumption itself is not necessarily the problem, but how much one consumes definitely is. While the quantity of our consumption can definitely make us happy, it only does so up to a point because eventually more does not equal better.

So why do Americans continue to consume when we are not any happier than other nations in the world, even though we are substantially wealthier in some cases?[9] Why do we willingly participate in an economy that practices "more equals better"–style consumption? One reason is that we define prosperity solely by our ability to consume goods and services. Economic growth allows us to amass wealth quickly, which in turn gives us the capacity to consume, and thus we think prosperity has more to do with luxury and opulence than anything else. This can be seen no more clearly than in our overwhelming societal belief that GDP is an accurate indicator of the strength of our national economy. Yet, this has nothing to do with the things that economic prosperity could really bring about: education for citizens, healthcare for those who need it, the infrastructure that allows for clean air and water, or even biodiversity conservation. We shall return to this topic below.

Another reason we consume so much is that the priests of the neoclassical worldview employ a sophisticated cadre of advertisers and marketers who shape consumer desire. Vincent Miller persuasively argues that consumer desire is influenced heavily by seduction and misdirection. Consumers are seduced not by the accumulation of lots of things, but by the constant search to accumulate. "Consumer desire is neither about attachment nor enjoyment. . . . Seduction is not about *having* the perfect outfit, piece of jewelry, or CD. It is about *seeking* the perfect one, about ensuring one has access to just the right one for just the right time."[10] The constant search for gratification did not need to be created by advertisers and marketers as a

8. McKibben, *Deep Economy*, 1.

9. See World Happiness Report, "World Happiness Report 2016," http://worldhappiness.report; Happy Planet Index, "Measuring What Matters," http://www.happyplanetindex.org.

10. Miller, *Consuming Religion*, 127; italics in original. See also Cavanaugh, *Being Consumed*, 33–58.

gimmick to buy more stuff; for Christians, we recognize it as an intrinsic part of the human condition. As Augustine famously wrote in the opening lines of *Confessions*, "You have made us for yourself, and our heart is restless until it rests in you."[11] Humans are creatures who are made to search for something. Advertisers and marketers do not have to convince us otherwise. The fact that consumer desire is so closely related to our search for the divine perhaps signifies why humans are so easily fooled by advertising campaigns. We are already pointed in the correct direction; all we need is a little push.

According to Miller, "Misdirection evokes and sustains desire for commodities by associating them with unrelated human needs and desires."[12] He goes on to say that "the decline of traditional social and cultural markers of identity and belonging, the rise of advertising, and the increasing complexity of commercial products" are all critical factors in the misdirection of desire.[13] This misdirection is considerably profound as we think about how advertisers and marketers are especially adept at compelling us to blur the line between needs and wants. They do this in two ways. First, they remind us constantly of a true claim: the differentiation between needs and wants is decidedly relative. For example, is a mobile phone really a necessity for life; is it a need? In one sense, the answer is of course no; human beings existed for thousands of years without mobile phones and seemed to do just fine. But if you are living in the United States in the twenty-first century and have regular access to electricity and telephone service, one could make the case that a mobile phone is a need. Granting for a moment that having a mobile phone is a certain type of need, the next question is even more difficult: What kind of phone do you need? Does it need to have the ability to send and receive texts? Does it need to be a smartphone? If you are a teenager or college student these may seem like silly questions, and yet that is the point. Our context often, if not always, determines perceptions about need and want. With technology evolving so quickly and new types of phones making their ways to the market so rapidly, we as consumers find ourselves asking a new kind of question: Do we *need* to upgrade to the newest version or do we merely *want* a newer phone? The line between needs and wants is easily blurred because humans are masters of rationalization. As small children, one of the first things we learn to do after we learn the difference between the words "need" and "want" is to manipulate the adults in our lives. My grandparents have often told the story about when I was a small child that

11. Augustine, *Confessions*, 3.
12. Miller, *Consuming Religion*, 116.
13. Ibid., 119.

I did not *want* blueberry muffins for breakfast, but instead I *needed* them. While perhaps we require no additional assistance blurring the line between needs and wants because of our seemingly innate capacity to rationalize, advertisers and marketers prey upon this human trait in more innovative ways than the average consumer is consciously aware of or can even imagine. And once we become convinced that a want is actually a need, we make ourselves believe that we are unable to make sense of our lives without it. In our most honest moments, we can hear ourselves saying, "How could I ever go without my mobile phone?" It is a very short step from asking this question to saying that these "needs" that provide order and meaning in our lives now play a moral role that justifies our actions. We end up using our new needs to justify substituting previous notions of right and wrong.[14] Mobile phone production and waste is environmentally destructive and in most cases systematically unjust to the humans who put together the products, but we cannot imagine our lives without our phones.

The priests of this worldview also promote this blurring by claiming that humans are naturally insatiable.[15] This assertion goes all the way back to the great prophet of economic growth, Adam Smith, who argues that human desire is "altogether endless."[16] If we are truly insatiable, then it only makes sense to continue to produce goods and services at an ever-accelerating rate, which consequently feeds economic growth. And if our insatiability is truly natural, why would we advocate for restraint of any sort? In fact, restraining our wants that we have convinced ourselves are actually needs may be psychologically destructive to our natural proclivity, and thus what was once seen as vicious is now understood to be normal, as we justify our behavior by calling it "rational." We find ourselves saying, "The sin of avarice cannot be overcome; therefore it should be used 'rationally.'"[17] It is not merely a vindication of our vices, but a profound alteration of what we believe it means to be human. The priests of economic growth work hard to make us believe that those who suffer from being unable to fulfill their "needs" are not fully human. We might hear ourselves saying, "What kind of parent are you if you do not give your eight-year-old child a mobile phone?" In this perverted context, "To want more is a sign that we are alive and more deserving than those with fewer needs."[18] This, however, is a claim that Christians must wholeheartedly reject or our faith in God is ultimately

14. Meeks, *God the Economist*, 166. See also, Bell, *Economy of Desire*, 102–3.

15. Ibid., 160–62.

16. Smith, *Inquiry*, 1:183.

17. Meeks, *God the Economist*, 168.

18. Ibid., 172.

futile because not even the divine could ever satisfy us. The consequences of this sort of misdirection are especially pernicious as the inability to distinguish appropriately between needs and wants can further separate those with wealth from those who have little to none. Our inability to discern what sufficiency actually might be is ultimately damaging to oneself, one's neighbors, and the rest of creation. Finally, this blurring of the need/want distinction prevents us from entertaining seriously the possibility that any sort of economy that does not rely on neoclassical principles could be effective because, for our supposedly insatiable selves, more is always better than less, faster is always better than slower, a newer upgrade is always better than an older model.

Miller also argues that consumer desire is potentially threatening to two components of Christian eschatology. The first is the radical notion of hope that critiques the present and offers good news to the oppressed, which we discussed in chapter 2. "The synthesis of deferral and anticipation that marks seduction is likely to reduce eschatological hope to an impotent desire for improvement that, because it is by nature not invested in any particular object or program, can envision nothing new, only endless superficial changes in the present order."[19] He goes further, contending, "Since desire is sustained by being detached from particular objects, consumer anticipation wishes for everything and hopes for nothing . . . Consumer anticipation is at heart a way of accommodating the endless repeat of the same, of finding pleasure in a world without hope."[20] This is antithetical to the gospel of Jesus Christ. The resurrection hope should stimulate an imaginative faith that endeavors to impart novel possibilities inspired by divine grace; it is not like the newest technological upgrade that is sold to us as if it will transform our lives, if only marginally, until the next upgrade become available. The resurrection is hope. The second component Miller proposes is that consumer desire can jeopardize the Christian commitment to seeking justice. "The absorption of concern for the other into commodification, likewise threatens to route the disruptive power of the eschatological and apocalyptic desire for justice into shopping."[21] This can be seen no more clearly than in the current strategies of environmental care encouraged by the neoclassical priesthood. If consumers want to pay more for fair-trade coffee or eco-friendly cleaning supplies, then the market will provide and it will contribute to economic growth. The assumption that "the market will provide" is a tacit acceptance of the status quo and does little to ascertain

19. Miller, *Consuming Religion*, 130.

20. Ibid., 132.

21. Ibid., 130.

whether or not injustice is occurring. For instance, should one purchase fair-trade coffee because conventional coffee supports unjust wages for farmers and fieldworkers? Should one purchase eco-friendly cleaning supplies because conventional ones necessarily pollute waterways and other sensitive ecosystems?

Controlling consumer desire is not the only way that the priesthood maintains the idol's prominent position in our society. Another way is through the claim that economics does not depend upon ethical presuppositions and can hence be considered an objective science. From Nobel Prize–winning economist Milton Friedman, "Positive economics is in principle independent of any particular ethical position or normative judgments . . . positive economics is, or can be, an 'objective' science, in precisely the same sense as any of the physical sciences."[22] This claim is indefensible. Russian Orthodox theologian Sergei Bulgakov's critique is especially piercing: "The science of economics belongs to the most contingent and philosophically least independent of disciplines; yet it has accepted the dominant role assigned to it by our wealth-conscious epoch, striving to become the regal legislator of thought and expanding its influence far beyond its own horizons."[23] We live in a society that makes so many decisions based upon whether economic growth will be increased or not. Consider just a few examples of things our society willingly accepts in the name of sound economic decision-making: many industries are less safe to work in today than they were in the past due to a host of deregulating influences; many industries have moved their manufacturing centers to developing-world nations in order to pay their labor force less and to boost profit margins; many industries have lobbied strenuously against environmental regulation because it purportedly makes the cost of business prohibitive.

Economics has indeed expanded its influence beyond its own horizons by making vast anthropological, political, and even theological claims. One such claim is that manufactured capital can satisfactorily be substituted for natural capital.[24] For instance, take the world's wetland systems: they protect populations from flooding and from wave activity caused by hurricanes; they can also serve as a filter for a certain amount of polluting runoff that would otherwise go directly into our oceans. Due to the massive elimination of the world's wetlands, many nations have been forced to build levees and wastewater treatment plants to do the jobs that wetlands used

---

22. Friedman, *Essays in Positive Economics*, 4.

23. Bulgakov, *Philosophy of Economy*, 44.

24. For more on this, see Daly and Cobb, *For the Common Good*; Ekins, *Economic Growth*.

to do for free. For adherents of neoclassical economic thought, levees and wastewater treatment plants can at some level replace what healthy wetland ecosystems used to do for no cost. But why do we believe so strongly that natural capital is basically interchangeable with manufactured capital? One chief reason goes back to our idol. We can account for manufactured capital in our calculations of GDP in an effort to determine quantitatively what economic growth has supposedly given us. It is easy to conclude that this is why manufactured capital is intrinsically prized over natural capital in neoclassical economic thought. Measuring economic growth by indicators like GDP is highly flawed, however, since all externalities are not factored into the measurements. For example, while our intuition would tell us that any indicator that counts the cleanup of an oil spill in the Pacific Ocean positively is askew, that is exactly how environmental disaster cleanups are calculated by the neoclassical priesthood. Any goods and services that contribute to economic growth are counted in the positive ledger regardless of whether "cleanup" is actually possible or successful, or whether ecosystems and the species within them have been irrevocably harmed. As long as goods and services are added to the economy, growth occurs.

The neoclassical economic worldview also presupposes that humans are individuals who make rational decisions based upon self-interest. Self-interest itself is not necessarily a vice. Alexis de Tocqueville, the great French sociologist who documented nineteenth-century America, maintains that self-interest properly understood was a driving impetus behind the American sense of civic virtue. This idea was not peculiar to the American experience, but one that Tocqueville believed was rooted universally in the lives of American citizens: "Man [sic] helps himself by serving others and that doing good serves his own interest."[25] He goes on to say, "[Americans] do not, therefore deny that every man [sic] can pursue his own self-interest but they turn themselves inside out to prove that it is in each man's interest to be virtuous."[26] And that sense of virtue is seen in light of the broader American community. "Every American has the sense to sacrifice some of his [sic] personal interests to save the rest."[27] For Tocqueville, then, nineteenth-century Americans understood that it was in one's self-interest to practice a least a modicum of virtue in order that the rest of the community might have the opportunity in some way or another to flourish. It is hard to see this sense of civic virtue, as limited as it may be, within the daily sermons we are bombarded with by the neoclassical priesthood. They tell us, "The economy

25. Tocqueville, *Democracy in America*, 610.
26. Ibid.
27. Ibid., 612.

prospers the most when the individual consumer is free to seek the self-interest of the individual consumer." If that includes the sacrifice of one's individual well-being for the good of the community or other creatures or even the planet, then that is for the individual to decide. It may even be virtuous to do so, but it is not a requirement of economic self-interest to be minimally virtuous. This anthropological presupposition is economic dogma for this allegedly objective science. "[I]f the laws that structure markets are properly defined, if essential goods and services are provided to those who cannot provide them for themselves, if most people and organizations live out a lively morality that readily goes beyond the minimum requirements specified by law, and if civil society is vibrant, we can typically count on self-interest in markets to be constructive and not morally offensive."[28] It is doubtful that these four ifs can ever be met and therefore it is a stretch to believe that self-interest can be constructive and not morally offensive. On this point, Douglas Meeks is entirely correct. "Economic theory claims to be the most 'realist' of all theories. But in point of fact much of modern economic theory has a utopian cast. It tries to make the economy conform to human and social conditions that could exist only in a nonhistorical world."[29] This is even more the case if we consider environmental conditions, too.

Tocqueville's description of the American experience is not nearly as naive as that offered by the neoclassical priesthood—he was keenly aware of the downfalls of self-interest improperly understood. "We must, therefore, expect private self-interest to become more than ever the principal, if not the only motivation, for human actions, but it remains to be seen how each individual will interpret this private self-interest. If, on the achievement of equality, citizens were to remain ignorant and coarse, it would be difficult to predict what ridiculous excesses their selfishness might commit and one would not be able to foretell to what shameful depths of wretchedness they would plummet for fear of sacrificing something of their own wellbeing to the prosperity of their fellow man [sic]."[30] We have not achieved equality and our selfishness appears boundless. And this is where we find ourselves today: economic decisions are not truly governed rationally by self-interest, but instead by selfish desires that have very little, if anything, to do with the well-being of our community or the rest of creation even though this pursuit is supposed to make us happy.[31] This sort of selfish behavior prevents us from truly loving our neighbors as ourselves, whether that neighbor is

28. Finn, *Christian Economic Ethics*, 220.

29. Meeks, *God the Economist*, 9.

30. Tocqueville, *Democracy in America*, 613.

31. This is not merely a theological critique. See Marglin, *Dismal Science*.

human or otherwise. And yet, it is even more than this: "The emphasis on self-interest entails a rejection of any substantive notion of a shared purpose or common good that unites humanity."[32] That said, how do we as a human civilization use economics to mitigate or adapt to climate change if by anthropological presupposition we cannot engage in a common good? While some Christian economists reject this notion of shared purpose or common good in a large society,[33] Milton Friedman rejects the notion outright. He maintains, "Few trends could so thoroughly undermine the very foundations of our free society as the acceptance by corporate officials of a social responsibility other than to make as much money for their stockholders as possible."[34] If Friedman is correct, why would corporations ever voluntarily be helpful in mitigating or adapting to climate change? After all, it will not always be beneficial financially to engage in mitigation and adaptation efforts. It is not just that Tocqueville's prediction has gone unheeded by many economists, but that many economists still assume that humans make rational decisions based upon self-interest when in fact we make decisions for many different reasons, many of which have little to do with supposedly rational thinking.[35] For instance, if Friedman is correct and economics has no ethical moorings, then economists have no way to distinguish between good and evil self-interest. Without a proper understanding of what sort of self-interest might be good or evil, economics is rather hopeless as it fails to do much more than facilitate the whims of individuals who happen to have the capacity to consume as they see fit. Moreover, Christians must not be so quick to believe that rationality is ever the only thing that dictates our decision-making. As sinners, we know firsthand that the apostle Paul's assessment of the human condition is entirely accurate: "I do not understand what I do. For what I want to do I do not do, but what I hate I do."[36]

Another fundamental presupposition of economics that keeps the idol strong is that scarcity is pervasive and fundamental. Economics, then, is the science that supposedly assists in a society's allocation of goods and services under such scarce circumstances. This premise is axiomatic for economists. Some Christian enthusiasts of our current system contend that scarcity propels humans to creativity and productivity. "Creation left to itself is incomplete, and humans are called to be co-creators with God, bring forth the potentialities the Creator has hidden. Creation is full of secrets

32. Bell, *Economy of Desire*, 101.

33. Hill and Lunn, "Markets and Morality," 627–53.

34. Friedman, *Capitalism and Freedom*, 133.

35. Finn, *Christian Economic Ethics*, 224–28.

36. Rom 7:14.

waiting to be discovered, riddles which human intelligence is expected by the Creator to unlock. The world did not spring from the hand of God as wealthy as humans might make it."[37] The problems with this viewpoint are numerous. This supposedly self-evident notion should compel Christians to ask this question: If God created the world and desires for us to live an abundant life, then is scarcity really the pervasive and fundamental fact that economists claim it to be? God's provision of manna to the Israelites in the wilderness, Jesus' multiplication of the fish and the loaves in the feedings of the multitudes, and the eucharistic meal shed light on an essentially different reality. "*If* the righteousness of God is present, there is always enough to go around."[38] The problem is not that God created a planet wherein humans and other creatures must fight with each other over the barest of necessities because God promises to provide, even if the work is difficult or the Earth does not always bear fruit easily. The problem is this: "Scarcity is not a natural condition but the consequence of sin."[39] Scarcity is not the problem; sharing resources justly is. Human sinfulness prevents us from sharing with each other and other creatures in ways that might demonstrate basic Christian virtues like generosity, equity, and charity. Additionally, the allegedly unassailable doctrine of scarcity legitimizes our desire for more as we believe that our own personal security and well-being are at stake if we do not satisfy our desires before the resources that it takes to satiate them are used by someone else. But, it is even more than that. "Scarcity is the more general hunger of those who want more, without reference to what they already have."[40] The failure to recognize the fullness of God's blessings that sustain our very existence and provide for our needs is the source of this notion of scarcity and its attendant ills. Moreover, this idea suggests a heretical view of God. "In this way, God is cast as a kind of sadistic cosmic Easter bunny, hiding stuff from humanity so that in the conflict and competition to find it, individuals will develop various traits and capacities. This is a sadist's game because not everyone succeeds in developing and finding."[41] Christian witnesses of the resurrection hope must stand firm in their assertion that this God is not the God who provided manna in the wilderness or blessed the loaves and fish for the multitudes. Instead, this portrayal of God is a blasphemous one; it is a deity who is conjured up to justify the hard work of "winners" of the neoclassical system against the "losers" who are

37. Novak, *Spirit of Democratic Capitalism*, 39.
38. Meeks, *God the Economist*, 12; italics in original.
39. Bell, *Economy of Desire*, 180.
40. Cavanaugh, *Being Consumed*, 90.
41. Bell, *Economy of Desire*, 116.

allegedly not ingenious enough to find the Easter eggs that God left behind to be discovered. The dogma of scarcity preached in a world that is created by God is a mark of the hopelessness of our present economic system and demonstrates the lengths the economic growth idol would go to in order to preserve its hegemony.

With the overemphasis of the rights and the supposed freedoms of the individual plus the doctrine of pervasive scarcity, it should come as no surprise that competition between humans, and eventually between corporations, is another basic anthropological presupposition that upholds the idol of economic growth. If there are only so many resources to go around and the individual's wants/needs are more important than any sense of shared purpose or common good, then it only makes sense that intense competition, if not all-out war, is the neoclassical priesthood's description of the basic interaction among humans. The sad fact is that Christians often do not question whether this description of reality is accurate. In other words, is competition really the only way that humans relate to each other in the economic sphere? Furthermore, what have we given away by implicitly acceding to this anthropological assertion? This emphasis on competition has led to the commodification of human relations in the economic sphere.[42] Thus, the question of an employee's worth is characteristically conceived only in monetary terms. Those who "cost" more are supposedly producing more and perhaps harder to replace than those who "cost" little and hence can be viewed as highly replaceable. This is the basis of what is often referred to as "human capital." This leads exactly to the perverted logic represented by the famous confidential memorandum from the chief economist of the World Bank: "Just between you and me, shouldn't the World Bank be encouraging MORE migration of the dirty industries to the LDCs [less-developed nations]? . . . The measurements of the costs of health impairing pollution depends on the foregone earnings from increased morbidity and mortality. From this point of view a given amount of health impairing pollution should be done in the country with the lowest cost, which will be the country with the lowest wages. I think the economic logic behind dumping a load of toxic waste in the lowest wage country is impeccable and we should face up to that."[43] Why should developed-world citizens who maintain a higher standard of living through education, technological consumption, medical services, etc., not send their trash to a lesser-developed nation whose citizens have not been invested in as heavily and thus do not cost as much to replace? We should all have to share the burden of health-impairing waste even if we did not create it or benefit from it, right?

42. Ibid., 103–9.
43. From Lawrence Summers, quoted in Pellow, *Resisting Global Toxics*, 9.

If humans can be commodified into monetized units, then why not the rest of creation as well? Recent attempts at monetizing ecosystem services like oxygen production, carbon sequestration, local atmospheric cooling, pollination of food crops, etc., represent the laudable effort to convince people of the vast services that nature provides for us that we would have to commit large segments of our GDP toward if nature was not doing it for free.[44] The mathematical sophistication required to compute "ecosystem services" or "natural capital" is impressive and it is a commendable enterprise to demonstrate in real-world dollars what nature does for free in hopes of convincing our society that we should protect these systems more vigorously. However helpful this exercise may be to showing economists, politicians, and other world leaders that we cannot afford to live without these services, it relies upon three troublesome presuppositions. First, it relies on a very healthy approximation of human ingenuity and its ability to calculate the vastness and multitudes of these services correctly. One must cautiously wonder if this is more an exercise in hubris than humility than we care to admit. Second, this sort of economic calculus still operates under the assumption that we are not only in competition with each other, but with nature as well. Once we have calculated natural capital accurately, we can then win the competition with nature by choosing to protect those services that maximize our wins and minimize our losses. This not only supports the neoclassical priesthood's sacrosanct idea of competition, but also furthers our sense of hubristic omniscience as it feeds the belief that we can actually know ecosystem functioning well enough to choose the winners and losers. Finally, it also supports the neoclassical belief that economic evaluations can adequately express the value of something. This should trouble Christians greatly when we consider using the terms "human capital" as well as "natural capital." The belief that an economic evaluation is satisfactory, if not preferable, is an egregious slander against the divine proclamation in Genesis 1 that everything God created is very good.

Daniel Bell Jr. contends that another important presupposition of neoclassical economics is that the freedom to choose is both formal and negative.[45] It is formal in the sense that the neoclassical priesthood is interested only in making the freedom to choose paramount, while the goal of such choice is undefined. As long as the consumer is free to choose, then the priesthood applauds the structures in place that allow for individual choice and therefore soundly discourages any economic or political entities

---

44. E.g., Daily, *Nature's Services*; Kareiva et al., *Natural Capital*; Heal, *Nature and the Marketplace*.

45. Bell, *Economy of Desire*, 98–99.

that might impede that choice. This supports the notion that we exist more freely as a nation of sovereign choosers,[46] which empowers us to maintain an aura of individuality that does not depend on anyone or anything else. Secondly, the freedom to choose is negative because it is a "freedom from" rather than a "freedom for." It is a freedom from coercion by an outside entity like the government or a freedom from the community encouraging our participation in the pursuit of a common good. This is the sort of freedom that Friedman and other priests of economic growth believe is at stake if humans restrain their wants to attain a common societal good, because the invisible hand cannot direct the market if any other sort of freedom exists. "Individual freedom cannot be reconciled with the supremacy of one single purpose to which the whole of society must be entirely and permanently subordinated."[47] And so again we are left with a fundamental dilemma: How can a collective, global response to climate change not appear as an affront to individual freedom?

It should not surprise us, then, that distributive justice has little to do with neoclassical economics, as this sort of justice is seen potentially to impinge on an individual's self-interest and ability to exercise choice. Instead, Bell maintains that the priesthood is interested only in commutative justice, or transactional justice, between individuals.[48] This type of justice is concerned with enforcing the terms of voluntary, contractual arrangements that are central to the flow of goods and services, which lead to economic growth. It cares nothing of the broader health and welfare of a society. This particular notion of freedom, as well as the insistence upon commutative justice, should cause Christians to be especially wary. First of all, the freedom to choose with no purpose other than one's self-interest in sight is destructive to any notion of the "love your neighbor as yourself" ethic that is fundamental to the Christian life. Second, the lack of appreciation for any notion of distributive or social justice should disturb any Christian who is interested in loving her neighbor as herself, since justice—not just the sort that governs voluntary, contractual arrangements—is essential to the Christian notion of neighborly love. Moreover, the claim that only commutative justice matters shows that nonhuman creatures have no inherent value in the neoclassical scheme since nonhuman creatures are incapable of entering into voluntary, contractual relationships.

The neoclassical worldview also presumes much about the role of technology in a developed economy. In particular, two claims are significant

46. Cavanaugh, *Being Consumed*, 53.

47. Hayek, *Road to Serfdom*, 206.

48. Bell, *Economy of Desire*, 109–10.

to our analysis. First, neoclassical priests proclaim that economic growth always generates useful technology. Second, they declare that technology can always solve our problems. While the neoclassical priests are fond of saying that technology of any sort eventually trickles down to all, it is not altogether clear that useful technology actually does affect people in similar manners. Many neoclassical priests often conveniently sidestep the critical question of who actually benefits from technology. Life-saving medical technology used in the developed world too often finds its way into the developing world only after it becomes cost effective or becomes a hand-me-down lifeline to those in need. This sort of situation is particularly exacerbated with environmental problems wherein "clean" or "green" technology lies in the hands of developed-world nations, but needs to be part of the daily lives of developing-world citizens immediately if environmental issues like climate change have any chance of being ameliorated quickly. It is true that humans are quite innovative and have created numerous technological fixes to problems of our own making; it is also very true that we have the ability to forget our many failures. While the priests of neoclassical economics shout from the mountaintops about humanity's many technological triumphs, our history with technology is a bit more ambiguous. With every insight into the very building blocks of atomic and subatomic reality, we have been able to generate new life-saving cancer treatments as well as sophisticated weapons of mass destruction. This should not catch Christians by surprise, as we of all people should recognize our incredible ability to rationalize away our failures. This ability to focus simply on our technological successes is what the Christian tradition calls "hubris." Must we be reminded that some environmental issues are irreparable (e.g., extinction events) or that the scope of some problems makes it nearly impossible to coordinate the simultaneous international cooperation needed to address them (e.g., climate change)? Finally, worse than this is that as the neoclassical priests fan the flames of our hubris, we come to believe that any reasonable discussion about behavioral change is irrational since it seemingly discounts the role of technology in solving the world's problems. Anyone who dares ask how much electricity an American household should reasonably consume rather than how we can make 70-inch flat-screen television screens more energy efficient is branded a Luddite (if not something more unsavory), a damnable heresy according to the neoclassical priesthood.

It is far too facile to say that the priests of economic growth are unconcerned about environmental problems like air and water pollution, biodiversity loss, and even climate change. Many of the priests argue that they are concerned about these critical problems, but without sufficient wealth a society finds itself helpless to act effectively and build a clean future.

They are disciples of Simon Kuznets and the environmental Kuznets curve, which maintains that there is a direct relationship between environmental degradation and per-capita income.[49] The famous U-shaped curve demonstrates that economic growth may in fact cause short-term environmental degradation because market inefficiencies, low political and societal will, and insufficient wealth often thwart environmental cleanup efforts. In the long-term, however, a higher per-capita income will create a more efficient market, the political and societal will to advocate actively for a cleaner environment, and the wealth to accomplish these goals. The neoclassical priests often point to cleaner skies and drinking water in developed-world nations, after they have gone through their industrializing birth pangs and the accompanying inevitable pollution periods, as evidence of the validity of Kuznets's hypothesis. It is this perceived inevitability that should strike us. Must economic growth be environmentally degrading? Or is it just a failure of the human imagination to think of more creative, non-destructive solutions? Or is it perhaps that humans are particularly attuned to short-term thinking, especially when it comes to creating wealth? Christians must also ask a subsequent question: How long will the dirtiness of industrialization take before we see any potential fruits from a cleanup or a cleaner economy? The priesthood employs a rather high-stakes "means to an end" argument here. If we want a clean future, we must be able to live in the muck in order to build up enough wealth to choose a different option. And yet, look at the sacrifices that must be accepted, and perceived as normal, in search of a cleaner future: polluted air that is difficult to breathe, dirty water that is unhealthy to drink, eroded topsoil that fails to yield nutritious food, biodiversity loss that can never be replaced, and billions of people living in utter poverty while a select few control much of the world's wealth, to name just a few. Clean air and water, to say nothing of environmental justice, have instead become luxury items for those who possess the necessary wealth to obtain them. This seems like a far cry from the prophet Amos's proclamation, "But let justice roll on like a river, righteousness like a never-failing stream."[50]

An Economic System Stricken by Hopelessness

In light of the overwhelming dominance of neoclassical economics and its devotion to the idol of economic growth, what are Christians to do?

49. Kuznets, "Economic Growth," 1–28. For critiques of the environmental Kuznets curve, see Stern et al., "Economic Growth," 1151–60; Essay et al., "Integrated Framework," 1421–34; Bagliani et al., "Consumption-Based Approach," 650–61.

50. Amos 5:24, NIV.

THE IDOL OF ECONOMIC GROWTH

Christians living in the radiant light of resurrection hope must critique the injustice of our culture for what it is and then offer a hopeful alternative inspired by the novel possibilities revealed by divine grace. The demise of most communist regimes after the fall of the Iron Curtain, as well as the tyranny of many leaders who have risen in socialist and communist-leaning nation-states, has only strengthened the declarations of the neoclassical priesthood that their version of economics is the only viable, and even moral, one. According to Sallie McFague, however, neoclassical thought misses a key point. Neoclassical economics is a model of reality, not a description of reality as such.[51] It is a system that believes that economic growth is the goal of economics and it uses the short-term self-interest of individuals and scarcity of natural resources as its guiding suppositions to attain that goal. In other words, economics is a very sophisticated and helpful means to a particular end. Economics, by Friedman's definition, cannot determine the endpoint since it is an objective science with no philosophical presuppositions; but by now we realize that this is entirely untrue. We may dictate the goal of economics if we so desire. The end of economics could be the just distribution of resources or ecological health and integrity, or both, but these sorts of goals are too communal in scope for neoclassical thought, which prizes individual self-interest as one of its guiding principles. If economics is really a means to an end and the end is not necessarily economic growth, as supposed by the neoclassical priests, then Christians may have something consequential to inject into the dialogue. McFague argues, "[Faith communities] know that economics is about human well-being, about who eats and who does not, who has clothes and shelter and who does not, who has the basics for a decent life and who does not. Economics is about life and death, as well as the quality of life. It is also about the life and death not just of human beings but of the planet itself and all its life-forms. Economics is not just about money; rather, it is about sharing scare resources among all who need them. Economics is a justice issue."[52] We intuitively know this. By hope, let us courageously act upon it.

Ultimately, the neoclassical priesthood would have us believe that their idol provides us with a definitive vision of hope. With the proper sacrifices, economic growth promises to give us all that we could ever ask for or imagine. Only very, very few participate meaningfully, though, in the fruits of this vision and most of them have sacrificed very, very little in the way that other humans, nonhumans, and the Earth have in order to make that vision

51. McFague, *New Climate*, 83. For more on her understanding of model versus description, see McFague, *Models of God*.

52. McFague, *New Climate*, 82. See also McFague, *Life Abundant*; Davis, *Scripture, Culture, and Agriculture*, 101–19; Horsely, *Covenant Economics*.

a reality. Developed-world citizens continue to consume resources in vastly disproportionate ways, which allows us to live luxurious lives that fail to discern the real difference between needs and wants. The idol of economic growth has instead delivered a false hope. Many believe that neoclassical economics is the best economic system that humans can participate in, and some even accept that it is divinely sanctioned because it takes into account the extensive nature of human sin better than any other.[53] This is what the priests of the idol of economic growth work hard to make us believe, as they remind us that alternatives (by which they mean communism or socialism) have already been tried and failed, and any mention of them is blasphemous. Our complete devotion to economic growth, however, should be characterized for what it is: the hopelessness of presumption, the perverse anticipation of the fulfillment of hope. It is the self-deceptive reliance on a security that is not genuine and based upon anthropological presuppositions that Christians must fundamentally reject. We are not insatiable creatures, but rather sinful ones who fail to make rational decisions consistently. While some resources may be scarcer than others, scarcity as a foundational principle is a rejection of the affirmation that God is sufficient for us and created the Earth to be sufficient for our needs. And yet, after more than half a century of neoclassical principles applied worldwide, we find more wealth centralized in the hands of fewer people and more environmental degradation than we could possibly imagine. We American Christians tacitly, if not explicitly, believe that the good life as defined by neoclassical economic principles takes us closer to a vision of the kingdom of God advocated by Christ.

Some American Christians, though, recognize that the sacrifices to the idol of economic growth are egregious, immoral, and unjust, but are at the point of despair because there appears to be no hope of changing the system as a single consumer, even one who wishes to be as conscientious as possible when consuming. Despair robs a person of the ability to act as one falls prey to apathy and indifference. We must remember that at the root of this despair is sloth. We display neither the courage nor the will to exercise novel possibilities that might exhibit hope to those oppressed by the economic growth idol and its legions of priests. The situation is doubly difficult because many American Christians benefit (some a great deal) from the system the way it is and therefore they are implicitly, if not explicitly, reluctant to change it. Others are paralyzed by their guilt, as they acknowledge that they have prospered like few others have in the history of human civilization while the Earth and the poor continue to be sacrificed to this

---

53. E.g., see Novak, *Spirit of Democratic Capitalism*, 82–88.

idol. Whether it is through apathy or indifference due to paralysis, many of us have become accustomed to the status quo even if we do not intend for our good fortune to disenfranchise others and simultaneously denude the planet. We fail to address the considerable needs of "the least of these"[54] even though we do not desire for them to suffer.

The idol of economic growth causes despair because of how it measures success. As discussed above, economic success is measured positively by the transformation of natural resources into something that can go through the market. Human-made things are the only things deemed to be of value. From a Christian perspective, this is a gross misunderstanding of God's declaration at the end of the first creation story in Genesis 1 that all of creation is very good. The goodness of creation is signified directly by the divine proclamation, not by the human ability to transform natural capital into something else. Furthermore, any indicator of economic success that measures environmental disaster cleanup as a net gain because it creates jobs or other products that can be exchanged on the market is fundamentally flawed and causes hopelessness. Disasters like the Exxon Valdez incident in Alaska and the Deepwater Horizon oil spill in the Gulf of Mexico must not be measured as possible benefits to our economy. Such ways of thinking cause us to lose our ability to appreciate the actual devastation brought on by profound tragedy.

Neoclassical economics is also full of despair because it assumes that the invisible providential hand of the market is sovereign, not the living God of Abraham, Isaac, and Jacob. A Christian acceptance of this neoclassical belief causes us to separate the economic aspects of our reality from the loving, sovereign God of Jesus Christ and the redeeming influence of the Spirit. Some even suggest that the incarnation of God in the flesh of Jesus of Nazareth should cause us to moderate our expectations of justice and redemption, because Christians of all people know that even Jesus could not change the human condition, so why concern ourselves mightily with this sort of critique?[55] Moreover, the neoclassical priesthood praises the fact that the market as presently constituted actually reduces the need for compassion, solidarity, and neighborly love.[56] None of this provides hope to the least of these who clamor for relief; it only supports the status quo for the minority currently "blessed" by the idol of economic growth.

54. Matt 25:40.

55. Novak, *Spirit of Democratic Capitalism*, 340–44.

56. For a positive recognition of this, see Benne, *Ethic of Democratic Capitalism*, 136–55. For a cautionary examination of this, see Daly and Cobb, *For the Common Good*, 89–95.

This economic system leads to despair because it is difficult to see how it can be leveraged meaningfully in such a way to address climate change. Mitigation and adaptation to climate change will require that humans commit to a common good or at least a shared purpose, which stands in stark juxtaposition to a seminal anthropological presupposition of this system: the individual's freedom to choose must be defended at all costs. Corporations must eschew the common good in order to make their shareholders maximal profit. While it is perhaps possible to imagine that a corporation could deploy mitigation and adaptation strategies as part of long-term profit maximization for its shareholders, what if such strategies do not stimulate profits? The system is also despair inducing because it is difficult to imagine how a collective response to climate change does not appear offensive to neoclassical priests' very limited notion of individual freedom. Lastly, it strains the imagination to see how the environmental Kuznets curve will be helpful in the age of climate change. The perceived inevitability of a dirty industrialization phase that leads to technological development and wealth creation that lead to an eventual shifting of political and societal will is too naive to rely upon since climate change is happening now and its consequences are presently being felt in tragic, consequential ways. Moreover, those who trumpet the significance of this curve as a historical model for environmental cleanup neglect significant factors, chief among them the fact that political and societal will is shaped by corporate funds in implicit and explicit ways that the world has never before seen. Even if the priests are correct, we may not have the luxury of time needed to see if they are right: Will the various self-interests of more than 7 billion humans produce the societal will necessary to move us in a direction that staves off the worst of the known consequences of climate change and prepares for the unknown ones as well?

Christians are called to do more than merely identify the problem for what it is. The prophetic message is one of hope as much as it is one of judgment. And yet, what is the individual Christian or even the local church to do to combat the hopelessness created by the idol of economic growth and its legion of priests and devoted adherents? We need a way of living hopefully, a way that places our trust in the correct God. We need a way of acting that allows us as economic agents to build relationships with our neighbors and provides the opportunity to stand in solidarity with the oppressed. We need a way of participating as consumers that does not merely lessen the effects of environmental degradation, but prizes ecological health and integrity. To do this, we must think about what we want our economy to do.

7

An Economy of Hope

No well-meaning Christian wants to denude the landscape and contribute to further species extinction and environmental degradation. We would prefer to breathe clean air, drink clean water, and eat food from land free of toxins now and allows generations of our neighbors to do the same in the future. And yet, as we saw in the previous chapter, we do not live as if we actually desire these things meaningfully. Instead, we fall into the many snares of the economic growth idol and participate in patterns of hopelessness that mark our present global economic order. Sometimes our participation is willful, while other times it is ignorant, but it always dramatically impacts our neighbors and the Earth. If we want to be recognized as faithful followers of Christ, though, we must practice economic decision-making that builds healthy relationships with our human and nonhuman neighbors, while at that same time allowing us to stand in solidarity with the oppressed around the planet. We desperately need to model an economic system that does not positively value the cleanup efforts of horrendous environmental disasters, but instead prizes ecological health and biodiversity. Such an economic vision signals resurrection hope. To get to such a place, Christians should lead the public, global discussion about what it is we really want from our economy.

What Is Our Goal?

What is the end or *telos* of an economy? Seemingly unbeknownst to modern economists, the *telos* of economy can be whatever a society deems it to be. It is apparent that the goal of the neoclassical economic enterprise is solely economic growth for the sake of economic growth. Any environmental, social, or personal benefits that come as a result of that growth are peripheral advantages, while the disadvantages of this idol, including climate change, are chalked up to being miscalculated externalities just waiting for the market to account for more accurately. But, what if the goal was something else? What if the goal of our economy was justice or sustainability or eco-logical health and integrity or climate change mitigation and adaptation? A hopeful Christian witness must include the public proclamation that the goal can and should be something other than economic growth. The hege-mony of the neoclassical priesthood must not dissuade us from this hopeful message. While some economists, and Christian ones at that, are extremely wary of theologians poking their noses into their business, I find a theologi-cal voice needed in the marketplace now more than ever.[1]

Does a Christian critique of the neoclassical scheme necessarily imply a Christian replacement? In other words, is it a "Christian" form of econom-ics that we should be advocating for and practicing instead that will get us to our particular goal? I believe the answer to be unequivocally no, but that should not be seen as an attempt to lower the expectation of what a theolog-ical imaginary might inspire us to think about and endorse economically. Instead, it is a recognition that we are living in the time of the Spirit, a time of the "already, but not yet." There is no perfect economic relationship to be practiced this side of the eschaton.[2] However, we should be looking for and practicing economic models that are, according to McFague, at least "pale reflections, but reflections nonetheless, of what Jesus meant by the kingdom of God."[3] Put another way, we need to find a way to conduct necessary eco-nomic activity that might be considered an explicit part of our worship to God.[4] What a theological imaginary can surely do is spur us to conceive of what sorts of presuppositions and ideas might make up such an economy of hope. This is the sort of imaginative exercise that Christian hope demands.

First and foremost, a hopeful economy must take the admonition of Jesus seriously: "No slave can serve two masters; for a slave will either hate the one and love the other, or be devoted to the one and despise the other. You cannot serve God and wealth."[5] We cannot worship both God and eco-nomic growth. The consequences of climate change are revealing this to us in dramatic ways since we cannot seem to figure it out on our own. While the priests of economic growth have demanded that the dignity and welfare of humans along with the vitality and stability of ecosystems are necessary sacrifices, an economy of hope begins with the notion that our economic life is essential to our worship of God. Jesus' recognition of the link between

---

1. E.g., see Young, *Environment, Economy, and Christian Ethics.*
2. For more on this, see Bell, *Economy of Desire,* 188–91.
3. McFague, *New Climate,* 37.
4. Wirzba, *Paradise of God,* 159–60.
5. Matt 6:24; Luke 16:13.

love of God and love of neighbor and the prophetic tradition's insistence that care for the widows, orphans, and aliens is what it means to be just should set a particular tone for what it means to be Christian economic agents.[6]

In the Gospel of John, Jesus says that he came into the world so that we might have an abundant life.[7] While the Gospel writer is undoubtedly leaning toward a more spiritual interpretation of abundance, we cannot forget that Jesus' healing ministry, in particular, witnesses to God's notion of an abundant life now, not just in the future, since the kingdom of God is upon us presently. The all-too-common feature of overspiritualizing the kingdom of God in American Christianity makes us think that the abundant life has no present economic implications. Yet, as Albino Barrera asserts, "What is important to note is the hallmark quality of a God so lavish and persistent in bestowing gifts upon gifts on humans. And if God is so prodigal in dispensing such blessings, it would be uncharacteristic of divine liberality to limit its bounteous gifts only to the spiritual realm and not to the material conditions of human life."[8] Sufficiency of needs for humans as well as nonhumans should be considered a fundamental starting point for any discussion about the abundant life God desires for us. The abundant life may mean that some of us will have to sacrifice much if we want other humans and nonhumans to participate in this divine desire. In other words, there are particular consequences to our decisions and they will undoubtedly affect those around us, both human and nonhuman, sometimes dramatically. Climate change is teaching us this lesson even as the neoclassical priesthood encourages us to believe that future generations will be able to solve the problems we now cause. A hopeful economy will earnestly accept the reality that our economic decisions have intentional and unintentional consequences on those around us that we see, and especially on those we do not see.

Let us return for a moment to the example about which model of the economy intuitively makes sense: Is Earth a subset of the greater economy or is the economy constrained by Earth? Any economic model that is to be a witness of hope must answer this question correctly. The Earth must be appreciated seriously, both in the way it functions and the amount of renewable and nonrenewable resources that it might have. While the way the Earth functions and the amount of resources it has is believed to be a considerable constraint by the neoclassical priesthood, Christians should acknowledge this as part of the gift God has given to those who call this

6. Matt 22:39; Mark 12:31; Luke 9:24. See also 1 Cor 10:31.

7. John 10:10.

8. Barrera, *Biblical Economic Ethics*, 237.

planet home. A recognition that this planet works in a certain intelligible way is a reminder that a covenant graciously undergirds the universe that God created. Ecological integrity and human justice are intricately linked in this place that bears the divine imprint. This is radically affirmed in the Noahic covenant as all creatures are called by God to be fruitful and multiply. A hopeful economy must explicitly appreciate the vast interdependence and interconnectedness of creation and hence consider seriously ways of allowing nonhuman creatures to flourish. Therefore, economic activity that destroys ecological integrity and promotes unjust working conditions should be deemed sinful and cannot be considered to be worship of the Creator. Such an economy will thus have to listen carefully to the limits of creation and choose development strategies built upon our best understanding of these limits, which often become apparent through sound scientific knowledge. These sorts of parameters will help us understand more fully what the abundant life is that God desires for us. Additionally, an economy of hope will also resist the fundamental assertion made by the neoclassical priests who accept the assertions of the environmental Kuznets curve as gospel truth. The dual "inevitability" of a dirty industrialization period followed by clean air and water, for example, promised by the idol of economic growth, is false hope proclaimed to billions of humans in developing nations and the even more numerous nonhuman creatures throughout the world. This inevitability is merely a recognition of the "creative destruction" that the economic growth idol requires with no guarantee of success.[9] Instead, we must trust that the prophets were correct about the cosmic covenant: ecological health and human justice are marks of an abundant life.

Any admission by the neoclassical priesthood that Earth has a fixed amount of nonrenewable resources usually elicits two subsequent responses: one, a reaffirmation of the assertion that scarcity is pervasive and fundamental; and two, human ingenuity and technology will be able to extend resources until an alternative can be found. The suggestion that scarcity is pervasive and fundamental is antithetical to belief in the God of Jesus Christ. It strikes a blow to the affirmation of the very goodness of creation. It negates the central theme of the biblical witness summarized by the psalmist: "The LORD is my shepherd, I lack nothing."[10] It invalidates the lessons of divine mercy and abundance depicted in the Gospels when Jesus fed the multitudes.[11] Moreover, it denies the witness of the earliest

9. Schumpeter, *Capitalism, Socialism, and Democracy.*

10. Ps 23:1. Or "The LORD is my shepherd; I shall not want" (ESV). This is reemphasized by the apostle Paul in light of the incarnation in Phil 4:19.

11. Matt 14:13–21; 15:32–39; Mark 6:30–44; 8:1–10; Luke 9:10–17; John 6:1–15.

Christians who served all that came to their agape meals and sat at the eucharistic table. If God is truly the God of grace revealed in the person of Jesus of Nazareth, then any economic model that witnesses to the hope of the resurrection should begin from the starting point that the sufficiency of God's grace is more pervasive and fundamental than scarcity. While the common response to scarcity has been the hoarding of possessions in light of supposedly perpetual insecurity and injustice toward both human and nonhuman neighbors alike, the response to divine grace should be something else entirely. Norman Wirzba states it compellingly: "The response to grace, as the witness of God's faithful has repeatedly shown, is cooperation, the commitment to the equitable distribution of the gifts of creation, but also frugality, the recognition that we should not take what we do not genuinely need."[12] To start economic thinking from the vantage point of God's sufficient grace rather than scarcity is to acknowledge profoundly our creatureliness. We are truly dependent upon God, who sends rain on the righteous and unrighteous alike.[13] This is in fact a message of hope.

We must recognize the role of human ingenuity and technology more soberly than those within the priesthood who believe that technology will be our messiah. Human creativity is impressive and Christians should recognize this as creatures made in the image of a creative God. But our reliance on human creativity and its resulting technology to solve problems that are often linked to poor human behavior should be labeled for what it is. For example, instead of asking if the standard of living that so many American Christians enjoy is the cause of climate change, we wait for scientists and engineers to create new ways for us to live the same way, but more efficiently. This not only shifts the blame of bad behavior away from us and onto others, but it causes us to avoid the critique that hope inspired by the resurrection demands. We fail to ask the question of how many cars should we really have in our garages and instead we bide our time, polluting at unsustainable levels, until automobile manufacturers produce more fuel-efficient cars. Our reliance on ourselves and our technology is ultimately a misplaced hope that not only severs our relationship with the true source of hope, but manifests itself in the unjust maldistribution of technology that we see so frequently throughout human history. Technology created in a hopeful economy is done with a full recognition of the pervasiveness of human hubris and the commitment to using technology in a way that fosters fellowship within communities, especially by serving both the human and

12. Wirzba, *Paradise of God*, 164.
13. Matt 5:45.

nonhuman least of these. Only technology that brings us into solidarity with the least of these can be conceived of as part of a life in worship of God.

The accumulation of wealth in order to indulge in whatever goods and services one desires is not the goal of an economy of hope. Instead, wealth must be used to create healthy sorts of relationships because all things ultimately come from God. The thoughts of second-century theologian Clement of Alexandria are especially relevant to this discussion today. "Those concerned for their salvation should take this as their first principle, that all property is ours to use and every possession is for the sake of self-sufficiency, which anyone can acquire by a few things. They who rejoice in the holdings in their storehouse are foolish in their greed."[14] Self-sufficiency in this context connotes contentedness or independence. Commenting on the term "self-sufficiency," Charles Avila notes, "Generally it denotes a standard of living enabling one to lead a life consonant with human dignity." For Clement, then, greedy people are foolish because they do not understand that wealth is a means to an end.[15] As discussed in more detail below, Clement's broad theological affirmation is that God brought Godself into fellowship with us and through that act made all things in common; hence, no one should live in luxury while another lives in need. The goal of wealth is not only to gain a measure of self-sufficiency, but also to create fellowship with others so that those few who live in luxury are no longer distinct from the vast majority of those who have nothing. This will allow us to have the abundant life that God desires for us. The goals of self-sufficiency and fellowship should not just be for our human neighbors, but for our nonhuman neighbors as well. While the goals will naturally be adapted to fit the nonhuman context differently, a hopeful economy should be inclusive of all of God's creatures and ecosystems, not just the richest human few who happen to control most of the wealth. By highlighting a new way to think about our connection to our possessions, we will fundamentally shift the way we conceive of consumer desire. The seduction and misdirection that currently shapes consumer desire must be cast aside in light of the affirmation that all possessions ultimately come from God and are to be used in a way that fosters self-sufficiency and fellowship. At the same time, a consumer desire fed by this theological imaginary would be more intensely committed to the divine call for justice for both the human and nonhuman least of these. As much as buying eco-friendly products and fair-trade produce might be meaningful steps in a hopeful economy, we must strenuously resist the

14. Avila, *Ownership*, 35.
15. Ibid., 36.

urge to think that shopping is a substitute for seeking justice and acting righteously.

An economy of hope rejects the idea that individual self-interest is an adequate anthropological assumption upon which to build a just economy. This is because we are not individually autonomous agents as the neoclassical priesthood would have us believe. The apostle Paul argues this by suggesting that we are not individuals, but instead are members of the body of Christ.[16] This is demonstrated beautifully by the Christians who sold all they owned and laid the proceeds at the feet of the apostles.[17] We are meant to work together toward a shared purpose or the common good. This is an anthropological starting point for a hopeful economy. These are not naive statements about the human condition. Christians should be the first to acknowledge that sin prevents us from acting properly human; however, we are created to exist in a way that models the divine life as creatures made in the very image of God. If our economic life is to be viewed as an act of worship, then our economic thinking must begin from an entirely different place than self-interest. Additionally, the idea that we should accept avarice as a natural impulse and then build an economy that works around that flaw or maximizes it for the alleged benefit of the rest of society strikes at the heart of the Christian claim that divine action is presently efficacious and seeks to abolish sinful ways now. The resurrection of Jesus attests to that basic theological affirmation. Finally, as discussed above, there is no logical reason not to include nonhuman creatures and the rest of creation in our discussions about the spirit of community. This is recognition of our interdependence and interconnectedness witnessed to over and over again in Scripture. While conceiving of an economy that takes into account the common good of humans, nonhumans, and the rest of creation will undoubtedly be difficult, it is not oppressive to set aside self-interest as a guiding economic principle as the neoclassical priesthood would have us believe. This sort of imagination speaks to the kind of humans that God created us to be. We are created to be in solidarity with others and that should make us more hopeful and courageous rather than anxious about the perceived threats that scarcity and competition can engender.

While I ultimately disagree with Tocqueville's belief that "self-interest properly understood" with Christianity's assistance, can make the American experiment successful, his insight into why this might be possible is telling. He readily saw the "this-worldly" emphasis Christianity had on many nineteenth-century Americans. "It is true that Christianity teaches

16. 1 Cor 12.
17. Acts 4:32–37.

us to place others before ourselves in order to gain heaven; but Christianity also teaches us to do good to our fellow men [sic] for the love of God. What a magnificent expression; man uses his intelligence to penetrate the mind of God and sees that God's aim is order. He freely joins in this grand design and, sacrificing his private interests to this admirable order of all creation, he expects no other reward than the joy of contemplating it."[18] We may choose to sacrifice some of our own desires for no other reason than to participate in the shared purpose that God has for creation. Simply reconceiving of economics in light of God's grace will not bring justice to the least of these or ecological health and restoration to portions of creation that desperately need it. As creatures made in the image of God, Christians need to be active in our pursuit of loving our neighbors, both human and nonhuman, as ourselves. We must exhibit a living hope that breaks us free from the debilitating forms of hopelessness and liberates us to consume and live in hopeful new ways. The first step forward is the explicit practice of one specific virtue that can help us live more hopefully because it is an activity of imaginative faith and represents the courage inspired by the resurrection hope. It allows us to participate more joyfully in God's purposes for creation. That virtue is frugality.

Frugality: The Subversive but Hopeful Virtue

While American Christians once viewed frugality as a virtue of paramount significance, it now seems to be a value of a bygone era. In its simplest form, frugality denotes temperance, moderation, and a satisfaction with material sufficiency. Being frugal might also mean being cost-effective or using natural resources efficiently. For Christians, though, frugality is much, much more. James Nash, the foremost twentieth-century Protestant voice on this subject, argues that frugality is an expression of both love and justice, especially since justice is merely one dimension of love. "The essence of frugality, from a Christian perspective, is sacrifice for the sake of Christ's cause of love, including justice. But it is a form of sacrifice that promises to bring fullness of being in solidarity."[19] Furthermore, "Frugality . . . is an expression of love—seeking the good or well-being of others in response to their needs and to the God who is love. The source of the sacrificial dimension in frugality is love of neighbor, for love always entails giving up at least some of our self-interests and benefits for the sake of the welfare of others in communal

18. Tocqueville, *Democracy in America*, 614.
19. Nash, "Ethics," 56.

relationships."[20] Being frugal then can effectively reformulate our thinking about economics to see the value of our neighbor, who is next door to us or on the other side of the planet, over against the supposed collective value of the economic system controlled by the invisible providential hand of the market. Being frugal also allows us to reconceptualize our relationship with our nonhuman neighbors and the rest of creation, which I discuss further below.

Frugality might appear to some as a form of austerity or asceticism that calls one to sacrifice a standard of living that is viewed as a birthright by many developed-world citizens, especially citizens of the United States. Some Christian thinkers frame frugality more in terms of giving up something, even if it is for a beneficial end, than gaining a new way of living.[21] Nash contends, however, that living frugally is not about idealizing the rural lifestyle of a bygone century or convincing people to move to monasteries on the outskirts of cities, but rather is about the quest for an abundant life. "It is a quest for being more rather than having more—that is, a qualitative rather than quantitative enrichment."[22] This virtue sharpens our focus as we contemplate our relationship to material possessions, primarily as we ask more pointed questions like, "What is a good quality of life, and what kinds and amounts of goods are necessary or valuable for it? Are various goods significant benefits or liabilities to personal, communal, and ecological enhancement? How should we distinguish needs and wants? How much is enough in quantity to sustain a reasonable quality of life and to ensure that the rest of humanity and other species, present and future, have similar opportunities?"[23] Naturally, these are the sorts of questions that the priests of economic growth would rather we not ask because they challenge principal notions that the economic growth idol holds sacrosanct. For instance, it is the Christian position that we can actually discern the difference between sufficiency and excess, especially when we confess our sinful rationalizations. Being frugal compels us to ask whether the *telos* of economics is economic growth or something else entirely, e.g., ecological health and integrity or the equitable distribution of goods and services.

As one can imagine, a nation or a planet of frugal citizens would impact our global economy dramatically. For that reason, frugality is ultimately a "subversive" virtue.[24] It strikes at the core of the idol of economic

20. Ibid.

21. E.g., see Theokritoff, *Living in God's Creation*, 114.

22. Nash, "Subversive Virtue," 427.

23. Ibid., 426.

24. Nash, "Ethics," 50–51.

growth as it impugns our cultural belief in the idol's innate goodness and capacity to deliver on its many promises. Frugality considers how ethically conscious production and consumption must take into account the bio-physical parameters of the Earth. It is also subversive because it rejects one of the primary claims of the neoclassical priesthood: human happiness is defined by an unrelenting commitment to material accumulation because we are naturally insatiable. Being frugal exhibits a different reality. It asserts that humans can live content lives through moral decisions that control our consumptive ways and give us a significantly more abundant life—a life that is defined by the strength of relationships in one's community rather than the weight of stuff in one's garage and off-site storage unit. Finally, frugality is subversive because it refuses the temptation to go after bigger, better, faster, newer, more attractive state-of-the-art products. "By resisting these temptations, frugality is again a witness to the fact that humans are far more than manipulable consumers. It is an affirmation of human dignity—our moral potential, our deepest yearning, our status as ends, not simply means—against the onslaught of mass manipulation."[25] Simultaneously, it is through this subversive virtue that we exhibit a way of hopeful living on this side of the resurrection. It is no wonder that the priests of economic growth do not want us to be frugal.

While Nash gives us an excellent entry into the benefits of being frugal, the church fathers, while not using the term "frugality" explicitly, spend a considerable amount of time elucidating the relationship between humans and their possessions, which sheds further light on how frugality might be applied to our current context. First, from Clement of Alexandria, who defines goods in this way: "Goods are called goods because they do good, and they have been provided by God for the good of humanity."[26] On the correct use of possessions: "God has given us the authority to use our possessions, I admit, but only to the extent that it is necessary: [God] wishes them to be common. It is absurd that one man [sic] lives in luxury when there are so many who labor in poverty. He who holds possessions holds them as gifts of God . . . and knows that he possesses them for his brother's sake rather than his own. . . . Such is the man who is blessed by the Lord and a ready inheritor of the kingdom of God."[27] Yet, it is not enough for Clement that we use our possessions in a just manner, but it is by using them in such a manner that we actually create a loving community that reflects the very character of God, who is love.

25. Ibid., 51.

26. Avila, *Ownership*, 43.

27. Krueger, *Cloud of Witnesses*, 35.

It is God himself [sic] who brought our race to a *koinonia* by sharing Himself, first of all, and by sending His Word (Logos) to all alike, and by making all things for all. Therefore everything is common, and the rich should not grasp a greater share. The expression, then, "I own something and I have more than enough; why should I not enjoy it?" is not worthy of a human nor does it indicate any community feeling. The other expression does, however: "I have something, why should I not share it with those in need?" Such a one is perfect, and fulfills the command: "Thou shalt love thy neighbor as thyself."[28]

According to Basil of Caesarea, to take more than what one needs is to engage in injustice, as excess goods are not to be accumulated by those who already have enough. "If each one would take that which is sufficient for one's needs, leaving what is in excess to those in distress, no one would be rich, no one poor."[29] Basil goes on to define an avaricious person as "One who is not content with those things which are sufficient."[30] Furthermore, he contends that avarice is a particularly pernicious vice because it robs us of our humanity. "God has poured the rains on a land tilled by avaricious hands; [God] has given the sun to keep the seeds warm, and to multiply the fruit through His [sic] productivity. Things of this kind are from God: the fertile land, moderate winds, abundance of seeds, the work of the oxen, and other things by which a farm is brought into productivity and abundance. . . . But the avaricious one has not remembered our common nature and has not thought of distribution."[31]

For the famous theologian from Milan, there is a link between the limits of the Earth and the amount we need to live fruitfully. Ambrose suggests that even fish know the distinction between needs and wants.

> Fish know their own confines, which are not bounded by city walls, by gates, or by buildings; neither are they marked as in the boundaries of the fields. But each has a terminal limit of space in accordance with its need, so that only so much is given to each as to satisfy completely its wants—not so much as its unregulated greed can claim for itself. There is, if I may say so, a law of nature that one can seek only what suffices for nourishment and that the allotment "which thy fathers have set" (Prov. 22:28) should be in proportion to the need for food.[32]

28. Avila, *Ownership*, 37.
29. Ibid., 49.
30. Ibid., 50.
31. Krueger, *Cloud of Witnesses*, 83.
32. Avila, *Ownership*, 71–72.

Additionally, he strongly maintains that our inability to control our wants not only allows a scarce few to prosper while many others' needs are insufficiently met, but also that the Earth itself is harmed by our unjust ways. "Why do the injuries to nature delight you? For everyone has the world been created, which you few rich are trying to keep for yourselves. For not merely the earth, but the very sky, the air, and the sea are claimed for the use of the rich few. How many people can this air feed which you include within your widespread estate?"[33] Ambrose also employs the familiar patristic theme about God providing Earth as a common gift to all. "God has ordered all things to be produced so that there should be food in common to all, and that the earth should be a common possession for all. Nature, therefore, has produced a common right for all, but greed has made it a right for a few."[34] And yet, he stridently condemns those who might become proud of their charitable acts, as he links charity more strongly with justice than love. "The earth belongs to everyone and every living thing, not just to the rich; but fewer are they who do not use what belongs to all than those who do. Therefore in giving alms, you are paying a debt, you are not bestowing what is not due."[35] Besides, "It is not from part of your own goods that you give to the poor, but rather from what belongs to them. This is because you have appropriated to yourself what was originally given for the use of everyone. The earth has been given for the whole world and not merely for use by the wealthy."[36]

The eminent homilete John Chrysostom considers the human relationship to possessions in a similar manner to his patristic brothers. "God never made some people rich and others poor. God gave the earth to everyone. The whole earth belongs to the Lord, and the fruits of the earth should be available to all."[37] He puts our refusal to share in the starkest of language: "This is robbery not to share one's resources. Perhaps what I am saying astonishes you. Yet be not astonished. For I shall offer you the testimony of the sacred scriptures, which say that not only to rob others' property, but also not to share your own with others, is robbery and greediness and theft . . . for the robbery of the poor is in your houses."[38]

---

33. Krueger, *Cloud of Witnesses*, 107.

34. Ambrose of Milan, "Duties of the Clergy," in Schaff and Wace, *Nicene and Post-Nicene Fathers*, 23.

35. Krueger, *Cloud of Witnesses*, 107.

36. Ibid.

37. Ibid., 122.

38. Ibid., 123.

Finally, the famed bishop of Hippo maintains that the work of Christians demonstrates the very presence of the divine. "God gives the world to the poor as well as to the rich. Will the rich person have two stomachs to fill because of being rich? Consider, and see to it that from the gifts of God the poor sleep satisfied. He [sic] who feeds you feeds them also, through you."[39] Augustine echoes a common refrain from this early church period when it comes to understanding who is the source of all possessions and how that should determine the human sense of ownership: "those who do not wish to share what they have with the needy . . . should understand that God commands [this] sharing not as being from the property of them whom he [sic] commands [this sharing], but as being from his own property; so that those who offer something to the poor should not think that they are doing so from what is their own."[40] Additionally, Augustine understands a particular relationship between correct ownership and justice. "For even among human beings themselves, each must be said to possess something [only] when he or she uses it well. For what a person does not treat justly, that person does not possess rightly."[41]

There are significant themes that emerge from this group of early Christian theologians that are still exceedingly pertinent today. First, there is the common idea that all possessions are ultimately owned by God, distributed by God, and are to be used in the service of the work of God, which is to serve one's sisters and brothers in need. Charity is viewed fundamentally as an act of justice and sharing our possessions with others witnesses to God's understanding of ownership. Second, related to the first theme, there is strong agreement among these thinkers that God not only created the Earth, but created it with sufficient resources for all of its inhabitants, not just the wealthiest few. Third, engaging in an excessive lifestyle (being unable to distinguish properly between needs and wants) is a dehumanizing one, as it not only impinges upon the dignity of the one who does not have enough, but also on the one who engages in luxurious excess. The first is incapable of living the abundant life God desires for us, while the latter chooses to pursue the supposedly abundant life dictated by the neoclassical priesthood—not God. Finally, for those who might say, "How do I know when enough is actually enough," Ambrose suggests that even the fish of the sea know when they are being greedy. While we might successfully rationalize away the distinction between needs and wants due to our sinfulness, it is

39. Avila, *Ownership*, 115.

40. Ibid.

41. Ibid.

clear to these theologians that we have the ability to discern exactly where that line might be.

While any person, whether part of a faith tradition or not, can be frugal, this virtue is of particular necessity for a disciple seeking to demonstrate Christ's love. Even though one could be coerced to act frugally due to external circumstances (e.g., a global financial crisis), I argue that a Christian must make frugal decisions as optional choices, not obligatory ones, if being frugal is to be a virtuous act. But perhaps more importantly, if frugal behavior is to be understood as a Christian expression of love, then it must be born out of a voluntary exercise of sharing. How can you truly love your neighbor if you are obliged by external pressure to do so? Additionally, guided by the understanding of the patristic theologians, Christians must ask: How can you truly love your neighbor without acting justly toward that neighbor? Since many contemporary Christians consider an act of charity to be motivated by a sense of neighborly love, the patristic theologians' understanding of charity emanating from justice rather than love might seem disjointed at first. Is this merely a matter of theological semantics or an important insight to meditate upon in our contemporary situation? As discussed above, Cavanaugh contends that the economic doctrine of scarcity dictates that goods are not held in common and thereby consumption is a private matter. "This does not mean that charitable giving is forbidden, but it is relegated to the private realm of preference, not justice."[42] Once again, the neoclassical priests seek to remove theological reflection further from economic thought as they banish charity to the realm of the private. While a private Christian impetus for charitable activity may indeed be neighborly love, which is still a virtuous starting point for charity, we must not forget the link between love and justice, the connection between the private and the public. Sharing with one's neighbor by exercising frugal forms of consumption is in fact an explicit expression of God's sense of justice. Christians in the United States must be particularly intentional to engage in frugal behaviors that will place them in the immediate situations of their neighbors, both domestic as well as international. These behaviors must be sacrificial as well, as it is difficult to imagine love or justice, especially as we think about the examples of Noah and Jesus, without some sort of sacrifice.

Frugality is a virtue that disciplines us to distinguish between needs and wants, both at the individual level as well as the societal level. The ability to discriminate between needs and wants focuses our attention sharply onto what is really part of the abundant life that God desires for us to live and what is not. For instance, does the abundant life include building familial

42. Cavanaugh, *Being Consumed*, 91.

and community relationships, or working 12-hour days in order to pay off credit-card debt used to purchase the latest technological widget? Is ecological vigor and stability marked by clean air, clean water, and healthy soil a need or a want? This capacity to differentiate between needs and wants will transform us into a new type of people. Meeks asserts, "God's destruction of scarcity through God's righteousness creates a new human being, the creature who finds satisfaction in God's righteousness and justice. Faith in the God of 'enough through justice' does not relieve the human being of all hungers but transposes them into the hunger after righteousness. The purpose of human life is not to consume or accumulate but to do justice. All needs should be defined in relation to that."[43] This is indeed the witness of hope.

This virtue does not need to be viewed solely as an anthropocentric pursuit. If being frugal is a form of justice, and there is no compelling reason that prohibits Christians from extending a form of justice to nonhuman creatures and the rest of creation, then we must consider carefully how being frugal can help us imagine the needs of nonhuman creatures and share with them, too. Building on the thought of Basil, if avarice causes us to forget the common nature that exists between humans, it also causes us to forget the theological and evolutionary "common nature" that exists between humans and nonhumans. This forgetfulness is deleterious to both humans and nonhumans alike. We are all neighbors within God's creation, from single-celled bacteria to the blue whale. If frugality allows us to be joyful with sufficiency, then more is left to allow other creatures to be fruitful and multiply and praise God in the ways they were created to do.

Exercising frugality also allows us to oppose courageously the current Western cultural idea that by simply waiting for per-capita income to rise to the level that we can then buy eco-friendly products we will fix our environmental woes. While purchasing such products may in fact be better than purchasing non-eco-friendly products, the idea of buying our way out of our global environmental mess only feeds the economic growth idol and keeps us from manifesting authentic hope.[44] Christians must learn to desire the abundant life and understand its explicit links to ecological health and integrity, and consequently our common nature with everything God has created. The abundant life is tied to the cosmic covenant that the prophetic tradition believes undergirds the universe. We cannot have a sense of justice when persons of color in America breathe disproportionate amounts of polluted air. We cannot have strong communal ties when only some have access

43. Meeks, God the Economist, 177.

44. This is not a Christian argument only as Hamilton argues persuasively for a secular version of this. See Hamilton, Requiem for a Species, 77–81.

to clean water. And we cannot claim to be concerned with biodiversity preservation when we continue to cause the extinction of species while we build
more strip malls and larger mansions.

Being frugal not only allows us to leave more resources for developing
nations to reach a level of dignified human existence, which is a good thing
in itself; it does much more. As Nash suggests, frugality is not solely an in-
dividualistic concept; it must take into account the health of a society. "The
measure of frugality is solidarity—the moral response to the fact of interdependence, the commitment to the common good, socially and ecologically,
nationally and internationally."[45] Living frugally becomes one important
means by which we can stand in some manner of solidarity with the poor in
our nation and across the world as they live "frugally" as a means of survival
rather than as a voluntary act. Again, it allows us to remember our common
nature with those who the neoclassical priesthood deems unclean because
they have not sacrificed enough. By refraining from the constant indulgence
in excessive luxury, American Christians can create space that is necessary
to be charitable neighbors with the world's poor, as we exercise frugal practices as a means of sharing justly. Only through sharing justly can we claim
to follow the command to love our neighbors as ourselves, since justice is
the minimum that love requires. Therefore, one must live frugally so that
one's distant neighbor has equitable access to resources, which reflects the
belief that the world is really God's and resources are common to all just as
the Earth is a common possession of all. The kind of intentional sacrifice
a frugal life demands is demonstrative of God's love and God's desire for
justice and subsequently strikes at the idol of economic growth in how has
failed to look after the least of these.

Frugality essentially questions whether the idol of economic growth
actually alleviates the problems of the least of these and declares the mal-
distributed economic growth that exists in the world today to be patently
unjust. And yet, the least of these should not be limited to our human neighbors. The economic growth idol has failed our nonhuman neighbors as well
and so we must stand in solidarity with them if we as Christians are to honor
God's affirmation of their goodness and their role in God's creation. According to Clement, how we use our possessions is even more than an expression of solidarity. A frugal use of resources allows for not only the sufficient
needs of others to be met, but the manifestation of the presence of a type
of community or fellowship that reflects the very Trinitarian life of God.
Clement is a precursor to the formal Trinitarian thought characterized by
the later patristic period as he points to the *koinonia* within the divine life as

45. Nash, "Subversive Virtue," 424.

well as the *koinonia* between those whom God created through the Logos. "God has made the human being a social being, to live in necessary *koinōnia* with others. To act in a way that is *anthrōpinon*, or properly human, one must act in a way that is *koinōnikon*, 'social,' or in a spirit of community."[46] This Christian affirmation is especially illustrative and yet simultaneously dissonant with our culture's insistence upon the self-made person who acts fundamentally according to self-interest. Living in the post-Darwinian context that we do, we now know that this "spirit of community" is even more profoundly interdependent than Clement could have possibly imagined.

Basil's words "Why do the injuries to nature delight you?" are still perspicacious today as developed-world nations have not taken the significant steps needed to address environmental problems like climate change and biodiversity loss, but instead wait for technology to deliver a panacea that will forestall any meaningful change to our overly consumptive behaviors. This stems from an inflated evaluation of ourselves, which is constantly reinforced by the neoclassical priesthood. This rather faulty anthropological assessment, along with our amazing ability to rationalize away our past failures and focus solely on our triumphs, is hubris of the worst sort. This hubris is fervently nurtured by the economic growth idol as it hides what actually is happening to the Earth and nonhuman creatures while at the same time promising that grand solutions will be readily available in the foreseeable future. Practicing frugality not only allows us to live more justly, but it can simultaneously stand as a notable guard against this destructive false theology and anthropology that encourages our desire for luxurious excess and our proclivity to be hubristic.

Much is at stake for the economic growth idol if Christians begin to practice the subversive virtue seriously. We will question whether or not we need as much stuff as the idol claims that we do in order to live an abundant life. We will question whether or not the idol can sincerely deliver on its promises to raise standards of living for all, significantly alleviate poverty, and provide relief to those suffering from climate change. We will ultimately question whether or not the economy should be based upon what the arth can actually provide, regardless of how sophisticated our technology is. As we question these things, we can expect the idol's promises to become grander and a call for even more significant sacrifices. We can expect the priesthood to label those who challenge the idol's sovereignty to be blasphemers. But this is the critique that hope demands. The courage inspired by resurrection hope permits us to challenge the false hope sold by the priesthood, which actually leads to the hopelessness of despair and

46. Avila, *Ownership*, 41.

presumption. Christians who choose to be frugal are the first to remember that God is the ultimate provider of goods because all things belong to God, who then gives them to us so that we might mirror the divine image and bless others. Frugal Christians are living reminders of our creatureliness. We depend on God for everything that we have because the Earth and all that is in it belongs to God. Subsequently, Christians exercising frugal means because of their recognition of God's ownership of the Earth manifest a fundamental rejection of the neoclassical priesthood's presupposition of scarcity and its insistence that goods are not held in common and that the consumption of goods is a private experience subject to the personal ethics of individual consumers. Frugality, then, is the Christian expression of hope in a God whose abundance is sufficient if we are willing to live in such a way that distinguishes needs from wants, which creates the space to share with others and then stand in solidarity with them. Our reprioritization of needs and wants to include the understanding that ecological health and stability is the basis of the abundant life God desires for us signals hope to the rest of creation, too. Through this, we can live the magnanimous lives that God created us to live. By committing ourselves to practicing this subversive virtue in novel, courageous, and imaginative ways, we start the process of manifesting an economy of hope.

8

The American Association with Food

Our nation's primary conventional food-production model does two things very, very well. First, through the results of decades of scientific research, technological innovation, government subsidies, foreign policy, and political lobbying, Americans live in a country that produces a lot of food. As Christopher Cook describes it, "It's like a miraculous gastronomic democracy—Roman Empire-style excess readily available to the common man and woman."[1] We produce so much food, in fact, that Americans waste nearly half of it without running out of items to choose from in their refrigerators, and we are still one of the most obese nations on the planet. Second, due to the same above-mentioned forces and more, Americans spend very little of their total disposable income on their purchase of all of this food. The case can easily be made that we throw away so much food because it literally costs us very little do so. This conventional food-production model, however, is not only unsustainable, but has also proven over the last 100 years to be incredibly destructive to humans, nonhumans, and the Earth alike.

Due to this system, which relies on the gross use of artificial fertilizers and the nearly ubiquitous use of monocultural farming, soil is eroding faster than it can be replaced. Millions of acres of monocultures have denuded the soil of the various micronutrients that healthy soil needs to remain vibrant and life-giving, which means that food grown now is less nutritious than it was just a few generations ago. Food is not only less nutritious than it used to be, but it is also less diverse. Americans eat only a small amount of the total number of edible species on our planet, and far less so than previous generations, which leads to species extinction and crop vulnerability. This is ironically tragic because rich biodiversity is our best chance to adapt to climate change. The air near farms and surrounding towns is often polluted,

1. Cook, *Diet for a Dead Planet*, 4.

as clouds of chemical pesticides float from field to field before they finally
settle on both intended and unintended destinations, like homes, schools,
and playgrounds. Water sources that farmers rely upon to irrigate crops are
being depleted faster than they can be replenished, and when they are not
being depleted they are being polluted significantly. Fertilizer and pesticide
runoff alone pollute water so rampantly in the United States that the idea
of drinking clean water from a river or spring is a rural dream of a bygone generation. If water is not being polluted by fertilizer runoff, then it
is being polluted directly by animal waste and effluents from one of our
nation's many confined animal feeding operations (CAFOs) or oft-called
"factory farms." This is to say nothing of the host of human injustice toward
farmworkers that comes from feeding Americans the way we currently do.[2]
Moreover, this nearly monolithic model of food production has resulted in
a host of woes that we now realize signal a definitive systemic problem that
not only causes climate change, but also is strikingly exacerbated by it.[3]

And yet, when it comes to food there is a critical disconnection, as
many Americans have spent much of their lives always having food while
living on a planet where much of the rest of the world faces food insecurity
daily. For Americans, the perceived lack of want lends credibility to the
notion that the current food system must be working and hence must be
the solution to having too little food, or food that takes up too much of
one's budget. But the disconnection is even more profound because most
Americans do not live on a farm, no matter how big or small, and so do
not have a fundamental understanding of where their food comes from or
how its production impacts the Earth or the humans that grow and pick it.
In a very real sense, then, food is not considered to be a subject of moral or
theological consideration. Food is just food; it is not moral or immoral, but
rather amoral. How did we get to a place where this sort of disconnection
is the status quo for so many in our country? And how did we get to a place
that food is seen more as a collection of calories than something that tastes
good and brings people together in creative and mutually beneficial ways?

Roots of the Problem

First, many Americans no longer treat food as items with deep social, ecological, and cultural roots as most humans throughout history have. Instead,

2. For more on the treatment of farmworkers, see Rothenberg, *With These Hands*;
Thompson and Wiggins, *Human Cost of Food*; Bowe, *Nobodies*; Shipler, *Working Poor*.

3. For excellent introductions into perils of the Western food system, see Cook,
Diet for a Dead Planet; Carolan, *Real Cost*; Roberts, *End of Food*; Lappé, *Diet for a Hot
Planet*; Elton, *Consumed*.

many, if not most, Americans have become devotees of nutritionism. Nutritionism is a paradigm that involves a reductionistic way of thinking that disconnects food from its social, ecological, and cultural contexts.[4] Food is reduced merely to the level of the effects individual foods might have on bodily health. Eventually this sort of reductionism goes all the way down to the nutri-biochemical level: the attempt to analyze individual nutrients and their effects that they have on the human body. The accompanying assumption is a sort of determinism in which we assume vitamins are vitamins regardless of what food they happen be in when we actually ingest them. Food that is socially, ecologically, and culturally greater than the sum of its parts cannot be labeled and manipulated effectively in a laboratory. Food that is conceived of as a sum of nutrients can, though, and can be done so dramatically. This paradigm has had a profound impact on the American diet and our association with food even if the vast majority of Americans are unaware of it, whether that is through sheer ignorance or actively putting our heads in the sand. One of the ways that we show our devotion to nutritionism is through our constant association of food with calories. The "calorie-ization" of food may have begun in the nineteenth century when European scientists first started measuring the energy within food, but Americans have become fascinated with the notion as it has come to dictate food policy and the American diet vernacular.[5] If food is merely energy that can be measured by calories, then food has little, if any, relationship to its initial social, ecological, and cultural contexts.

Another of the ways that nutritionism shapes American eating is the rise of bio-fortification.[6] If food is merely a sum of nutrients, then why not add nutrients to supposedly low-nutritionally yielding staple crops or perhaps to processed foods? For example, there have been many attempts to address vitamin A deficiency in parts of the world by American scientists attempting to add vitamin A to rice and thus transform it into so-called Golden Rice. Or, what if the process of manufacturing the white bread that so many Americans are enamored with strips it of many, if not most, of wheat's vital nutrients? Food scientists can merely add nutrients back into the sort of bread that we really want—bio-fortify it if you will—and voilà, we have "Wonder Bread."[7]

Second, it would be easy to think that even in a culture like ours where food is more about calories and bio-fortified food products, the taste of food

4. Scrinis, "On the Ideology of Nutritionism," 39–48.
5. Carolan, *Real Cost of Cheap Food*, 58–61.
6. Ibid., 64–65.
7. Pollan, *In Defense of Food*, 106–14.

might dictate our food purchases; yet, this does not seem to be the case. The idea of enjoying our food for the quality of its taste is often seen as passé, or worse, elitist, in a culture that prizes efficiency and is so impatient that multitasking is seen as an essential skill. If taste, or more generally speaking, the quality of the food, is not often a determinative factor for what Americans eat regularly, what is? Price. We tend to believe that five tomatoes for five dollars are better than three tomatoes for five dollars without ever asking the relevant question: But what do they taste like?[8] Questions of quality have been subsumed by questions dictated by the economy, as if price is the definitive factor in deciding what should be on our plate for tonight's dinner. Most Americans do not believe that they should be expected to pay very much money for their food. We spend only about 10 percent of our disposable income on food, which is less than any other industrialized country in the world.[9] We tend to have very little trouble using our disposable income to purchase luxury items like big-screen televisions, automobiles, and mobile devices that keep us "connected" with our friends and family, but we whine incessantly and vociferously when the price of milk goes up or ground beef is no longer on sale. Whether one has great financial means or is a participant in a government-sponsored food assistance program, the price of food seems to affect the American psyche more than many other aspects of our lives. This is bizarre behavior, especially in light of how much food Americans annually waste. Some have suggested that the cheap nature of American food prevents consumers from understanding exactly what is being wasted.[10]

Third, perhaps our aversion to questions of taste and quality can be derived from our tendency to treat food as if it is a commodity rather than food. Most of us treat food as a commodity rather than as something that has social, ecological, and cultural significance. "Commodity" is not just technical economic jargon for a good that satisfies a need or a want of someone willing to buy or trade for it in the marketplace; it also refers specifically to a good that has full or partial fungibility. The market prizes fungibility of this sort because commodities can be treated as equivalent entities regardless of who produces them and the location and context of their initial production. A tomato is a tomato is a tomato, no matter who grew it or where it was grown or how it arrived at the grocery store. The commodification of food is perhaps most illustrative in the American association, and curious

8. For more on this, see Pollan, *Omnivore's Dilemma*, 136.

9. United States Department of Agriculture, "Food Prices and Spending"; Cook, *Diet for a Dead Planet*, 220–22.

10. Stuart, *Wasted*, 78.

fascination, with corn. A head of corn, or even a single kernel of corn for that matter, is more desirable in our market for what it can be transformed into rather than whether it is an edible product or not. Corn is transformed into high-fructose corn syrup, feed for animals, ethanol, and preservatives; it is a material used in batteries, diapers, cosmetics, deodorant, cough drops, paints, candles, fireworks, drywall, sandpaper, dyes, crayons, shoe polish, antibiotics, and adhesives; it is even the source of vitamin C in most of the vitamins we take in pill form.[11] In 2011, American farmers harvested 84 million acres of corn, with cash receipts from sales of $63.9 billion. According to the National Corn Growers Association, domestic and overseas livestock, poultry, and fish consume 80 percent of all American-grown corn. Moreover, each American consumes 25 pounds of corn annually, while only roughly 12 percent of the U.S. corn crop ends up in foods that humans either consume directly (e.g., corn chips) or indirectly (e.g., high-fructose corn syrup).[12] Michael Pollan aptly describes us as "processed corn, walking."[13] If food is primarily viewed as an economic entity, then it truly has lost its significant connection to deep social, ecological, and cultural roots. Paul Roberts contends that herein lies one of the basic problems with our view of food: "But this is the paradox of the food economy and, in my view, the source of most of its current problems: for all that the food system has evolved like other economic sectors, food itself is fundamentally not an economic phenomenon. Food production may follow general economic principles of supply and demand; it may indeed create employment, earn trade revenues, and generate profits, sometimes considerable profits; but the underlying product—the thing we eat—has never quite conformed to rigors of the modern industrial model."[14]

Fourth, one of the reasons that we no longer see the social, ecological, and cultural dimensions of our food is because most Americans no longer know the farmers that grow, pick, and sometimes process our food. As our society has urbanized, fewer and fewer of us live next to farms or have even been to a farm. We have little to no understanding of the work and ingenuity it takes to be a farmer. Moreover, we have little appreciation of the honorable vocation that farming can be. Some even argue that there has been a systematic effort by multiple forces and administrations in the U.S. federal government to move the work force out of the traditional agrarian professions and into the labor forces of the city, whether that is the manufacturing

---

11. Cummans, "What Is Corn Used For?"
12. Environmental Protection Agency, "Agriculture."
13. Pollan, *Omnivore's Dilemma*, 23.
14. Roberts, *End of Food*, xiv.

sector of the mid-to-late twentieth century or the white-collar workforce of the twenty-first century.[15] The larger the gap in geographical space between us and those who grow and pick our food, the less likely we are to reflect morally on the issues faced by those who grow and pick our food. When was the last time that you met the person who grew the food you ate for dinner? When was the last time you considered the wages and the working conditions of the person who picked the food that you took with you in your bag lunch? The host of justice concerns that are a daily reality for farmers and farmworkers are distant from our normal space of moral evaluation because we no longer buy directly from farmers nor live close to farms and because we have severed the social ties that have been connected to food for millennia. Food is just calories; it is not actually connected to a human being who grows it, picks it, and brings it to the market.

Finally, while food production may not seem like a moral issue to many, it is definitely an issue of political concern for the nation's dominant food corporations and elected officials. Food production obviously is benefited greatly by the transportation and distribution infrastructure that government provides the funds to build and maintain. For instance, food corporations, no matter how large, and farmers, no matter how small, rely on the railways and roads built with taxpayer monies to distribute their goods to consumers. But food production has also become more "political" in the partisan sense of the term that seems to pervade our national consciousness. Food corporations and agribusiness have spent hundreds of millions of dollars annually in lobbying efforts and campaign support of political candidates whom they believe will vote for legislation that will promote their agenda, e.g., the continued subsidization of the price of food production, guest-worker programs that are skewed to benefit agribusiness, or bills that preclude farmworkers from being paid overtime. During the 2012 election cycle alone, the agribusiness sector is estimated to have spent more than $90 million supporting candidates at the federal level. In the last 20 years, the agribusiness sector has contributed approximately $625 million to federal-level campaigns, with roughly 70 percent of that going to Republican candidates.[16] Moreover, the federal government has paid out billions of dollars in direct and indirect subsidies to farmers and agribusiness since the Great Depression. It is estimated that between 1995 and 2012 the U.S. government paid out $292.5 billion in subsidies related to the agricultural sector, with $177.6 billion in commodity subsidies alone. Ten percent of farms collected 75 percent of all available subsidies, with 62

15. Hauter, *Foodopoly*, 11–37.
16. Vendituoli, "Agribusiness."

percent of farms not collecting subsidy payments at all.[17] Since American-born workers seem highly unwilling to pick fruits and vegetables, migrant and undocumented foreigners have become the majority of the farmworkers in the United States. Some research indicates that billions of dollars in crop losses are due to the lack of labor to pick these crops and bring them to the market.[18] Therefore, immigration reform and inevitably partisan politics have become terribly important components of the national discussion about our domestic agricultural policy.

Theological Roots of the Problem

Food not only has deep social, ecological, and cultural roots, it has profound theological ones as well. Humanity's problems with eating go back to the very first narratives of Scripture. In Genesis 3, the writer describes a harmony that existed between God and the rest of creation, both human and nonhumans, within the garden of Eden. That harmony was fundamentally disrupted by a human act of disobedient eating. The first humans decided that God's instruction to refrain from eating from one particular tree was not worthy of their obedience. They put their own desires over the good desires of the Creator. This perennial truth articulated by the author of Genesis is still valid today. We prefer to follow ourselves or other idols rather than devote ourselves fully to God. This can be seen no more clearly than in our association with food. While many Christians might think that the issue of sacrificing food to idols is passé in this century because our culture generally denies the existence of deities traditionally associated with the idols of the past, we should not be so easily dismissive. Norman Wirzba contends that we have given food production and consumption over to the modern idols of control, efficiency, and convenience.[19] But how is this unholy trinity manifested precisely?

Control is attempted in every aspect of the food production industry, from control over how quickly an animal grows through genetic modification of certain traits to the sorts of legal arrangements that contract chicken farmers are allowed to sign. Let us consider three types of control that might be especially illustrative. First, look at how food gets to the typical local supermarket. There are 10 to 20 companies that dominate the food input market, i.e., seeds, fertilizer, herbicides, etc., who eventually sell products to the nearly 2.2 million American farms. Those farms then sell their

17. Environmental Working Group, "United States Farm."
18. White House, "Fixing Our Broken Immigration System."
19. Wirzba, *Food and Faith*, 11.

agricultural produce and animals to the approximately 25,000 food processors and manufacturers, who then sell products to the approximately 32,500 food wholesalers, who then seek to sell to the approximately 112,000 food and beverage retailers, who then sell to 300 million–plus consumers.[20] It is not an exaggeration to say that a tiny cross section of American society is choosing what to grow for the vast majority of Americans. As Paul Roberts argues, by the latter half of the twentieth century, "Food companies had in effect become the rulers of a supply chain that stretched from farmers to consumers, or from 'dirt to dinner,' and through which more than 95 percent of calories flowed."[21] If we look at the concentration ratio (CR) of supermarkets in America, we see the CR4 (i.e., the top four supermarket chains: Wal-Mart, Kroger, Safeway, and Costco) is approximately 50 percent, which means that only four supermarket chains own about half of the grocery market in the United States.[22] If we look more closely at the five largest retail U.S. markets (Atlanta, New York, Dallas, Chicago, and Los Angeles), the control is even more profound. The CR4 ratio in Atlanta is 81.9 percent, in New York 63.8 percent, in Dallas 63.7 percent, in Chicago 60 percent, and in Los Angeles 59.1 percent.[23] If we dig just a bit deeper into a type of food that Americans enjoy now at an unfathomably lower price than ever before in human history, we see even more control. Witness the reality of the animal meat market. The CR4 of the beef market is 80 percent, of the chicken market 50 percent, and of the pork market 60 percent.[24] So what do these percentages mean precisely? Generally speaking, when the CR4 reaches 20 percent, the market is considered concentrated, 40 percent indicates a highly concentrated market, and above 60 percent is evidence of a distorted market.[25] While control of a market is not necessarily a bad thing, it does beg the question whether or not our food security should depend on so few corporations.[26]

Another type of control is the capacity to dictate the flavors that actually register as tastes on our tongues. The flavors of much of the processed food most Americans eat (to say nothing of vitamins and minerals) have been heavily eroded by a variety of elements during the manufacturing process. Putting flavor back into food is critical because Americans generally

20. Carolan, *Reclaiming Food Security*, 101.

21. Roberts, *End of Food*, 35.

22. Richards and Pofahl, "Pricing Power."

23. Ibid.

24. Roberts, *End of Food*, 74.

25. Carolan, *Real Cost of Cheap Food*, 198.

26. For why this might be an extraordinarily bad idea, see Carolan, *Reclaiming Food Security*.

want their processed breakfast treats, for example, to taste like the straw-
berry- or blueberry-filled items that they are advertised to include. The food
engineering business is as fascinating as it is lucrative.[27] With the dash of
a chemical here or the addition of an amino acid there, Roberts explains,
"Breads can be made to taste more bread like; orange juice orangier; canned
meats meatier; pork more porklike."[28] Food engineers are able to trick our
brains, through our tongues, into believing something is what it is actually
not, and the corporations that employ the most talented of these engineers
make billions of dollars annually. Perhaps it should not surprise us that so
much tastes like chicken.

One more example of control is how we feed and slaughter animals.
Let us take chickens, for instance. The American desire for chicken breast
meat has spurred scientists to genetically engineer and breed chickens that
metabolize most of their energy into large breasts. In order to maximize
this sort of metabolism, most chickens in America no longer are allowed
to walk around looking for food that they have eaten traditionally on the
farms of American generations past; instead, they are fed a precisely engi-
neered diet of starch, amino acids, and antibiotics, which helps grow large
breasts quickly. This sort of control allows most chickens to grow at basically
the same rate, which subsequently allows for a sophisticated automated
slaughterhouse to process chickens of essentially the same size. This sort of
control allows many Americans access to just the sort of meat they desire
at prices that generally fit well within a food budget that we do not want to
see swell to a point that it disrupts expenditures on other "necessities," like
mobile phones, high-speed internet access, and streaming entertainment
services. This sort of control does not come without cost, however, as the
massive amount of energy that is now metabolized into breast meat causes
at least two significant problems for the modern broiler chicken: one, the
mere weight of the chicken's breast is often too much for the chicken to
handle and thus its hips and legs tend to break if not slaughtered first. Two,
because so much of its metabolic energy is being spent on muscle development, the average chicken that Americans eat is producing fewer antibodies
that might protect it from diseases it is more likely to contract living within
a confinement chicken coop. But do not worry, scientists are attempting
to genetically engineer disease-resistant chickens to combat this problem.[29]

27. To the tune of a $23 billion industry. See Leffingwell and Associates, "2011–
2015 Flavor & Fragrance Industry Leaders," http://www.leffingwell.com/top_10.htm.

28. Roberts, *End of Food*, 46.

29. Ibid., 66–77.

Linked to control is the idol of efficiency. As discussed earlier, efficiency is so prized by American industry that we presume that any lack of efficiency, no matter in what phase of our lives, means a loss of profit. Why eat lunch with colleagues when you could get work done while you eat? Why not genetically engineer a plant to be a uniform size so that it can be picked by a machine rather than a human being? In a world where the phrase "time is money" has such cultural cache, it is no wonder that slowing down to eat seems like a considerable waste of time, and thus money. This mantra is manifest in myriad ways in the food-production industry, where the downward price pressure can only be met by the cost-cutting that comes through more efficient means of production, whether that be more efficient workers, equipment, or even inputs of food. "With rapid advances in breeding, production, and shipping, a ham or a chicken can now be manufactured as uniformly and precisely as the frozen pizzas or fast-food burritos they wind up in."[30] Why should plants and animals not be grown or raised to be as efficient as *we* want them to be? As we shall discuss below, the idea of efficiency even creeps into the amount of time we spend eating.

The last member of this profane trinity is convenience. If it is a perceived waste of time to eat lunch with colleagues, then it is certainly inconvenient to come home at the end of a long day and make dinner for the family. The rise of fast food, drive-thru restaurants, frozen dinners, ready-made meals, and so-called convenience stores demonstrate that when we actually do eat, we want the meal to be as convenient as possible. The rise of convenient food is driven as much by producers as it is by consumers. From the vantage point of producers, Roberts asserts, "In a food economy geared toward ever lower prices, selling convenience has become the food industry's most important means of making money."[31] And as many Americans have moved further away from their workplaces and "live" so many hours a day in their cars on their way to some event, we have been willing to exchange homemade meals for less-flavorful and less-healthy items because of "their cheapness, uniformity, relative safeness, and huge convenience."[32] Thus the rise of items like meal-replacement bars and single-serve yogurt in a squeezable tube, because who really has the time to be bothered by the time it takes to eat an actual meal or to eat yogurt out of a single-serve cup? While you can go to a supermarket and purchase the ingredients for a meal, if you lack the time you can purchase any number of ready-made meals that only require reheating, if that. And if you find yourself in a pinch, you can

30. Ibid., 59.
31. Ibid., 31.
32. Ibid., 32.

always buy a "meal" for the family in the convenience store that is managed by your local gas station on the way home from work. But, as Wendell Berry argues, it is more than this: "We have made a social ideal of minimal involvement in the growing and cooking of food. This is one of the dearest 'liberations' of our affluence."[33] In a culture dominated by these idols that prescribe this sort of liberation, cooking from scratch may very well be a subversive act of the profoundest sort.[34]

The efforts of these three idols have created more calories at a cheaper price than human civilization has ever seen. While this should signal a decline in starvation and food insecurity around the planet, it in fact has generated a massive amount of food waste with no end of starvation and food insecurity in sight. Americans, for example, waste nearly 40–50 percent of all of their food.[35] This refers to food that has been knowingly discarded or destroyed—food waste that might be inedible to humans but could be fed to livestock—and inadvertent spoilage or destruction (e.g., due to shipping or lack of refrigeration).[36] This does not even account for the amount of scarce freshwater around the planet that is being wasted in the process[37] nor that in the U.S. organic waste is the second highest component of materials in landfills and is the largest national source of methane emissions.[38] These simple factors alone beg moral and theological reflection, but due to our devotion to convenience the situation is actually more appalling than we would care to admit. For example, let us look at a farmer who provides carrots for a large supermarket chain. According to this farmer, the chain insists that the carrots be so straight that "customers might be able to peel the full length in one easy stroke." After the carrots are picked, they are washed and sent through incredibly expensive machines that detect the brightness of the color of the carrot, potential blemishes, and the carrot's curvature. Whatever carrots the machines do not push to the wayside are then scrutinized by employees of the farmers and then a representative of the supermarket chain. This farmer concludes that 25–30 percent of his carrots fail to meet the chain's standards; about half of those are rejected for "defects" that are related to aesthetic criteria prescribed by the chain, while

33. Berry, "Waste," 128.

34. Pollan, *In Defense of Food*, 200.

35. Stuart, *Waste*; Gunders, "Wasted"; Gustavsson et al., "Global Food Losses"; Buzby et al., "Estimated Amount"; Donlon, "Food and Climate"; Nellemann, "Environmental Food Crisis."

36. Robin Roy, quoted in Stuart, *Waste*, 315n4. He also talks about relative waste: the inefficient use of food (like grain) in feeding livestock instead of people.

37. Nellemann, "Environmental Food Crisis," 32.

38. Ibid., 29.

the other half may have small defects that could be removed by employees on the production line or by the consumer. None of this has to do with the actual quality and taste of the carrots themselves. While some of this "waste" can be sold to food processors (e.g., to be transformed into so-called baby carrots) or for livestock feed, neither of these secondary sources matches the revenue generated by selling food for human consumption.[39] This is just one example of many that could be used to demonstrate how control, efficiency, and convenience not only dictate our aesthetic sensibilities, but lead to an overwhelming amount of waste.

The sort of wastefulness is not merely endemic to producers; like supermarket chains, consumers are significantly wasteful, too. Tristram Stuart argues that undergirding our wastefulness is a distinct anthropology. "A well-stocked larder has, in many cultures since antiquity, been a principal signifier of status and affluence. Anybody who is entertaining guests or even just cooking for the family would rather cook more than enough than run out. In this way, we operate a bit like a supermarket: projecting an image of unlimited abundance. Anything less and we might appear stingy, or too poor to offer enough food."[40] Sadly, he goes on to say, "Wasting money on excess food may actually be something that comforts consumers. It is the very fact that we can afford to buy food even if we may not want to eat it which subliminally gives us a sense of affluence—a cozy buffer between us and hunger. Having surplus, even in excess of what is ever likely to be needed, can be reassuring. It is a normal phenomenon, but one which can become pathological: at that point it is called greed."[41] What Stuart deems potentially pathological, Christians must definitely regard for what it is—sin.

But why is wastefulness sinful? The reasons are similar to those discussed in the previous chapter about material excessiveness. If God is indeed the creator of life and the giver of all blessings, and those blessings are to be used to serve our sisters and brothers, then to waste food is failing to serve our sisters and brothers in our neighborhoods both near and far who desperately crave good, nutritionally dense food. Whether we call this service an act of charity or justice, it is an act that is needed in just about every community on the planet. Just as living a materially excessive lifestyle is a dehumanizing for both the one who has little and the one who has much, so too is living a life of wasting food. For those who are food insecure, their dignity is intrinsically degraded by a society that would prefer to

---

39. Stuart, *Waste*, 103–5. While this example hails from the United Kingdom, it could very well be from the United States.

40. Ibid., 73.

41. Ibid., 78.

throw away food that ultimately contributes to climate change, which likely further harms those who are food insecure, than to creatively imagine solutions to distribute aesthetically unpleasing carrots or day-old bread to those who are in critical need of nutritionally dense food to signal the hope of the abundant life promised by God. For those who are wasting food regularly, it is dehumanizing, because when we participate in a system that deems less-than-perfectly straight carrots to be inappropriate for human consumption, we become prideful and lose our sense of creatureliness that should define us as humble human beings and thus cause us to model the gratitude we should have for the abundant life God wishes for us to enjoy. Moreover, the sort of wastefulness that deems worthy only carrots straight enough to be peeled in one sweep of the peeler demeans the honorable work of the farmers and workers who grow and pick our food, which is ultimately a profane statement about what the land is giving us through the blessing of God, who stands behind the whole system as the original farmer/gardener.[42] Also, from our earlier review of the patristic theologians, recall that there is strong agreement that God not only created the Earth, but created it in such a way that there are sufficient resources for all of its inhabitants.[43] If this is the case, then we have a fundamental sharing problem. In terms of eating, the question of how much is enough is pivotal and we shall examine that below, but suffice it to say, presently, the God of Jesus Christ who desires us to have an abundant life would see our food waste while billions of people are food insecure to be similar to the cry of the ancient Israelites seeking reprieve from slavery so long ago. Those of us seeking to witness to the resurrection hope must hear the sufferings of those crying out today. Finally, perhaps the most corrosive aspect of the sin of wasting food is that we are in fact wasting life. Eating should remind us of how costly it is for a creature to participate in the gift of life that God has bestowed upon us,[44] and hence wasting food is to profane that gift. If sin is our alienation from ourselves, from our neighbors (both human and nonhuman), and from God, then wasting food does nothing to signal the reconciliation to be found in Christ and the hope we find in the resurrection.

Wastefulness is not the only sin that Christians must consider when it comes to our perverted relationship with food. In her concise introduction to the subject of gluttony from the vantage point of Western culture, Francine Prose maintains, "However flawed and partial, the idea that overeating

42. Wirzba, *Food and Faith*, 195.

43. The UN FAO proposes that there is roughly 3,000 kcal available per person on the planet today and that number will last until 2050. See http://www.un.org/en/development/desa/policy/wess/wess_bg_papers/bp_wess2013_millennium_inst.pdf.

44. For more on this, see Wirzba, *Food and Faith*, 1–11.

is symptomatic of a psychological disorder somehow seems (at least to the secular mind) more logical and comprehensible than the notion that glut- tony should constitute a crime against the divine order."[45] Once known as one of the seven deadly sins, it is hard to remember the last time gluttony was seriously considered to be sinfully pernicious in the American church. This was not always the case; for centuries, Christian thinkers beseeched their parishioners to remain vigilant against the ills of gluttonous behav- ior. In the Roman Catholic tradition, St. Thomas Aquinas' reflections on the subject are still the catechismal standard. He contends that gluttony is the inordinate desire to eat; by "inordinate," he means leaving the realm of rational thought.[46] Relying upon St. Gregory the Pope,[47] Aquinas contends that gluttony comes in five forms: 1) eating food that is too costly or exotic; 2) eating too much food; 3) eating food that is too daintily or elaborately prepared; 4) eating at the wrong time, in the sense of too soon after the last meal; and 5) eating too eagerly or greedily. Both Aquinas and Gregory provide us with much to think about regarding the nature of the conse- quences of this specific sin. As for Aquinas, he asserts that by eating too much, one's brain is disturbed by the "fumes of food," which subsequently causes one to lose the ability to think rationally.[48] In other words, gorging oneself on food subsequently prevents clear thinking. This, of course, is of primary significance to Aquinas because it is only by thinking clearly that one can make virtuous decisions and exhibit Christian living. While Gregory may be more famously known for saying the appetite of the belly must first be conquered in order to fight spiritual battles successfully,[49] he makes a rather subtle, but profound, distinction between pleasure and ne- cessity that I believe is still illustrative for our era. Gregory contends that the fundamental human problem when eating is to distinguish when one is eating for necessity and when one is eating for pleasure. He presumes that eating out of necessity is virtuous, while eating for pleasure is gluttonous. "For at that time, when the demand of necessity is paid, because pleasure is, through eating, blended with necessity, it is not known what necessity demands itself, and what (as has been said) pleasure secretly demands. But we frequently both distinguish them, and yet, from knowing that they are mutually connected together, take pleasure, when hurried beyond proper

---

45. Prose, *Gluttony*, 12.

46. Thomas Aquinas, *Summa Theologica* II.II.148.

47. Gregory the Pope, *Books of the Morals*, vol. III, pt. 6, bk. XXX, xvii, 60.

48. Ibid., article 6.

49. Ibid., 58

bounds, in being wittingly deceived: and whilst the mind flatters itself on the necessity, it is deceived by pleasure."[50]

While Aquinas and Gregory are both helpful in this analysis, it is a church father from the second century who may be even more instructive. Clement of Alexandria contends, "Excess, which in all things is an evil, is very highly reprehensible in the matter of food. Gluttony, called *opsophagia*, is nothing but excess in the use of relishes (*opson*); and *laimargia* is insanity with respect to the gullet; and *gastrimargia* is excess with respect to food—insanity in reference to the belly, as the name implies; for *margos* is a madman."[51] While Clement does not categorically explain why the excess of food is so reprehensible, it is imaginable after the above exploration to understand this at least in the context of our present century. The personal and societal wastefulness of food is especially telling as we live on a planet that still has billions who are either starving or food insecure daily. Clement argues that the gluttonous are unbounded in their search for items to satiate their desire. "'Whatever earth and the depths of the sea, and the unmeasured space of the air produce,' they cater for their gluttony. In their greed and solicitude, the gluttons seem absolutely to sweep the world with a drag-net to gratify their luxurious tastes."[52] Living in a country that imports exotic food from all over the planet and a vast amount of its produce so that it may have summer fruits and vegetables year-around, Clement seems almost prescient. He goes on to make a fundamental distinction between sufficiency and its relationship to love and the damages that gluttony causes due to a lack of love. "For love is a good nurse for communication; having as its rich provision sufficiency, which, presiding over diet measured in due quantity, and treating the body in a healthful way, distributes something from its resources to those near us. But the diet which exceeds sufficiency injures a man [sic], deteriorates his spirit, and renders his body prone to disease."[53] He then maintains, "Appropriate designations of such people as so indulge are flies, weasels, flatterers, gladiators, and the monstrous tribes of parasites—the one class surrendering reason, the other friendship, and the other life, for the gratification of the belly."[54] He then draws a connection between the famous parable of the prodigal son and our love of certain foods. "For it were not seemly that we, after the fashion of the rich man's son in the Gospel, should, as prodigals, abuse the Father's gifts; but we should

50. Ibid., 62
51. Clement of Alexandria, *Paedagogus*, bk. II, ch. 1.
52. Ibid.
53. Ibid.
54. Ibid.

use them, without undue attachment to them, as having command over ourselves. For we are enjoined to reign and rule over meats, not to be slaves to them."[55] Finally, he exhorts those who are wealthy to be on the lookout for their gluttonous ways. "If a person is wealthy, yet eats without restraint and shows himself [sic] insatiable, he disgraces himself in a special way and does wrong on two scores: first he adds to the burden of those who do not have, and he lays bare, before those who do have, his own lack of temperance . . . it is abundance that blinds in the matter of gluttony."[56]

So what might we learn from these theologians? While Clement, Gregory, and Thomas most likely saw gluttony as a sin of the individual, our worship of the idols of control, efficiency, and convenience have made gluttony a societal sin as well.[57] Gluttonous behavior disconnects us from our capacity to think clearly. Eating ourselves into a "food coma," as my students are known to say, hinders serious rational contemplation. We know this is the case because as difficult as it is for American Christians to distinguish between eating out of necessity and eating for pleasure, it becomes even more problematic the more food we are shoving down our gullets. While Aquinas and Gregory perhaps err on the side of divorcing all of the pleasure from eating in order to remain vigilant against gluttony, I believe it is possible to enjoy the taste of food and still exhibit a devoutly Christian lifestyle. We shall turn to that in the evaluation of the Eucharist in the next chapter. That said, there seems to be little doubt that being gluttonous causes one to think about the needs of the belly and not the needs of others. Moreover, gluttony not only thwarts clear thinking, but also causes the loss of friendship and life. In our context, this plays out in at least three ways. One, while one form of gluttony for these three theologians has to do with eating food that was too costly, we must now consider the notion of eating food that is produced too cheaply. Efficiency in American food-production systems has caused food to become cheap, though at a considerable price. Much of the food of the American diet is so cheap because it surrenders friendship and life. We fail to pay the farmers and migrant workers who grow and pick our produce a wage that would allow them to live dignified lives. We fail to pay the full price of our meat as our nation's rivers and water sources are polluted with slaughterhouse effluent and the air above CAFOs is toxic to breathe. We fail to grow nutritionally dense food that nourishes and satisfies our bodies, whether we are wealthy or poor. Two, we have created such an efficient system of creating cheap food that we are actually overproducing calories that

55. Ibid.
56. Ibid.
57. See also Wirzba, *Food and Faith*, 139–40.

are literally decomposing in landfills and contributing to climate change, and there still is a vast amount of starvation around the globe. At the same time, we find ourselves on a planet where approximately a billion people are obese. The bizarre tragedy that has arisen simultaneously out of this is that most of these obese are malnourished because they are eating too many empty calories.[58] Our abundance has truly blinded us to our gluttony. Three, through this loss of friendship and life, gluttonous behavior continues to obscure the capacity to reflect individually or societally on the failures of the American diet. Thus, the admonishments from centuries ago are eerily contemporary: our gluttony, and in particular our ability to self-rationalize pleasure into necessity, has profound impacts on our relationships to other humans, nonhumans, and the planet around us. Do our bellies rule us or do we rule them?

A System Marked by Hopelessness

Ultimately, the American food system is marked by profound hopelessness. On the one hand, the system is riddled with the hopelessness of presumption. Rather than question the root of the problem, which takes into account our relationship to food and our behavior toward it, we presume that since human ingenuity and technology have solved so many food problems in the past, we will figure a way out of it again. We tend to believe, whether explicitly or implicitly, that we need even more control over and efficiency from our food systems, which signals the need for more technological solutions. I remain skeptical of relying on human ingenuity alone to solve our problems because the root of the issue is not technology per se, but placing our hope in it, and consequently ourselves, rather than in God, which prevents us from thinking essentially about our behavior, both personal and societal, and listening for the sorts of novel solutions that divine grace provides. More sacrifices to the idols of control, efficiency, and subsequently convenience are not the answer because we have already sacrificed too much. We have, in Clement's words, surrendered friendship and life of many kinds. The source of this presumption is a *perversa securitas* derived from a lack of humility that causes us to see ourselves as more divine than creaturely. This is one of the principal lessons of the Tower of Babel narrative: we revel in our ability to create technology because we believe it makes us more godlike.[59] Instead, Michael Northcott contends that we should turn to the Noah story in order

58. Roberts, *End of Food*, xvii. For more on this, see Patel, *Stuffed and Starved*; Levenstein, *Paradox of Plenty*.

59. Gen 11:1–9. See Noble, *Religion of Technology*.

to understand our proper relationship to technology and combat our own hubris, where we find that "humility and a preparedness to change direction in response to the clear signs of impending dange" are deemed virtuous.[60] The idols of control, efficiency, and convenience blind us to the virtuous nature of humility and its role in defining our relationship to God and listening for the novel possibilities of divine grace that are the source of hope.

At the same time, an odd sense of despair has crept in for many, as we ponder the prodigious failures of the American food system, which not only contributes heavily to climate change, but also is staggeringly exacerbated by it. As we witness droughts become more dramatic and lengthy or topsoil continue to erode at a pace that cannot be replaced in many lifetimes, we may begin to think that there is nothing that God can do to help us, and no novel solutions left to inspire us to be courageous in the face of the seemingly indomitable status quo maintained by the various principalities and powers. While this sort of despair may even manifest itself occasionally as being reasonable, Christians must resist this form of hopelessness, too. Despair is not only existentially threatening, but as the result of sloth it legitimates apathy and indifference. By surrendering to sloth, we fail to acknowledge and live the magnanimous lives that God created us to live.

This system has been so successful, in a sense, because most Americans give little, if any, thought to the theological, moral, social, ecological, and cultural aspects of food. Our thoughtlessness about something we do so regularly allows us to support a deleterious status quo and the hopelessness it produces. This is tragically ironic for Christians in particular since we participate in a ritualistic meal that in some manner or another affirms the presence of God. If Jesus is the Bread of Life,[61] the theological and moral dimensions of food should be on the forefront of our minds. The good news, though, as Alexander Schmemann argues, is this: "Centuries of secularism have failed to transform eating into something strictly utilitarian. Food is still treated with reverence. A meal is still a rite—the last 'natural sacrament' of family and friendship, of life that is more than 'eating' and 'drinking.' To eat is still something more than to maintain bodily functions. People may not understand what that 'something more' is, but they nonetheless desire to celebrate it. They are still hungry and thirsty for sacramental life."[62] In other words, even though nutritionism dominates American thinking about food, every time we actually sit down to the dinner table with family or have lunch with our friends, we know that something more than merely

60. Northcott, *Moral Climate*, 79.

61. John 6:35.

62. Schmemann, *Life of the World*, 16.

ingesting calories is occurring. And if we could pinpoint what exactly that something is, we know that we desire for it to happen more regularly. Let us turn to chapter 9 and determine what that is.

9

Eating as a Christian
Act of Hope[1]

In a culture that continues to separate food from its theological, moral, social, ecological, and cultural roots as it descends into the hopelessness of despair and presumption, it can become difficult to listen for the imaginative possibilities that divine grace offers us. Thankfully, God does not call us to reinvent the wheel, as it were, when it comes to mealtime, but rather to remember what it is that we do when we participate in one of the central rituals of the Christian faith. The Eucharist (or the Lord's Supper or Communion, or whatever your particular tradition might call it) is *the* principal model for eating hopefully. For more than two thousand years, this meal has been central to the Christian life, but the meal on Sunday is detached from the eating we do the rest of the week more so now than ever before. Let us explore what the Eucharist means to the Christian life and then connect that to a form of hopeful eating we can participate in daily.

Eating Hopefully

The prominent anthropologist Mary Douglas argues that eating teaches us something about ourselves, especially the values that we, as families and societies, hold dear.[2] For example, in some churches older folks are encouraged to go through the potluck line first, while in other congregations the little kids are allowed to fill their plates before everyone else. Or during holidays, some families have staunch traditions about who gets to sit at the adult table and who remains tethered to the kid table. So what might American eating habits tell us about ourselves? For most of the history of human civilization, eating has been viewed as a deeply social event. It is only recently that eating

1. The ideas in this chapter originated in an article entitled "Eating as a Christian Act of Hope," *Interdisciplinary Environmental Review* 16.2–4 (2015) 193–205.

2. Douglas, *In the Active Voice*, 82–124.

alone has become a habitual part of American life. We often believe that eating with someone else takes up too much time or that we can accomplish more if we work while we eat lunch. There is a sense that our deep-seated value of efficiency is somehow being violated if we slow down to eat with others. After all, food is just calories and calories can be consumed efficiently while performing other purportedly more important tasks. Even when we do eat together, we are not really eating together because we are often eating completely different items. How many times do we see a parent making a special meal for a defiant child unwilling to eat the same food as the rest of the family? Michael Pollan poignantly notes that even when his family is physically together in a car going through the drive-thru of a fast-food restaurant, they each order different meals and are ultimately eating alone.[3] In contrast, when we participate in the Eucharist (with the exception of my gluten intolerant sisters and brothers), we eat and drink the same things, and we do so together as a family. We not only participate in this eucharistic meal with our Christian sisters and brothers, but we do so with Christ, as Christ invites everyone to break the bread and drink the wine together. Eating the eucharistic meal together should remind us that God calls creatures to be together in community in the divine presence; we are not meant to be alone. The meal is the ultimate symbolic and physical representation of God's plan for all of creation to participate in God's gracious redemptive scheme.[4] Everyone is invited to the table; no one is excluded, which I believe has dramatic consequences for our understanding of the sort of community that Jesus was intending to build through the Eucharist.

Many Protestant faith traditions tend to think of the Eucharist as more of a symbolic meal, almost to the point where the idea of the meal somehow mediating divine grace seems nearly a foreign idea. Perhaps there is much we can learn from other Christian traditions that tend to reflect consciously upon God's grace being present, in some form or another, in the bread and the wine. For instance, meditating on God's grace being present in the meal might help us to remember in a real way that we ultimately depend upon God because it is only by grace that our very being is held in existence. Moreover, by considering our ontological dependence upon God we open

---

3. Pollan, *Omnivore's Dilemma*, 110.

4. "We can see Eucharistic eating as manifesting God's heavenly kingdom because it *participates* in what it manifests. By eating at the Lord's Table, people are given here and now a glimpse of heaven as the sort of life God desires for the whole creation. They are invited to turn from sinful ways that profane and fragment the world, and instead commit to a comprehensive reorientation in which all life is restored and made whole by the communion Christ's loving ways with the world make possible." Wirzba, *Food and Faith*, 153; italics in original.

ourselves to the opportunity of becoming more grateful for who God is and what God does to substantiate every moment of our existence. This sort of thankfulness represents more literally what the Greek verb *eucharisto* connotes,[5] from which we derive the noun "eucharist." Additionally, since the Eucharist is in some way a manifestation of God's grace, it should represent a distinct reminder that God is sufficient to meet our needs, which I believe has profound ethical, political, and social implications that beg to be examined.

Partaking in the Eucharist is not merely an act of internal reflection; it is also a political act, even if many contemporary Christians fail to recognize it as such. The proclamation "Jesus is Lord," affirmed by the Eucharist, does not seem as radical today as it was to followers of Christ in the earliest centuries of the church. Two thousand years ago, this declaration was interpreted by the Roman authorities to signify that one did not believe Caesar was sovereign. The depth of meaning of this affirmation was tested just decades after Jesus' resurrection. One of the earliest struggles for the church in Corinth was the decision about whether to eat meat previously sacrificed to the Roman gods. The apostle Paul argues that it is not immoral to eat meat sacrificed to idols because the idols do not in fact exist, but at the same time he includes an intriguing caveat: do not allow the eating of the meat to be a stumbling block to those who may not have the ability to understand the distinction he just made. In fact, he says that he would give up meat altogether if that was the cause of even one person to fall.[6] This is a keen reminder that eating is indeed a deliberative moral, theological, and even pastoral exercise in the Christian life and is directly related to one's life within the *polis*. This is no clearer than in the industrial meat-production system to be examined shortly.

At the same time, the Eucharist is about hospitality. Jesus invites everyone to the table.[7] According to L. Shannon Jung, Christian hospitality is about welcoming others to the table, not just your friends or family, but strangers and even enemies. Being hospitable means recognizing the dignity and value of those at the table, especially that of strangers and enemies. Theologically and existentially, hospitality reminds us of who God is and how we are to act as creatures made in the divine image.[8] "We eat and drink both in acknowledgement of common loyalty and in anticipation of being strengthened for discipleship."[9] Hospitality is acutely political as

5. E.g., Matt 26:26; 1 Cor 1:4; 10:30; Rom 1:8.
6. 1 Cor 8.
7. E.g., Matt 22:1–14; Luke 14:15–24.
8. Jung, *Sharing Food*, 45–50.
9. Ibid., 134.

well since the church restores dignity to those that a given *polis* might deem undesirable. Those farmers and fieldworkers who grow and pick our food should be invited to the table, especially since they are so often castigated and discarded by our society. Our dismissal of farmers and fieldworkers is doubly tragic since they can represent the image of God in a special way.[10] Those who emulate the vocation of the first caretaker of the garden of Eden should be held in the highest esteem as they model the divine work highlighted in Genesis 2. Hospitality is not without the sharing of food, and the sharing of food is ultimately about sharing the good news of Jesus. Wirzba argues, "To invite others to one's table and share food with them is to communicate that life is not a possession to be jealously guarded. To share food is fundamentally to share life."[11] This is exactly what we see in the stories of Jesus feeding the multitudes.[12] For Angel Méndez-Montoya, this sharing of life reveals God's character. "God's sharing of food, and self-sharing *as* food, is the source of divine goodness that heals spiritual and physical hungers, but in addition urges us to share with and care for one another."[13] To share food, and consequently life, is a fundamental rejection of the sins of wasting food and gluttony, and a hearty embrace of the virtue of sufficiency, which we see demonstrated so vividly in Jesus' feeding of the multitudes. It is this sufficiency, according to Clement, that is required to measure truly the love of one's neighbor.

Wirzba goes even further and argues that eucharistic eating is not just about hospitality, but reconciliation as well. "If the scope of God's reconciling work extends to the whole creation, then it becomes evident that eating, understood as our most intimate joining with the bodies of creation, must be a primary site and means through which this reconciliation becomes visible. In our eating we are not simply to be reconciled to fellow human eaters. We must also be reconciled to what we eat. How we prepare to eat, as well as the character of the eating itself, demonstrates whether or not we appreciate the wide scope of God's reconciling ways with the world."[14] Moreover, he maintains, "[To be reconciled] is to commit to an economy and a politics in which the care of each other is our all-consuming desire."[15] Christians in the earliest centuries saw how profoundly the hospitality of the Eucharist affected the economic and political aspects of their lives. It is

10. Wirzba, *Food and Faith*, 195; Davis, *Scripture, Culture, and Agriculture*, 104.

11. Wirzba, *Food and Faith*, 121.

12. Matt 14:13-21; 15:32-9; Mark 6:30–44; 8:1–10; Luke 9:10–17; John 6:1–15.

13. Méndez-Montoya, *Theology of Food*, 122; italics in original.

14. Wirzba, *Food and Faith*, 175.

15. Ibid., 178.

time for American Christians living in the light of the resurrection to do the same now, centuries later.

Since most American Christians do not reflect morally or theologically on food, it stands to reason that even fewer consider carefully how the eating they do at the eucharistic table connects to the eating they do the rest of the week. Michael Northcott argues that this was not the case for the earliest Christians, who seemed to believe fervently that all eating is potentially an opportunity to eat with Christ since there is a moral continuum between the Lord's Table and the dinner table.[16] This is key to understanding that "something more" that we know is present when we eat. And yet, in an American Protestant climate, in particular, that is moving further and further away from the weekly practice of the Eucharist, we give ourselves less room to reflect upon the theological roots and implications of eating.[17] In other words, the frequency of partaking of the Eucharist can impact the frequency of our theological and moral reflection upon the food we eat daily, particularly as we begin to reflect on the sacrifices we make to the idols of control, efficiency, and convenience, as well as on the gluttonous behavior that pervades American life. If we are to resist our culture's attempt to separate eating from its moral and theological roots, then we must recognize that the Eucharist is the symbol for hopeful eating and therefore regularly participate in it and apply the eucharistic table manners to the rest of the week. Eating hopefully is a way for Christians to exhibit novel and creative possibilities inspired by divine grace that will allow us to overcome the hopelessness of presumption and despair. Let us examine six ways these eucharistic lessons can be connected to daily eating and transform us into more hopeful eaters.

First, hopeful eating should remind us of our connection to the Earth. Humans are truly people of the soil; we are the *adam* of the *adamah*. The sometimes-cynical author of Ecclesiastes puts it this way: "Surely the fate of human beings is like that of the animals; the same fate awaits them both . . . All go to the same place; all come from dust, and to dust all return."[18] This fact is not only reaffirmed when we partake of the eucharistic elements, but every time we place food in our mouth because everything we eat has its beginning in the soil. No amount of chemical alteration, synthetic derivation, or technological sophistication in the food-production chain that serves the idols of control, efficiency, and convenience can alter this fundamental biological truth. Therefore, Christians should be the very first to contemplate

16. Northcott, *Moral Climate*, 255.

17. See also Northcott, "Eucharistic Eating," 153–54.

18. Eccl 3:19–20.

the moral and theological dimensions of our food, where it comes from, and how it got to our plates; instead, we are often the very last to do so.

Second, hopeful eating should remind us of our interdependence with the rest of creation. We cannot celebrate the Eucharist without the Earth's capacity to bring forth wheat and grapes. The fact that we cannot create our own energy by absorbing the rays of the sun and transforming them into sugars, like plants, means that humans, like many other creatures on the planet, necessarily depend on countless nonhuman creatures merely to survive from one day to the next. This should give us pause and compel us to think about food's moral and theological implications. And yet, through the priests of advertising who speak for the idols of control, efficiency, and convenience, we implicitly believe that we rely on the supermarket for our food, not a farmer, and certainly not other creatures, especially the tiniest ones that make the soil bring forth food. Through deeper contemplation we perceive not only our interdependence, but also the costs associated with biological life on this planet. "All life becomes a sign and sacrament of God's love, a witness to the costliness and mystery of life and death, and so becomes the inspiration to greater attention and care."[19] We must not take for granted that something must die in order for something else to live, whether it is plant or animal. We should also be reminded that this interdependence is not merely biological. The cosmic covenant that undergirds the universe links us together as well, since ecological health and justice for the oppressed are not mutually exclusive on this planet, but instead are constituent of God's good creation.

Third, hopeful eating should remind us of the nature of our ontological dependence. Just as the Eucharist reminds us on Sundays of the divine grace that sustains our very existence, daily eating should cause us to be cognizant of this in a very specific way. While we may grow plants to eat and thus believe that we have done something to maintain our existence, the truth is we did not create the sun that provides the energy that allows plants to be the basis of the food system upon which we completely depend. The question of who or what created the sun that gives plants the energy that is the basis of our food system should prompt us to ask upon whom we ultimately depend. Thinking that we ultimately rely on the grocery store or seed companies or fertilizer manufacturers or even farmers for our food misses the ontological mark. For Christians, each meal should be a reminder that we depend upon God, not human ingenuity or technology, for every bite that we take. This is one of the principal lessons that God providing manna in the wilderness was supposed to teach the Israelites and it was reemphasized

19. Wirzba, *Food and Faith*, 158.

by Jesus feeding the multitudes.[20] Unfortunately, too many contemporary Christians have too easily forgotten this lesson. As Wirzba puts it, "To approach food with a concern for its theological depth is to acknowledge that food is precious because it has its source in God."[21] Additionally, as Ellen Davis states, "[F]ood is, more than anything else, an expression of God's sovereignty over creation and generosity toward humankind."[22] Food, then, is also a fundamental reminder that God is the sovereign and generous author of the cosmic covenant that is part of the very fabric of the universe that God has created. Good food is enjoyed when we appreciate that ecological integrity and human justice are intricately linked. Food that does not degrade the environment and is purchased at a price that allows the farmers and fieldworkers to earn a dignified living honors God.

Fourth, hopeful eating should remind us to be humble. The Eucharist exhorts us to be humble as we recognize our sin and celebrate the work God did in the resurrection of Jesus to conquer death and redeem us back to God. Every meal we eat can be a reminder of this and more. Remember, the fact that "human," "humus," and "humility" all share the same Latin root is etymologically illustrative of the ontological link made in Genesis 2 between the *adam* and the *adama*. As any farmer will tell you, no amount of technological innovation derived from the collective genius of humanity can make the soil bring forth life. We do not control whether or not a seed sprouts or when the sun shines or the clouds deliver rain. (This does not even take into account the hundreds of human hands that it takes to bring the food to us.) This reality should shape us into humble beings who are grateful for the very meal on our table (or perhaps even in our car). Being humble allows us to have knowledge of God. Davis argues, "Eating is a primary occasion for knowing the work of YHWH. . . . For those who draw near and offer themselves before God, satisfaction of hunger is neither an end in itself nor a wholly 'secular' event. In this economy, eating is worshipful, even revelatory; it engenders a healthful knowledge of God."[23] Our devotion to nutritionism and the rapt attention we give to its marketing, advertising, and scientific priests who trade on the notion that technology causes food to arrive at our table has prompted us to be less cognizant of our interdependence with the rest of creation, less aware of our utter dependence upon God, and less likely to believe that eating should develop humility within us.

20. Méndez-Montoya, *Theology of Food*, 122–42.

21. Wirzba, *Food and Faith*, 29.

22. Davis, *Scripture, Culture, and Agriculture*, 73.

23. Ibid., 74.

Fifth, hopeful eating should remind us of a particular peculiarity: humans are deeply moral creatures. The apostle Paul is keenly aware of this in his admonishment of those members of the Corinthian church who were making poor decisions about how much they ate and drank before their house church came together and what those decisions were doing to harm other members of that church.[24] Daily we engage in moral decision-making that allows us the opportunity to be either more or less Christlike, especially when it comes to eating. Whether we care to admit it explicitly or not, Pollan is absolutely correct: "Eating puts us in touch with all that we share with the other animals, and all that sets us apart. It defines us."[25] For the most part, and especially for many American Christians, we can decide what sort of food we want to place in our mouths on any given day. We can be strict carnivores, vegetarians, or even vegans with a penchant for raw chocolate. We can decide whether or not to purchase food from a grocery store or the local farmers' market. We can choose between fair-trade organic products or conventionally grown ones. All of these decisions shape us (literally) into the persons we are, whether we consciously admit to them or not. While there is perhaps no unadulterated, perfectly good moral choice to be made in any supermarket or from the list of your Community Supported Agriculture's spring produce, to neglect to recognize that the food decisions we make everyday shape us into virtuous or vicious people is foolhardy. These are not just individual decisions, but ones that collectively shape our society as well; this makes them political decisions, too. Christians must make deliberate choices that signify the work of the Spirit through Jesus' resurrection rather than implicitly and explicitly supporting a status quo that is permeated by so much violence, injustice, and destruction, even if the choices are admittedly compromised ones or ones where we cannot always see the full consequences. Christians must manifest signs of hopeful eating in a world that seems trapped in hopeless eating mired by presumption and despair.

Finally, hopeful eating should remind us that food is in fact revelatory. From the manna in the wilderness to the miraculous multiplication of the fishes and loaves, from satisfying the hunger of the lion to providing food for the raven's young,[26] food reveals the magnitude of divine benevolence toward humans and nonhumans alike. Jung goes further and says that through food's revelation we learn that God intends for us to enjoy

---

24. 1 Cor 10:17–22.
25. Pollan, *Omnivore's Dilemma*, 10.
26. Job 38:38–39.

food because in that delight we taste that God is good.[27] In an American food culture where food engineers add so much taste, it may be difficult to imagine that a ripe heirloom tomato right off the vine can tell us something about God's goodness. As we have already seen above, eating reveals much about the costliness of biological life on this planet as well as the profundity of the human condition. Therefore, it is quite fitting that the sin of humanity, which began with an act of eating, is redeemed in the Eucharist, which reconciles us back to God through a proper understanding of what eating in fact can be in all of its theological, political, economic, ethical, and pastoral splendor when God is seen as the source of life. That said, we return to Schmemann's notion that our culture knows that eating is not merely a utilitarian exercise; there is something more to it even if we do not entirely comprehend it because we hunger and thirst for the sacramental life. While the general definition of a sacrament is "a visible means of invisible grace," for the Orthodox tradition the idea of sacramentality represents something different. According to Schmemann, "[A] sacrament is understood primarily as a revelation of the genuine *nature* of creation, of the world, which, however much it has fallen as 'this world,' will remain God's world, awaiting salvation, redemption, healing and transfiguration in a new earth and a new heaven."[28] God invites human participation in the transformation of God's gifts into the divine life made fully manifest at the eschaton. A sacrament, then, is simultaneously cosmic and eschatological. It is cosmic in that it recognizes the goodness of all of creation, despite the depravity caused by human sin. At the same time, it is eschatological as it is oriented toward God's future that is still to come.[29] This is good news. No matter how much the priests of control, efficiency, and convenience manipulate food or how much the hopelessness of presumption and despair permeates our society, food can always remind us of who God is and how God desires for us to live courageously in the present. Through eucharistic table manners inspired by the resurrection, we can seek to make eating hopefully a reality, even if only in limited ways now.

Eating Meat

If eating hopefully is going to be a practical reality for modern American Christians, then we must analyze the American fascination with meat. We eat a massive amount of nonhuman animal protein yearly and expect to pay

27. Jung, *Food for Life*, 32–54.

28. Schmemann, *Eucharist*, 33; italics in original.

29. Ibid., 34.

very little for the opportunity to do so, especially when it comes to Americans' three favorite sources of protein: cattle, chickens, and pigs. Americans have a very curious relationship to meat. As Maureen Ogle observes, "Meat is the culinary equivalent of gasoline."[30] We expect to pay a reasonable price for gasoline, even though we have no clear way of defining what "reasonable" is. Americans frequently throw a fit whenever gasoline prices exceed that "reasonable" price, and they blame a host of parties that may or may not actually be involved in the pricing of gasoline. "When meat's price rises above a (vaguely defined) acceptable level, tempers flare and consumers blame rich farmers, richer corporations, or government subsidy programs. We're Americans, after all, and we're entitled to meat."[31] But just how much meat do Americans eat and how much do we pay for it?

The amount of meat that Americans eat is absolutely staggering. The average American consumes approximately 277 pounds per year.[32] Only the small country of Luxembourg consumes more than the United States; India consumes the least on average, at 7 pounds per citizen per year. The average American now eats roughly 107 pounds of meat more than the average American did 60 years ago. While it is difficult to discern exactly how much we pay for meat per se, for our purposes it is helpful to examine how much of our disposable income we spend on food as a whole. Americans, on average, use less than 10 percent of their disposable income on food, which is down roughly 4 percent in the last 45 years and is part of a continuing downward trend since the conclusion of World War II. This number is even more astonishing when one considers that 50 percent of the American food budget is spent eating outside of the home, which is up from 25 percent just 50 years ago.[33] But how is it that we can eat a product that takes so many inputs and so much labor to produce and yet pay so little for it? We pay so little for meat because of two consequential factors. First, the price of meat is so cheap because so much animal feed is heavily subsidized by the federal government. Those subsidies might come in the form of direct cash payments to agricultural corporations and farmers that actually enable the cost of corn, for instance, to drop below the cost of production. Subsidies provided to the fossil-fuel industry also artificially reduce the cost of grain, even if only indirectly. The price of meat and the price of fuel are interdependently linked in the heavily fossil fuel–dependent American fac-

30. Ogle, *In Meat We Trust*, xii.

31. Ibid., xiii.

32. United States Department of Agriculture, "Profiling Food," 15; Carolan, *Reclaiming Food Security*, 93; Tepper, "World's Meat Consumption."

33. Carolan, *Real Cost of Cheap Food*, 2.

tory-farming industry. Second, environmental costs like manure disposal, air and water pollution, soil erosion, and health-related illnesses that come from the industrial farms where these animals are raised are externalized to the broader taxpaying American public, whether they eat industrial meat or not, and are not captured in the initial costs of production and hence not calculated into the actual retail price of meat. This does not even count the lax environmental regulations that many CAFOs often fail to comply with, which also appreciably lower the price of meat.[34] Only where this sort of system is in place does a hamburger not only cost less than a veggie burger, but also frequently costs less than a head of broccoli.

In order to produce the amount of meat we do at the cheap price we do, most of the meat Americans eat is raised in CAFOs. The central aim of a CAFO is to produce as much meat as possible in the shortest amount of time with as little human labor as possible on the smallest amount of land. A few people can do the work of feeding and administering medication to thousands of animals daily if those animals are kept in confined quarters. Let us look at a brief snapshot of the living conditions of Americans' two favorite types of meat: chicken and beef. Broiler chickens, the ones grown to be eaten rather than lay eggs, are raised in tens of thousands at a time, often in large confinement barns. A vast majority of these birds never see the light of day; literally, a vast majority live their entire lives without seeing sunshine. Their beaks are filed down so that they do not harm one another when they peck at each other since they often exhibit violent behavior in such close quarters. It is almost impossible for CAFO-raised chickens to extend their wings fully without touching another bird. Through the alteration of the chicken's metabolic cycle, chicken breasts grow so large in such a short amount of time that their hips and legs begin to break under their immense weight if they are not slaughtered in roughly a month and a half after birth. Before their legs break or they are removed for slaughter, they meander around on the barn floor that is covered with their own excrement and is regularly drenched with ammonia to help eliminate the overwhelming stench. The ammonia also is sprayed in an attempt to mitigate the damage done by the likelihood of disease and vermin caused by these living conditions. Since male chicks are not needed at the same rate as female ones, hundreds of millions of males are merely thrown away each year in dumpsters outside of chicken-hatching facilities.

Most cows that turn into the beef we consume in America no longer eat grass for a majority of their lives, even though they evolved with

34. Pew Commission on Industrial Farm Animal Production, "Putting Meat on the Table," 6; Carolan, *Real Cost of Cheap Food*, 102–5.

digestive systems to do just that. While some are allowed to graze for the first hundred or so days of their lives, most are then transferred to CAFOs and fed corn or a combination of corn and grain for the remainder of their days, if they are lucky. Cows are often fed the ground-up remains of other cows and debris found on the farmhouse floor, which leads to devastating ailments like bovine spongiform encephalopathy, more commonly known as mad cow disease. The corn-based diet fattens up cows quite rapidly but, as ruminant animals, cows do not have digestive systems that can process corn and hence they are given a panoply of antibiotics to prevent their multiple stomachs from exploding before their slaughter date. A cow's stomach that is digesting corn is just the right place for *E. coli* O157:H7 (a lethal strain of bacteria linked to many food-related deaths) to propagate. Those bacteria then are excreted and live in a cow's manure that is often caked on the hide of the animal before it makes its way into a slaughterhouse. Since CAFO-raised cattle are not able to roam freely, they spend much of their lives literally standing in tons of their own excrement and that of their fellow cows. *E. coli* has been the source of the recalls of millions of pounds of beef in the U.S., as well as the death of a number of Americans, including toddlers and small children.[35]

This is to say nothing of the welfare of the humans that work in the slaughterhouses and process our cheap industrial meat. The circumstances of those who process our meat today are no better than their counterparts depicted in Upton Sinclair's *The Jungle* in 1906. The middle of the twentieth century represented a boon for meat processors, as salaries, pension packages, and relatively safe working environments made it an appealing middle-class profession. Since then, through the meat-packing industry's deregulation, a general erosion of meat-packing unions, and access to a new foreign labor force, this industry has become known for its low pay, little to no job security, and hazardous working conditions. Whether it be fingernails that regularly peel off their nail beds, repetitive-use injuries from cutting thousands of pieces of meat in the same fashion for hours at a time, severe bodily injury from knife cuts, or back and head injuries from slipping on animal effluent on the slaughterhouse floor and falling, processing meat at the prices that Americans desire to pay is a perilous task. While death due to the hazards in this workplace is not common, it is not unheard of in this line of work either. One of the reasons these conditions are possible is that an immigrant labor force of both undocumented and legal workers

35. For more on this, see Pew Commission on Industrial Farm Animal Production, "Putting Meat on the Table"; Foer, *Eating Animals*; Lymbery with Oakeshott, *Farmageddon*; Schlosser, *Fast Food Nation*, 193–222; Cook, *Diet for a Dead Planet*, 27–43; Pollan, *Omnivore's Dilemma*, 65–84.

performs much of the work done in these facilities. Transnational corporations have been known to advertise in countries like Mexico and provide financial assistance, transportation, and housing to bring foreign workers into their slaughterhouses. The financial assistance can only be described as the bare minimum, if it is not entirely based on loans that will be debited directly from the employees' paychecks without their sanction, and the housing is often in shanty-like structures that would often not meet basic requirements for urban rental situations. These corporations have frequently participated in backdoor agreements with the federal government to turn over undocumented workers occasionally. In this relationship, government officials appear to their constituents as if they are tough on illegal immigration, while the corporation never has to endure a shutdown of their production lines that a full-scale raid of a facility would entail.[36]

It takes a lot of resources to produce meat. Just the amount that these animals eat and drink is astonishing. Due to the fact that most animals raised to be slaughtered and eaten are raised in CAFOs, these creatures are not walking around in sprawling pastures looking for food, but are instead fed a mixture of cereal grains, mostly corn, daily. Feeding them grain has the added advantage, from the industrial meat perspective, of bringing animals to slaughter weight more quickly. According to the beef industry, it takes only 4.5 kilograms of grain to produce a kilogram of beef raised in a CAFO feedlot. Representatives from the U.S. government say it takes 16 kilograms of grain to produce that same kilogram.[37] It is difficult to know which group is accurate, but one way or another a vast amount of the world's grain must be diverted from human mouths to nonhuman ones to keep with our present scale of consumption. But just how much? Researchers estimate between 35 to 50 percent of the world's grain production is currently used to produce animal feed, while that number is expected to exceed 50 percent substantially by 2050 as meat production worldwide continues to accelerate, especially as China's rising middle class seeks to add more nonhuman animal protein into its diet.[38] Put another way, cattle, chickens, and pigs collectively consume about 50 percent of the world's wheat supply, 90 percent of the world's corn, 93 percent of the world's soybeans, and almost all of the world's barley that is not used for brewing and distilling.[39] Approximately one third of all

36. For more on those who process meat, see Schlosser, *Fast Food Nation*, 169–90; Cook, *Diet for a Dead Planet*, 187–216; Oxfam, "Lives."

37. Gold, "Global Benefits," 22; see also Friends of the Earth, "Healthy Planet Eating," 7.

38. Gold, "Global Benefits," 27; Nellemann, "Environmental Food Crisis," 26.

39. Colin Tudge, quoted in Carolan, *Real Cost of Cheap Food*, 85.

arable land on the planet is devoted to the production of animal feed.[40] Putting that in terms of land-use efficiency per usable protein yield, an acre of soybeans yields 356 pounds of protein, an acre of rice yields 261 pounds, an acre of wheat yields 138 pounds, while an acre of land yields *only* 20 pounds of beef.[41] Land is not the only resource that is needed to produce meat; it takes a massive amount of water as well. Raising livestock accounts for over 8 percent of global human water use, mostly in the irrigation of animal feed crops.[42] In terms of the amount of gallons of water it takes to produce a single pound of food: it takes 119 gallons of water to produce a pound of potatoes, 132 gallons to produce a pound of wheat, 449 gallons to produce a pound of rice, 468 gallons to produce a pound of chicken, and 1,799 gallons to produce a pound of beef.[43] So what does this mean, precisely? As good as meat might taste, meat is an incredibly inefficient way to transform scarce resources, like arable land and freshwater, into protein for humans. Ironically, as our society focuses more on protein consumption, which is what we believe the CAFO system is giving us cheaply and efficiently, the meat has actually become fattier rather than more intensely protein packed. Chickens, for instance, carry less protein today than they did in previous generations, while carrying more fat than ever before.[44] The alteration of the content of beef is even more profound if one compares the healthiness of the meat of grass-fed cattle to that of grain-fed factory-farmed ones.[45] Just how inefficient is this process, particularly in a world where meat consumption is accelerating rapidly? One estimate is that based upon an intake of 3,000 kcal per day, the total amount of cereal used for animal feed would cover the calorie needs for about 4.35 billion people. If we factor in the energy value of the meat produced using these cereal crops, then "the loss of calories by feeding the cereals to animals instead of using the cereals directly as human food represents the annual calorie need for more than 3.5 billion people."[46]

The industrial meat industry also creates a colossal amount of pollution, especially water and air pollution. As one might imagine, cattle, chickens, and pigs create quite a lot of waste in the form of manure. The U.S. Department of Agriculture estimates approximately 500 million tons

40. Nellemann, "Environmental Food Crisis," 25.

41. Gold, "Global Benefits," 23.

42. Food and Agriculture Organization of the United Nations, "Livestock's Long Shadow," xxii.

43. *National Geographic*, "Hidden Water." For more on this, see Mekonnen and Hoekstra, "Green, Blue and Grey."

44. Carolan, *Reclaiming Food Security*, 23.

45. Carolan, *Real Cost of Cheap Food*, 85–87.

46. Nellemann, "Environmental Food Crisis," 27.

of manure are produced annually by CAFOs, which is roughly three times
the estimate for the annual human sanitary waste produced in the United
States.[47] Compared to human waste, nonhuman animal waste is poorly reg-
ulated and much of it finds its way into rivers, streams, and other freshwater
sources for millions of Americans. The sort of runoff from these facilities
can be filled with antibiotics, heavy metals, pesticides, and synthetic fertilizers, which not only cause terrible problems with human drinking water
supplies, but also create "dead zones" in freshwater and eventually saltwater
fisheries. The air pollution that this industry contributes to climate change is
equally immense. The United Nations Food and Agricultural Organization
(FAO) estimates that the worldwide livestock sector, most of which is produced through factory farming, is responsible for 18 percent of greenhouse
gas production and 9 percent of anthropogenic carbon dioxide emissions
alone.[48] This means that livestock production causes more air pollution than
the entire global transportation sector. When taking into account more potent greenhouse gases than carbon dioxide, the data is even more dire. The
livestock industry emits 37 percent of anthropogenic methane emissions
and 65 percent of anthropogenic nitrous oxide emissions.[49] Much of this
comes from storing the vast amounts of animal manure in lagoons that are
directly emitting these gases into the atmosphere. However, the FAO's data
may be far too conservative. Some research indicates that livestock and their
byproducts may account for 51 percent of worldwide greenhouse gas emissions.[50] It is extraordinary, but true: what one eats contributes far more to
climate change than what one drives.

From a Christian perspective, one of the first questions we must ask
is: Is eating meat from an industrial farm an act of gluttony? As we have
already discussed, determining whether or not behavior is gluttonous is a
matter of degree, not kind. It is a matter of discerning what is too much or
what is too elaborate or when is too soon. That said, it strains the imagination how one could *not* describe the voluminous meat eating in America as
gluttonous. Recalling Aquinas, it is easy to believe that our inordinate desire

47. Pew Commission on Industrial Farm Animal Production, "Putting Meat on
the Table," 23.

48. Food and Agriculture Organization of the United Nations, "Livestock's Long
Shadow," xxi.

49. Ibid.

50. Goodland and Anhang, "Livestock and Climate Change," 10–19. For sake of
scale, the estimate of greenhouse gas emissions of the agricultural industry is often
cited at 11 to 15 percent, but if one factors in the effects of deforestation, processing,
packaging, transportation, refrigeration, retail energy use, and food-waste emissions
from landfills, the estimate is between 44 to 57 percent of anthropogenic greenhouse
gas emissions. Donlon, "Food and Climate."

for meat daily has caused us to leave the realm of rational thought as we consider the needs of other humans and the global food system in general. The vast amount of resources, like water and grains, that are diverted from humans into the mouths of cattle, chickens, and pigs should give us pause in a world that has not only a gross amount of obesity, but also a vast and growing amount of humans who are in daily need of food. Our cultural desire for meat that is cheap has also led to the abhorrent mistreatment of nonhuman animals in our nation's CAFOs as well as those who slaughter them in the processing facilities. Additionally, due to the vast amount of subsidies the federal government uses to keep meat artificially cheap, we fail to pay the true price of our eating habits, which includes not only environmental devastation, but also a national obesity epidemic. This does not even take into account the vast climate change implications that eating meat has that we find loathsome to admit. To say that producing industrially farmed meat the way that we currently do is done with rational thought is farcical to say the least.

Living in a culture that follows the precepts of the priests of nutritionism with religious devotion, many Americans find themselves looking for one particular nutrient in their food whenever they go to a supermarket counter or their refrigerators: protein. Protein is the singular nutrient that Americans currently surmise that they need more than any other. In a culture where, on the one hand, a governmental agency claims that protein should take up between 10 and 35 percent of one's daily caloric intake, which might be as much as 56 grams daily for the average male,[51] and on the other hand, popular fitness magazines recommend that an 180-pound male who works out regularly needs at least 80 grams and as much as 139 grams daily,[52] you can see why deciding what is necessary can seem rather complex. While undoubtedly the discernment of necessity is a perpetually difficult task, Ambrose says that even the fish of the sea know when enough is enough.[53] That said, we are once again left to ponder Gregory's insight from 15 centuries ago: Does the consumption of industrially produced meat prevent us from distinguishing thoughtfully between necessity and pleasure? It must, since we are consuming more and fattier meat than generations before us who did not consume factory-farmed meat, as we continue to become less healthy than our forefathers and mothers. While we undoubtedly crave the richness of the taste of meat, we are probably craving the fat in the meat more so than the actual protein content. While gaining pleasure from eating is not the

51. United States Department of Agriculture, "Supertracker."
52. Steiman, "Truth about Protein."
53. Avila, *Ownership*, 71.

problem, pleasurable eating that brings with it all of the consequences we have discussed is exceptionally problematic. Moreover, if we fail to discern clearly between necessity and pleasure in a seemingly banal activity like eating, how are we to make even more complicated decisions in other aspects of our lives?

Remembering Clement's reasoning, we need to consider whether or not we have surrendered reason, friendship, and life in the pursuit of filling our bellies with cheap, CAFO-raised meat. It is quite evident that we have surrendered reason as we use a worldwide dragnet in the daily import of meats from around the world, but have we lost friendship and life as well? On the human side, it strains the bounds of credulity to argue that American Christians exist in any sort of friendly relations with those foreign, migrant, and often undocumented workers who most commonly populate the meat-processing facilities of our nation. They are employed because they work for wages below anything that would approximate a dignified living for American citizens and then are often turned over to the federal government for deportation when they are no longer "needed." This does not account for the substantially debilitating injuries, or even deaths, that come as part of the hazardous task of producing cheap meat that Americans believe they are entitled to consume daily. These workers, implicitly at least, have become just as fungible as any other part of the food production chain. On the non-human side, the production of industrially produced meat at CAFOs allows us to reinforce the belief that cattle, chickens, and pigs are just as fungible as any other product in the food-production system. This desecrates the idea that life should be respected in some manner, even if it is to be eaten, because it ultimately belongs to God. The sort of behavior that CAFO-style production encourages does nothing to help us remember that theological affirmation or make us more virtuous, but instead emboldens us to justify our gluttonous ways. Clement is exactly correct: we have deceived ourselves and become slaves to the cheap meat that comes from factory farming as we seek to fill our overextending bellies.

Finally, while eating food that is too costly has been traditionally considered gluttonous behavior by many Christian thinkers, today we must consider that eating food that is too cheap is gluttonous as well. By not paying the full price of meat we not only contribute dramatically to the sense we Americans are entitled to have meat whenever we so desire, but we also show how we have divorced ourselves from any understanding of what food production does or does not do to those humans, nonhuman animals, and ultimately the Earth upon which we all depend. By asking questions about how much slaughterhouse workers are paid or what conditions cattle are raised in or how the effluents affect the town that raises the chicken we eat, we begin to engage in a process that applies eucharistic table manners to what we do daily and transform eating from the hopeless act it so often is in the United States to one that models genuine hope.

As of now, the way that the vast majority of cattle, chickens, and pigs are raised and processed in our nation's CAFOs can only be described as hopeless. The hopelessness of presumption abounds as we presume that cheap meat will bring us the joy of a healthy life that we all desire so ardently. In fact, this form of hopelessness is so pervasive in our culture that we presume that the industrial meat-production model is the only way we can acquire the meat that we need in order to keep the rest of our household budget manageable. As more and more evidence mounts about the impact that livestock production has on climate change, the presumptive attitude of our culture says that we do not need to reevaluate our current path and possibly change direction, a la Noah, but instead we need to genetically engineer less polluting forms of livestock and create newer technologies that will hold and sanitize animal effluent. At the same time, since we presume that we are entitled to cheap meat, the supposedly fungible human labor that we sacrifice is of little to no concern. Additionally, this system of meat production is a source of despair as we fixate on how paying more for meat, for the protein that we ostensibly need so desperately, will impact our family budgets and our national economy. If we start paying more for meat, will that not put ranchers and meat packers out of business? This sort of hopelessness locks us into a pattern of slothfulness as we ask these types of rhetorical questions that demonstrate little creativity or sensitivity to those humans and nonhuman animals that actually endure the industrial system on a daily basis. We fail to live the magnanimous lives that God created us to live because we lack the courage to ask if eating meat is making us more virtuous Christians. If we are to listen for divine grace in this area, what are our options for hopeful eating?

One of the options to eating hopefully would be to become a vegetarian, if not a vegan. One of the most articulate voices for the contemporary Christian vegetarian movement is Andrew Linzey.[54] His argument for vegetarianism as a biblical ideal employs three points.[55] First, he argues that the divine permission given to eat animals in Genesis 9 is rather ambiguous because it does not seem easily reconcilable with God's original intent found in Genesis 1 and 2. The permission comes with the caveat that humans remember that all creatures belong to God; therefore, one is personally accountable to God for the lives that one kills, even those one kills to eat.

54. See also Webb, *Good Eating*; Young, *Is God a Vegetarian?*
55. Linzey, *Animal Theology*, 125–37.

Second, Linzey maintains that Genesis 1 and 2 cannot be read in isolation from Isaiah 11. In the eschatological vision of Isaiah, the violence that God judged as unholy through the flood is juxtaposed against a setting where peacefulness between humans and nonhumans is characterized as part of God's kingdom, both in Isaiah 11 as well as in Genesis 1 and 2. "Those individuals who opt for vegetarianism can do so in the knowledge that they are living closer to the biblical ideal of peaceableness than their carnivorous contemporaries. The point should not be minimized. In many ways it is difficult to know how we can live more peaceably in a world stricken by violence and greed and consumerism. . . . To opt for a vegetarian life-style is one practical step towards living in peace with the rest of creation."[56] In other words, violent killing for food is no longer necessary in God's kingdom of the future and can be witnessed to now through a vegetarian lifestyle. Linzey's third point is this: "But *where we do have the moral freedom* to live without recourse to violence, there is a prima facie case to do so. To kill without the strict conditions of necessity is to live a life with insufficient generosity."[57] For Linzey, giving up the eating of meat is an eschatological sign of God's reign that unites the vision of God's future kingdom of peace with God's original intent, signaled in Genesis 1 and 2, and lived in the present. In the context of the other factors that make up factory farming, a nation of Christian vegetarians would have a profound impact on the hopelessness of animals raised in CAFOs and likely change the circumstances of the employees that slaughter and process them.

As Christopher Southgate points out, however, one of the problems with Linzey's defense of vegetarianism is that it relies upon an understanding of God's original intent for the universe that diverges from the actual history of the universe.[58] Linzey implies that God's original intent for creation did not include predation, which as we know is fundamentally problematic if we accept the scientific account of Earth's history. Furthermore, Southgate questions whether or not vegetarians take into account how God ultimately redeems predation if it is not caused by the sin of humanity in a primeval history that led to a historical fall. What Linzey seems to disregard is that predation and death are written into the very fabric of the universe as we know it. In this universe, unless you have chloroplasts or some other way to convert direct or indirect solar radiation into usable energy, something must die in order for something else to live. While we long for a day

56. Ibid., 132.

57. Ibid., 135; italics in original.

58. Southgate, "Protological," 247–53. For other theological critiques of vegetarianism, see Barth, *Church Dogmatics* III/4, 352–56; Horrell, "Biblical Vegetarianism?," 44–59.

when the wolf will lie down with the lamb, it will not be a reality this side of the eschaton, no matter how much we may desire it.[59] Christian essayist Wendell Berry describes it succinctly: "To live, we must daily break the body and shed the blood of Creation. When we do this knowingly, lovingly, skillfully, reverently, it is a sacrament. When we do it ignorantly, greedily, clumsily, destructively, it is a desecration. In such a desecration we condemn ourselves to spiritual and moral loneliness, and others to want."[60] Meat eating is not immoral as vegetarians and vegans often presuppose because the shedding of blood is intrinsic to biological life in this particular universe. As I shall argue below, context matters immensely. For example, there is no doubt that factory farming sheds blood ignorantly, clumsily, and destructively and should be identified as the desecration that it is. However, I believe that Christians must still wrestle with the other two components of Linzey's argument because they do not necessarily rely upon this disputed point for their potential efficacy. In a culture where American Christians often feel hopeless against the status quo, choosing to refrain from eating meat, particularly meat from CAFOs, can practically witness to at least a small part of God's kingdom of peace. It is hard to disagree with this. The institutionalized violence that is directed toward both nonhuman animals and humans in the factory-farming industry is extensive and, whether we prefer to admit it or not, eating none of the meat that comes from those facilities makes a profound statement about what we affirm to be hopeful and what we do not. Thankfully, we can remove industrial meat from our tables whether we become vegetarians or not. This is a fundamental step away from violence. As for Linzey's third point about having a prima facie obligation to be vegetarian and to do any less would be to live a life of insufficient generosity, I think here again Berry's insight is quite incisive. We are participants in a universe that requires the daily breaking of the body and shedding of the blood of creation, and if that is indeed the starting point, then sufficient generosity must be weighed differently than Linzey suggests. Generosity is shown through how a creature is treated during its life rather than whether or not it is killed and eaten. Additionally, generosity is manifested explicitly by how we pay and treat slaughterhouse employees, who have for too long been treated as fungible units in a production chain.

59. Southgate wonders if the wolf lying down with the lamb actually transforms the wolf into something else entirely. Southgate, *Groaning of Creation*, 78–91.

60. Berry, "Gift of Good Land," 304.

What Should We Do?

Whether you are a person who enjoys rare steak for dinner daily or not, it is hard not to agree with Michael Northcott, who says, "The reality is that the industrial food economy is the most unholy form of agriculture invented by any civilization."[61] Both human and nonhuman participants in this system cry out, "My God, my God, why have you forsaken me? Why are you so far from saving me, so far from my cries of anguish? My God, I cry out by day, but you do not answer, by night, but I find no rest. . . . Do not be far from me, for trouble is near and there is no one to help."[62] It is clearly evident that the industrial meat system is devoid of anything that resembles hope. Michael Pollan is entirely correct: "Eating industrial meat takes an almost heroic act of not knowing or, now, forgetting."[63] Is it possible for a Christian to eat meat, especially meat from a CAFO, and still model hopeful eating? In a society that deems meat eating to be mandatory for protein intake and has invested billions of dollars in the form of subsidies to make meat very, very cheap, we must recall that eating is a daily reminder that we are in fact moral creatures. For many American Christians, we can decide on a meal-to-meal basis what exactly we *want* to eat. We entertain the notion of what we *need* to eat almost as an afterthought. As moral creatures we can decide what in fact we put into our bellies, and as Christians we should do so as thoughtfully as possible. That said, we must recognize that for the vast majority of American Christians meat is in fact a luxury and not a necessity for a healthy diet. While it is undoubtedly unpopular to say, it is quite true that most American Christians can gain their necessary daily protein intake from sources other than meat. I say this not to be flippant about the reality of our dietary needs, but to return us to a conversation that began in the early centuries of the church. Novatian, commenting on the relationship that Jews have with certain meats, states, "Luxury does not entertain the fear of God,"[64] to which he adds, "But from the fact that liberty of meats is granted to us, it does not of necessity follow that luxury is allowed us; nor because the Gospel has dealt with us very liberally, has it taken away continency."[65]

However, this is not merely an interpretation of one of the earliest Christian theologians. Ellen Davis argues that if we evaluate the story of

61. Northcott, *Moral Climate*, 258.

62. Ps 22:1–2, 11.

63. Pollan, *Omnivore's Dilemma*, 84.

64. Novatian, "On the Jewish Meats," 4.

65. Ibid., 6.

the Israelites in the wilderness receiving manna along with the story of the prohibition of the first humans from eating fruit from the tree of knowledge of good and evil, "[I]t is evident that if an adequate and even generous food supply may provide the occasion to know God (Exod. 16:12), then accurate knowledge of God, the world, and our place in it—in short, wisdom—is available only to those who eat with restraint."[66] In a culture that prizes moderation very little, especially when it comes to eating, the connection between restraint and how we view God is not entirely self-explanatory. Much as being frugal with our material and financial resources provides us the space to meet the needs of our neighbors in a loving manner, so too does restraint in eating. A hopeful eater is one who thoughtfully measures how many resources go into the production of food. For example, a hopeful eater recognizes that the amount of water and food that is fed to cattle, chickens, and pigs is quite sizable and must be taken into consideration if one desires for the sufficient needs of one's neighbor to be met as well. With an ever-increasing human population, it is difficult to satisfy the Christian call to love one's neighbor as oneself if the basic needs of sufficiency are not met for those we call neighbors. A diet that is high in industrial meat does not thoughtfully consider the needs of one's neighbors, both human and nonhuman.

A hopeful eater is concerned about a more equitable distribution of calories across the planet because friendship between neighbors can only exist after hungry bellies are satisfied. By refraining from an industrial meat–based diet, a hopeful eater has more resources to share at the table, which fundamentally means a greater possibility for the sharing of life. This sort of restraint also reminds us more deeply of the costliness of life that goes into the daily breaking of the body and blood of creation. Eating meat is not morally wrong, but when we consume meat ignorantly and without any thought of restraint, it can easily become an act of desecration. A hopeful eater contemplates Novatian's admonishment about luxury sedulously. As discussed in chapter 7, material excess separates one from understanding the plight of the poor and thus prevents us from having solidarity with the least of these. Similarly, meat is a luxury, no matter how inexpensive the industrial system has made it, and it can easily separate us further from those who need nutritionally dense calories the most rather than bringing us into solidarity with them. Finally, a hopeful eater considers how the consumption of this kind of meat continues to alter the climate and thus violates the cosmic covenant that links ecological integrity with justice for the poor. Hopeful eating examines these topics because only through

66. Davis, *Scripture, Culture, and Agriculture*, 78.

identifying these issues sincerely can one listen for the divine call to act courageously and eat differently.

If one decides to eat meat, the type of meat one eats is significant. By type of meat, I do not mean that eating chicken is somehow more virtuous than eating beef. A hopeful eater must be cognizant of what relationships may or may not have been built or supported as that nonhuman animal was raised and eventually became food on one's plate or in one's takeout container. In order to eat hopefully, a Christian should be aware of two broader considerations: the care of the nonhuman animal to be eaten and the welfare of the humans that raised it and slaughtered it. It is impossible to imagine eating as a hopeful act if the creature that is to be eaten was not treated well as it was raised. Was the animal given the chance to exist in an environment where it was able to move freely, be in the sunshine, and consume food that it was meant to ingest? Or was it raised in a confinement crate, in a barn that had the windows blacked out, and fed whatever was found on the barn floor and ground up as "food"? If Linzey is correct and we will be called upon to justify to the Creator of the universe how we treated the creatures that are God's and not ours, then the circumstances in which we raise and care for the welfare of these creatures should be reflections of hopeful living rather than those of hopelessness. To treat the creatures we intend to eat as if they are actually God's rather than ours would be to recognize factory farming for the desecration that it is. Generosity, to use Linzey's term, is measured precisely by how we treat these creatures when they are living.

Secondly, the apostle Paul's declaration to give up eating meat if it became a stumbling block for any of his Christian sisters and brothers in Corinth appears oddly anachronistic to modern Christians, if we do not cavalierly gloss over it altogether. But what if Christians took the heart of Paul's proclamation more seriously today? What if American Christians declared they would not eat factory-farmed meat if it disenfranchised even one worker on the slaughterhouse line? A hopeful eater must meditate on Paul's example in just this manner. Food that is produced using human beings that are treated as completely fungible and disposable units should be seen as the manifestation of hopelessness that it is. Hopeful eating should think of reconciliation as an act that commits to "an economy and a politics in which the care of each other is our all-consuming desire."[67] The hospitality of the Eucharist, which has such economic and political dimensions, is especially important to those who want to eat hopefully. Whether we are cognizant of it or not, the consequences are the same: industrial meat production dehumanizes thousands of workers a year, stripping them of basic

67. Wirzba, *Food and Faith*, 178.

aspects of human dignity, as consumers demand to pay even less for our meat and corporations attempt to increase their profit margins. A hopeful eater declares that this system is profane by not purchasing its meat because it says that only some humans are welcome to the sufficiency offered by divine grace at the eucharistic table. By rejecting this meat and the ignorant, greedy, clumsy, and destructive way it was produced, Christians demonstrate the courage that is needed to stand in solidarity with the poor and those who are not invited to the table.

Eating meat in the manner I am proposing will inevitably cost more in the United States. Let us remember, though, that the reason for the cost increase is that the principalities and powers that control the production of industrial meat have gained a significant pricing advantage due to decades of subsidies that artificially deflate the true cost of meat. Also, many Americans generally prefer to use their disposable income to purchase luxury items rather than nutritiously dense, quality food. Those who eat in the ways that I am describing here could easily be described (and some probably are) as elitist, separating themselves further from any possible solidarity with the poor by eating food that more often than not can only be afforded easily by those with significant financial resources. If we want good food, food that restores ecological health and promotes justice, then we must commit the financial resources to do so. American Christians, especially those who can afford to expand their food budget more easily, must be constantly mindful of this. And yet, American Christians of all economic demographics must consider carefully how each of our food purchases represents the eucharistic table manners discussed above. The lesson of Paul's exhortation to the Corinthian church is once again relevant for our contemporary situation. Just as Paul admonished the wealthier Christians of that church for arriving early and eating and drinking before the less-fortunate members (i.e., the slaves and working class) because it significantly disrupted the unity of that Corinthian body, so too should wealthy Christians today ask themselves whether or not they should overindulge on good meat that only they can reasonably afford. Once again, restraint seems to be a critical characteristic of the sharing that is so central to eucharistic table manners. For both those who are more financially secure and those who are less so, sharing food is essential if everyone is to be included at the table and hospitality is to be a central witness of the Christian life.

By eating hopefully, through the power of the resurrection, we exhibit a daily way of living that declares that the hopelessness of presumption and despair do not have the final say. We disrupt the hopelessness of presumption when we stop making the sacrifices to the idols of control, efficiency, and convenience that industrial meat demands. By recognizing the costliness of life and eating meat sacramentally, as Berry suggests, we engage in an exercise of humility that defeats the *perversa securitas* that is a source of presumption. Through acknowledging our proper place in the universe, we also combat the gluttony that is promoted by the industrial meat system and practice the restraint that is habitually necessary for hopeful eaters. Caring for creatures in a way that we could justify to our Creator also allows us to remember that we too are earthly creatures and no amount of technologically sophisticated and automated chicken coops will make us more godlike. If the universe is indeed created by the God of Jesus Christ and has a moral order to it that was affirmed radically over and over again by the prophets, then righteousness is defined not by how cheap the food is, but by how good it is, which means it promotes ecological health and is accessible, at the very minimum, to the poor. By eating hopefully, Christians also stand against the status quo in a way that calls attention to the despair that currently permeates the factory-farming system. Consequently, hopeful eating is deeply political because it declares that the current system is unholy and deserves to be undone. If we are to live the magnanimous lives that God created us to live, then we must not surrender to sloth. Too many nonhuman and human lives are affected by the apathy and indifference that American Christians have toward food in general and meat in particular. To bring hope to those in meat-processing facilities, Christians must be willing to pay more for their meat by demanding that they will only eat meat that makes dignity possible for the least of these.

Hopelessness, whether it be in the form of presumption or despair, robs us of the capacity to engage in the critique of the present that hope demands, while simultaneously preventing us from listening to the novel possibilities that God offers us that could actually transform the "not yet" into the "already" that marks a living hope. And even when we do successfully identify instances of environmental degradation and injustice caused by our current food system, we often lack the courage to act in ways that demonstrate the resurrection is truly the witness to the hope we have in God to deliver us because we are afraid of the shame or ridicule that we might receive for proclaiming that this system is genuinely unjust and unsustainable. The result of this is that the sloth-induced inaction that permeates much of our culture indicates that the principalities and powers have truly won and God's presence is nowhere to be found. Furthermore, when we embrace the American food-production system, whether implicitly or explicitly, we radically dismiss the obligation of greatness that God has bestowed upon us. The hope that stems from the resurrection should lead us to do uniquely transformative work in and for creation; it should give us the imagination and courage to confront the principalities and powers and witness to God's work now, in our present situation. Resurrection hope demands this sort of action and can be manifested daily by decisions that shape our Christian witness as we seek to decrease our impact on the environment and seek justice for those who grow our food. By reconnecting to the moral and theological aspects of eating through more frequent and intentional participation in the Eucharist, we can engage in a process of remembering how eating connects us to our neighbors, other creatures, and God. Through this, we can start to listen for the new possibilities grace provides that shape us both personally and as a society, as we seek to create a food system that is at least a pale reflection of the kingdom of God. The daily acts of remembrance at each meal can inspire us to be courageous as we contemplate what it means to live as if God has truly conquered the sting of death through the resurrection of Jesus. In this way, we find the potential to imagine, live, and eat hopefully each and every day.

10

The Church as a Beacon
of Hope: Part 1

I n the restless seas of hopelessness that we find ourselves in, the church
must be a beacon if it is to matter at all in the age of climate change. This
metaphor is appropriate for the age we are in precisely because of what a
beacon is. A beacon is an intentionally conspicuous device whose goal is
to attract attention. That is why a beacon is often on top of a mountain or
on the edge of a cliff next to a body of water. For centuries, beacons have
been used to warn communities that a threat is approaching. For example,
in times before calamity alerts sent via televisions and mobile phones, a
town's population might only know that trouble was near when the light in
the mountaintop beacon was ablaze. The beacon signaled when a legitimate
emergency was present and the community needed to respond immediately. A beacon can also be used in a navigational sense in order to help the
captain of a ship or the pilot of an aircraft find one's way amidst a treacher-
ous storm or in the darkness of the night. In this age of climate change, the
church needs to be a beacon of hope in both manners.

In the first sense, many, if not most, Protestant American churches
have failed miserably when it has come to warning their communities about
the imminent threat of climate change. Even though various governmental agencies, transnational corporations, news-media outlets, and countless other members of our society have failed to warn us as well, churches
cannot discount their role in the lack of information sharing and blatant
misinformation distributed about climate change. Churches should be vital
to their communities in helping congregants, and even the wider citizenry,
prioritize what should be taken seriously and what can wait until later to
deal with, but they frequently are not. I believe there is still time for Protestant churches to be these sorts of beacons in their local and global contexts, but action must happen now. Secondly, the church must be the sort
of beacon that allows people to find their way even amidst the hopelessness

of despair and presumption. The church will only be able to do that if it can offer something that is more than mere wishful thinking or sheer optimism. It must be able to inspire us to be courageous and stimulate us to provide novel solutions to the worst sorts of wicked problems that climate change poses. I believe the church can do this if it embraces its mission to be a beacon of hope in the age of climate change. In order to be this beacon in this era, we must accept the reality of our present situation and the future scenarios that science is depicting about our increasingly warming planet and share that information truthfully and willingly. We must assist our congregants in prioritizing the effects of climate change both in the near and distant future into the upper echelon of our finite pools of worry. We must then be places where people turn to when they seek the courage that will be needed to endure. Churches must also exhibit how hope is embodied in everyday life.

Becoming a beacon is not as easy as an erecting a lighthouse and flipping a switch at night. There is a bond of trust that exists both implicitly and explicitly between the beacon and the community it serves. It must be relied upon to function appropriately when tragedy threatens. The light it sends out into the darkness must be known to be trustworthy by those who use it to find a way to their final destination. Unfortunately, American Protestant churches have much work to do if we are to be beacons of hope. In order to become these beacons we must commit ourselves to developing better theological imaginaries. Theological imaginaries that demonstrate significant "ecological conversion"[1] are desperately needed if we are to inspire our congregants and regain the trust of those who are looking for a significant moral and theological response to our present crisis. We must move away from trite advertising campaigns and bumper stickers that encourage us to think of ourselves as "not of this world" in such a shallow manner that we purchase "Christian" merchandise that actually disconnects us further from the realities presently facing this world and cause us to dismiss the this-worldliness of Jesus' ministry. Additionally, we must resist the neoclassical priesthood's support of economic growth in many of the all-too-common top-ten lists that suggest by purchasing just the right car or an eco-friendly cleaning product environmental problems will be ameliorated with little change to our current behavior.

Instead, Christians must model creation-care thinking and behavior that is central to the hopeful witness of living this side of the resurrection. Our theological imaginary must inspire a new social imaginary that takes seriously the fact that injustices to the poor and the oppressed, to the

---

1. Pope Francis, *Laudato Si'*, 216–21.

widows, orphans, and aliens, and to those nonhuman creatures who have no voice will only be further exacerbated by climate change. Let me suggest six places to start that process in this chapter and the next.

Political Involvement

If the church indeed is to develop a theological imaginary that is suitable to our present crisis and thus be a beacon of hope, then we must reconceive of the relationship between Christian theology and politics, or perhaps better put, between our faith and the world in which we live. Much of Christian history in America is littered with those who believe that Christians should be intimately involved with the political processes that govern nation-states, whether domestic or those abroad. Many who hold this position, in some manner or another, think that Christians can wield power properly and consequently create more just, and maybe even loving, conditions for citizens in a nation-state like ours. In more recent American history, many Christians have forsaken a broader theological conversation about politics and instead have tacitly practiced a social imaginary that suggests that we believe that we are called upon only to vote on "Christian issues." Too often American Protestants think that engaging in political activity means voting for a measure related to gay marriage or signing a petition to make sure a nativity scene can be displayed on public land during the Christmas season. Our range of political engagement often revolves around issues that we believe in some manner or another infringe upon what we consider to be our religious liberties outlined in the First Amendment of the U.S. Constitution. Topics like creating conservation corridors or high-speed public transportation do not register even a blip at all on the average Christian's moral radar screen during election season. However, we must not allow political strategists and others hired by elected officials to dictate what we think is actually worthy of time spent in political deliberation, which often is defined only as casting a vote on election day. The emphasis on getting people to the polls to vote for supposedly moral issues reinforces a stereotype that Christians only vote in mass for a single political party on a very narrow array of allegedly important topics. While voting in local or federal elections is not the only way to conceive of one's political activity within a nation-state, it is a rather telling statement of what one considers to be the minimum responsibility one owes to the government and the *polis*.

There has also been a minority Christian voice throughout American history that has advocated intentionally staying away from the political process altogether, e.g., participating in elections or serving as a governmental official. Generally speaking, this group's concern has been that the political machinations of a nation-state are fundamentally about national self-interest and not the objectives of the kingdom of God. Additionally, political machinations are about compromise, if they are about nothing else, which seems to go against the gospel's uncompromising charge to love our neighbors as ourselves. The demands of love require sacrifice for the benefit of the neighbor, not sacrifice for the sake of political gain. This minority voice is undoubtedly an important critique and a witness to the ministry of Jesus that we should wrestle with constantly, but I fear it may be an untenable position if we are to advocate for meaningful solutions in the age of climate change.

I am concerned, however, that many Christians in the United States are becoming as disillusioned with the formal political processes that make up our nation as those who identify with another faith tradition or no faith tradition at all. For Christians who eschew the political process, there may be many valid reasons: too much corporate influence in the political process, the perception that elected officials no longer reflect a constituency's values, a division between our two dominant national political parties that is so great that no actual work seems to get done at the federal level, etc. These reasons cannot be discounted, but American Christians should think about politics much differently. Thoughtful Christians who are witnesses to the hope of Jesus Christ are not servants of a political partisanship that is ultimately self-seeking; instead, Christian heralds of hope understand that our actions are always political because we make demands upon a nation-state by proclaiming that the kingdom of God is at hand. Living out our Christian faith, whether in the marketplace, in the election booth, or in our neighborhoods, is a public act of worship. It is a witness to the public nature of a Christian faith that resists those agents, some secular and some within our own churches, who would prefer that the activities that define and manifest our faith remain private. A faith that remains within the bounds of the private sphere, however, is not the witness of Jesus, who ate with sinners, who healed those in need on the Sabbath, and who empowered the outcasts to recognize their own dignity because God recognized them as human beings.

When considering the relationship between one's faith and the world we live in, we raise a seminal theological question: If God is indeed sovereign, then is God involved in the political sphere? According to James Nash, any segregation of Christianity from politics is "theologically indefensible" because "[Our] God is also *political*, blessing the peacemakers, intervening in the affairs of governments and nations, and liberating slaves from the shackles of pharaoh. To be in communion with God the Politician, this 'lover of justice' and 'Prince of Peace,' is to struggle to deliver the community of earth from all manner of evil—private *and* public, personal *and* social, cultural *and* ecological, spiritual *and* material."[2] This is a crucial reminder not only of the nature of divine sovereignty, but also of the Christian mission proclaimed by Jesus. We are challenged by God to transform the "not yet" into the "already" through the work of the Spirit initiating the kingdom of God in our present world. Do not hear me wrong; I am not arguing for the establishment of a Christian theocracy or the instantiation of the kingdom of God through the executive, legislative, or judicial branches of American federal government. Instead, if Christians are truly inspired by hope, then we should see the injustices of the world differently than those who are not Christians and hence advocate for innovative solutions to the violence and cruelty we see precisely because we are confidently expectant of God's ability to act in novel ways through our response to grace.

As we have discussed already, so much of our engagement with environmental problems and solutions has been framed in terms of broader societal understandings about economics or the personal decision-making of individual consumers to choose "green" or "eco-friendly" items rather than polluting ones. For example, my students often ask me whether or not they should drink water from a reusable water bottle or convenient, disposable plastic ones. The answer is obvious: for myriad reasons, we should discipline ourselves to drink water from reusable containers, just as humans have been doing on this planet for thousands of years with very little environmental impact. (Lest we forget, plastic bottles are not biodegradable since they only break down into smaller and smaller pieces of plastic, and if the bottles do not make it to a recycling depot, they often work their way into our waterways and oceans and into the bellies of marine life, which is then caught, filleted, and fed back to us.) The personal decisions made by a single individual, however, can too often make us eco-self-righteous. It is amazing how drinking from a trendy reusable water bottle with a hip conservation phrase scribbled onto it or driving a hybrid vehicle instead of a gas-guzzling SUV or purchasing organic produce at a farmers market in walking distance from one's house can be a morally good act that turns into a self-righteous one rather quickly. Part of this is undoubtedly because the priests employed by the various principalities and powers have for so long made it a point to label those who are buying "eco-friendly" things as outside of the norm (e.g., tree-hugging hippies), but some of this is due to the human desire to be recognized for the good that we do. We would prefer to be honored by others, rather than for our charitable giving to be done without letting

2. Nash, *Loving Nature*, 193; italics in original.

our left hand know what our right is doing.[3] Nash, though, maintains that engagement in the political process is a potentially effective buffer against this sort of eco-self-righteousness. "The political process is the only place where the rules of relationship for a given society are officially established and where sufficient power might be mustered to match the current scale of the ecological crisis. An apolitical posture on contemporary ecological concerns, therefore, is righteous irrelevance."[4]

We must resist not only self-righteousness, but also the attempt of the principalities and powers to make us think that we can consume or purchase our way out of the consequences of climate change. Much effort has been mobilized and countless dollars have been spent in trying to convince developed-world citizens that one can do something about climate change and other environmental problems if each of us makes different consumer decisions. The message that we might be able to change our consumption patterns (i.e., consume eco-friendly items instead of severely polluting ones) and still hold onto our standard of living—which seems never to be at a loss for finding new ways to consume energy and resources—is an alluring one indeed. We desire to do good by not harming the environment, so we decide in the supermarket or the online store that it might actually be worth it to spend a few extra dollars on eco-friendly items. Clive Hamilton argues that this is a significant problem. "The danger of green consumerism is that it transfers responsibility from the corporations mostly accountable for pollution, and the governments that should be restraining them, onto the shoulders of private consumers."[5] This is not to say that buying eco-friendly products or putting solar panels on your rooftop is not an important step, because it is. It actually can be in some small measure a sign of hope. However, consumers do not exist alone. Consumers exist in a symbiotic relationship—a trinity of sorts—with producers and regulators, i.e., the government. While the priesthood of economic growth would have us believe that power flows evenly and freely between these three entities, the fact is this is far from the truth. In our present situation it is clear that producers, i.e., the world's largest transnational corporations, hold by far the most power when it comes to deciding on the production of eco-friendly goods and services or the release of greenhouse gases, while the governments of the world are in second place. The world's consumers exercise the least amount of power, all the while being told they possess the most.

3. Matt 6:1–5.

4. Nash, *Loving Nature*, 194.

5. Hamilton, *Requiem for a Species*, 78.

As Christians think more consciously about our political involvement, it is critical that we do not limit our activity merely to consumer responsibility because consumer choices are shaped primarily by producers and sometimes by regulators. Michael Maniates asserts that there exists a sad irony: as our awareness of environmental problems has become more global, the framing of environmental problem-solving has become decidedly and intentionally more individualized, which serves to benefit those who would prefer that developed-world citizens not think that these problems have relevant political solutions.[6] He goes on to argue that only collective citizen action, rather than individual consumer activity, can cause the relationship between producers, regulators, and consumers to be reconfigured in such a way that will create meaningful solutions to environmental problems.[7] Theologically, we might say that by giving in to the seduction of green consumerism, we exalt the role of the individual to a place that is hubristic. The attempt to make buying eco-friendly products alone our solution to climate change fundamentally rejects the idea of shared purpose or common good that might unite us. We must consider in all urgency how to reach for the common good rather than be guided solely by a perverted sense of self-interest. A reach for the common good can be expressed in profound ways by our churches as we seek ways to be beacons of hope in our communities. Another reason that environmental problem-solving through eco-friendly consumption is so appealing to so many developed-world citizens, like ourselves, is that it seems to be "apolitical and nonconfrontational, and thus ripe for success."[8] Americans crave solutions that lack a politically partisan edge in a contemporary moment when the politicians who occupy the halls of government disgust more and more people. We desire to be seen as tolerant and politically correct as possible and consequently want environmental resolutions that do not force us to confront our deepest-held views about our notions of entitled lifestyles and how they might actually impact the widows, orphans, and aliens. And yet, the ministry of Jesus shows us explicitly that the critique of hope should compel us to be politically relevant and confrontation with the principalities and powers will undoubtedly be a crucial part of our search for justice. The daily witness of a Christian church convicted by hope can seek no less.

Some Christians advocate strongly for Christians to participate in the political process because of the transformative effects laws can have on societal behavior as well as public values and attitudes. While acknowledging

6. Maniates, "Individualization," 58–59.

7. Ibid., 54

8. Ibid., 66.

that laws like the Endangered Species Act and presidential orders like Executive Order 12898 have been instrumental in changing the landscape of environmental regulation and enforcement, I remain skeptical of how much laws shape societal behavior rather than reflect it. Do laws really change our hearts and minds, or just ameliorate bad behavior in a society of relatively decent people? Yet, I desire to think of myself as pragmatic. We will not be able to incorporate climate change–mitigation and –adaptation strategies merely through consumer movements or grassroots campaigns or even through the church's examples of hopeful eating and economics, as critical as those will be in inspiring us to mobilize toward more sanguine endings. Ultimately, climate change will have to be addressed through local, regional, national, and global political means if we are to secure any mitigation and adaptation measures that are truly meaningful and efficacious. Political engagement not only can serve, then, as a way to limit our tendency toward self-righteousness, but can also provide us with another reminder that we are in need of divine grace. Even the best environmental regulation and climate change–adaptation schemes have unforeseen consequences that could end up being worse than the original problem. In the midst of our best-laid plans, we must remember that we are not omniscient; we are only human. Anything that reminds us of this basic theological, existential, and biological fact will help us make better decisions when it comes to addressing our present problems.

At the same time, while granting that our particular democratic republic exercises a certain measure of justice by the enforcement of law, whether that be at the individual or community level, Christians cannot allow the American notion of justice nor the election of a political representative to constrain our theological imaginary in our efforts to be just toward the poor and oppressed. Too often we can be heard saying, "How can I possibly make a difference in light of a political order that seems so corrupt at times or moves regularly at a glacial pace?" The prophetic voice that exhorts us to be just and righteous toward the widows, orphans, and aliens does not grant us the leisure to wait for the law of the land to catch up with what we know is God's call for us to be merciful. Jesus' ministry calls us to recognize the dignity of others person by calling them our neighbors and proclaims that this is an expression of God's love that makes a difference. Resurrection hope says our actions matter now. For instance, if frugality is the subversive virtue that I maintain it is and it consequently allows us to stand in solidarity with the poor, then our personal economic decision-making is a public, political expression of our faith. Additionally, if eating is really an activity that demonstrates how we appreciate the land, creatures, farmers, and fieldworkers, then it too is a public, political manifestation of our faith, whether we choose to be cognizant of it or not. Even though the various priests of the principalities and powers socialize us to think otherwise, these are conspicuous political acts as we live in a world and attempt to proclaim that Jesus is Lord. These are hopeful ways that can be counted as righteousness, no matter how limited, by those we connect ourselves with as we shop and eat. This kind of intentional political behavior can allow the church to be a beacon of hope.

Seeking Justice Now

If the church is to be a beacon of hope in the age of climate change, then it must be just toward the poor and the oppressed; it must be a righteous voice for the widows, orphans, and aliens. If justice and righteousness are the foundation of God's throne, then they should also be the bedrock of the church's outreach to a world ravaged by the hopelessness brought on by climate change. Working for environmental justice allows us to continue the work of the prophets and their plea to care for the widows, orphans, and aliens, and also the ministry of Jesus and his desire to bring good news to "the least of these."[9] A lively, hopeful witness must first critique present injustice by correctly identifying the problem. Let us remember that the root of much of environmental injustice in America is environmental racism, which refers to any policy, practice, or directive that differentially affects or disadvantages (whether intended or unintended) individuals, groups, or communities based on race or color. In other words, many white communities, whether intentional or not, receive a vast amount of environmental benefits without sharing the environmental burdens of living in an industrialized society like ours. We must acknowledge that environmental racism is a sinful behavior. In short, it is a failure to love our neighbors as ourselves. Whether intentional or not, it is a failure to treat our many Latino sisters and brothers in the fields as our neighbors when we allow them to be exposed to cancer-causing chemicals as they pick our fruits and vegetables that we ourselves would prefer not to be exposed to or to allow African American communities to be disproportionately impacted by asthma and other respiratory diseases because they are more likely to live next to train and bus depots. Environmentally racist thought and behavior is fundamentally dehumanizing as they affirm the dignity of one group of people while neglecting the humanity of the other. Such sin will eventually lead to alienation between ourselves and our neighbors, and ultimately alienation from God. As discussed in chapter 2, if we engage in the practice

9. Matt 25:40.

of "blaming the victim" for choosing to work in dangerous or unhealthy settings, we distance ourselves from structural dynamics that place Latino migrant fieldworkers in these sorts of situations to begin with and we relieve ourselves of any culpability we may have for supporting such injustice. This is not the hopeful witness of a neighbor, but rather a profound way of dehumanizing those who are impacted. Moreover, if we, like so many Americans, believe that people live where they do or waste facilities are sited where they are due solely to market forces, we engage in a form of self-deception at both the individual and the societal level that leads to the hopelessness of despair for those impacted in these communities. We preach a message of hopelessness to the poor and oppressed if we succumb to the historically descriptive question, "Which came first, the industry or the people?" instead of asking the normative question, "Should a school, no matter who attends it, ever be built next to a toxic release site?" Consequently, a hopeful Christian asks, "How might I stand in solidarity with those who are oppressed by these conditions and critique the principalities and powers that support them?"

For some of us, we might find ourselves saying, "I had no idea that schools were being built next to toxic release sites," or "Doesn't the government have laws that protect workers in the fields from being exposed to such dangerous toxins?" Our lack of knowledge of these sorts of situations does not mitigate our culpability, but instead highlights the reality of living in a world permeated by sinfulness. It should also serve as a distinct reminder that the principalities and powers who benefit greatly from injustice desire to keep us ignorant. A hopeful witness demands that we step out of the ignorance that leads so many people into despair and acknowledge the world that we live in daily. One way for us to do this is to conceptualize environmental injustice for the sin that it is, but also for the violent activity that it is. It is obviously not the violence manifested in war or the slaughters in our churches and schoolhouses or even domestic settings within families that is often so easy for the media to report in their quest for ratings. Environmental injustice is the product of what Rob Nixon calls "slow violence." "By slow violence [he means] a violence that occurs gradually and out of sight, a violence of delayed destruction that is dispersed across time and space, an attritional violence that is typically not viewed as violence at all . . . a violence that is neither spectacular nor instantaneous, but rather incremental and accretive, its calamitous repercussions playing out across a range of temporal scales."[10] He goes on to argue, "Slow violence is often not just attritional but also exponential, operating as a major threat multiplier; it can fuel long-term, proliferating conflicts in situations where the con-

10. Nixon, *Slow Violence*, 2.

ditions for sustaining life become increasingly but gradually degraded."[11] Finally, Nixon contends that the way our society tallies the casualties of slow violence is incredibly disturbing. "Casualties of slow violence—human and environmental—are the casualties most likely not to be seen, not to be counted."[12] This is a frighteningly accurate assessment of what environmental injustice is and what it does to those who are deemed by our society to be outcasts. Additionally, we must acknowledge that nonhuman creatures and the rest of creation fall into this category as well. They too are causalities that are unlikely to be seen and counted, especially since it is doubtful that we recognize their basic goodness as God does.

It is tragic that in many of the same communities that face environmental injustice daily, food injustice is a constant reality as well. As if the inequity of breathing polluted air or drinking dirty water is not damaging enough to the health and dignity of people in these communities, they also lack access to the basic necessity of nutritionally dense food. While there is enough consumer, producer, and governmental blame to be handed out, the situation is made even more deplorably tragic by the nearly unfathomable amount of food waste that is produced daily and fills our landfills. Food waste is an act of slow violence, too. Food waste is neither spectacular nor instantaneous. It is attritional, but its effects are exponential. It is harmful to the people that this food could be feeding who suffer daily from food insecurity and outright starvation. It is also harmful to us all as the methane created by the vast mountains and valleys of food waste contribute far more substantially to climate change than other greenhouse gases. And yet, the tragedy and violence do not stop there: food waste is also a waste of preciously scarce resources like arable land and potable water, and an offense to the farmworkers in the fields who are harmed in so many ways by the lack of care we extend to those in that profession. Food injustice and food waste stand as blatant examples of the hopelessness that continues to envelop us. While our theological imaginary should include the vision of the Israelite farmers leaving the corners of their field untouched during the harvest and leaving behind any gleanings as well as grapes that fell from their vines for "the poor and the alien," it does not.[13]

Many of the consequences of climate change can also be identified as products of slow violence. For most American Christians, the ravages of climate change on the citizens of low-lying island nations or nations with severe water-security issues are out of sight. It is often not viewed as violence

11. Ibid., 3.
12. Ibid., 13.
13. Lev 19:9–10; 23:22.

because most of the time nothing spectacular occurs to make it onto the media feeds of global news agencies. Island nations, like the Maldives, are slowly sinking into the oceans at a pace that is too protracted to notice in a sound-bite, news-consuming culture like ours. In the case of the Maldives and other low-lying island nations, the loss of a culture and the displacement of an entire population is not just attritional, but exponential. After becoming aware of the fact of rising oceans, it can take decades for an island and its culture to go underwater; yet, when that day comes there is no alternative but to leave behind all that allows you to identify yourself as a member of a people, as part of a culture. This is also the type of violent occurrence where the casualties are not seen or even counted. While it would be easy to say that these sorts of situations are happening on the other side of the planet and there is nothing we can really do, this sort of attitude only serves to support a status quo of the hopelessness of despair. As discussed in chapter 5, we cannot allow a perverted sense of humility to be used as a smokescreen to disguise willful ignorance and abrogation of responsibility. This would represent a sin of not acknowledging the magnanimous lives that God has created us to live. Michael Northcott states it succinctly: "The poor in the land who are already being excluded by climate change from enjoying its fruits are owed justice, but they also need mercy and compassion if they are to be enabled to adapt and survive."[14] What is needed is the good news of hope. This sort of good news will be needed for generations to come as hundreds of millions of people around the planet will become climate refugees in this new age. In an era of increasing nationalistic fervor across the globe, Christians especially will be judged by how they treat those who have become refugees due to climate change.

If the church is to be a beacon of hope, we must dignify all those who are ravaged by slow violence, whether they are human or nonhuman, by counting them as our neighbors and standing in solidarity with them as much as we can. We must also live in just and righteous ways that model what Micah, Zechariah, and the rest of the prophets exhorted the Israelites to do: be compassionate and merciful to the widows, orphans, and aliens, and to those nonhuman members of creation as well. Moreover, the church must be a place from which people can draw their courage, the ability to endure in the face of injustice and slow violence. To engage in this work is to participate in the creative theological imaginary provided by hope in the God who raised Jesus from the dead. This is the witness of a lively hope.

14. Northcott, *Moral Climate*, 162.

Is Climate Change Denial a Sin?

The denial of the reality of climate change and how it affects both human and nonhuman populations is profound, especially among the citizens of the developed world. Developed-world nations like the United States, the United Kingdom, Canada, and Australia have a robust industry of so-called climate change skeptics. While legitimate skeptics employ methodologies that seek to uncover the truth in any given situation, climate change skeptics demonstrate blatant disregard for and obfuscation of the truth that may be found. Climate change skeptics are not really skeptics, but deniers. Sociologist Stanley Cohen defines denial thusly: "Denial is understood as an unconscious defense mechanism for coping with guilt, anxiety and other disturbing emotions aroused by reality. The psyche blocks off information that is literally unthinkable or unbearable. The unconscious sets up a barrier which prevents the thought from reaching conscious knowledge. Information and memories slip into an inaccessible region of the mind."[15] According to Cohen, denial encompasses many aspects of what it means to be human. "Denial, then, includes *cognition* (not acknowledging the facts); *emotion* (not feeling, not being disturbed); *morality* (not recognizing wrongness or responsibility) and *action* (not taking active steps in response to knowledge)."[16]

Using Cohen's categories as a backdrop, Haydn Washington and John Cook contend that three types of denial are particularly evident when we think about those who deny that climate change is happening.[17] The first is literal denial, which refers to the claims of the fossil-fuel industry and think tanks funded by the fossil-fuel industry, either directly or indirectly, or by individuals who have often made their fortune from the fossil-fuel industry.[18] These groups financially support those who create elaborate conspiracy theories that implicate scientists and environmental organizations in obscuring the truth and lying to the public, stand as fake experts in place of legitimate climate scientists, hold science to impossible expectations that mainstream science does not accept as reasonable, engage in explicit misrepresentations and logical fallacies, and cherry-pick data that supports climate change "skepticism."[19] The second type is interpretive denial. The facts are not necessarily in question, but their interpretation is very

15. Cohen, *States of Denial*, 5.
16. Ibid., 9.
17. Washington and Cook, *Climate Change Denial*, 98–99.
18. For more on this, see Oreskes and Conway, *Merchants of Doubt*.
19. Ibid., 43–63.

much in question. For example, many world governmental leaders admit that climate change is occurring, but engage in very little policy-related action that reflects serious consideration of what climate science is telling us about the changing conditions of the planet. The third type is implicatory denial, which is the most common among the public.[20] We know that there is a problem but fail to convert that knowledge into action because in some way or another we cannot comprehend the implications of the truth about climate change. This sort of denial can manifest itself as distraction. We might consciously or subconsciously ignore pressing matters in our lives and replace them with something less serious or trivial in nature in order not to deal with reality as it is. Another manifestation of this sort of denial might be to lessen the seriousness of the problem altogether by saying that humans have solved complex problems before and so we should trust that we can do it again. We might exhibit implicatory denial when we attempt to shift the blame onto someone else. Why should the United States (the historical leader in emissions) limit its carbon dioxide emissions if China (the contemporary leader in emissions) will not?[21]

The question for Christians is not, "Does this sort of denial exist?"—because it undoubtedly does—but rather, "Is climate change denial a sin?" It is difficult not to call literal denial a sin. The effects of the deceitfulness and slander that have been promoted by those who trade in the literal-denial industry have only served to alienate us from our human neighbors, our nonhuman neighbors, and God. Those involved in these efforts have belittled and besmirched people who disagree with them by attempting to destroy their professional credibility and personal reputations. These acts must be labeled for the sins of commission that they are. This sort of denial is also an eco-sin in that it is a radical attempt to deny that there are limits to creation that we are to keep. It represents a denial of the interconnectedness and interdependence of our creatureliness and a rejection of humility along with an adoption of the *perversa securitas* that leads to the hopelessness of presumption. Those who peddle in literal denial reject the idea that humans are members of creation and instead argue that we are the apex of it and can fix any problem, wicked or not, that comes our way. Interpretive denial should be considered sinful as well as its effects also alienate us from our human neighbors, our nonhuman neighbors, and God. While this sort of denial, often manifested by global heads of state, could very easily be a sin of commission, it seems to exist more as a sin of omission: we know that we need to act so that the effects of climate change that are currently harming

20. For more on this, see Norgaard, *Living in Denial*.

21. For more on climate change denial, see Hamilton, *Requiem for a Species*, 95–133.

the poor and extinguishing species, for example, do not get dramatically worse, but we lack the political will to do so. Most global political leaders are not actively engaged in disenfranchising the poor or decreasing biodiversity, but it is happening due to their collective inaction. As an eco-sin, interpretive denial represents a failure to live up to our capacity to see the creation as a whole and a lack of humility to take responsibility for our actions within it. Interpretive denial leads easily to slothful behavior that benefits the status quo as it deprives the poor further and destroys creation even more. This sort of sloth eventually leads to despair, which is a form of hopelessness in the face of this crisis that we cannot afford.

Finally, is implicatory denial sinful? Is lacking the ability to connect knowledge of a problem with appropriate action sinful? There are typically three common behaviors that exhibit this sort of denial. Seeking to distract ourselves from weighty matters in order to evade their full implications can seem innocent enough or even occasionally needed to maintain healthy psychological boundaries, but the effects of this distraction can be dramatic if it causes us to disregard how the poor and the rest of creation are being impacted by climate change. Whether the distraction is intentional or not, our lack of attending to climate change alienates us from our human neighbors, our nonhuman neighbors, and God. Lessening the seriousness of climate change and relying on our past history of success in solving problems is also potentially sinful. We can be deceitful by denying the seriousness and the wicked nature of the problem. Moreover, we can become hubristic quickly if we do not look at our many failures in problem-solving as well. Being humble demands that we measure our triumphs and our debacles fairly. Shifting the blame to another party is sinful, too. While one waits for the other party to get its act together, further alienation from neighbors and God is occurring as the destructive status quo persists. Implicatory denial, then, really is an exercise in slothful behavior or an exercise in hubris, if not both; sadly, both can lead to hopelessness.

So while we engage in denial as a psychological attempt to ward off guilt, anxiety, or ultimately hopelessness, we ironically end up growing more hopeless in our attempt to avoid the truth that is clearly in front of us. Eventually, we cannot escape the cognitive, emotional, moral, and action-oriented features of denial. They impact our entire existence, our entire way of life. Therefore, we must acknowledge that climate change denial is a failure to live up to the human capacity to see the whole of creation for what it is. It is a rejection of our interconnected and interdependent creatureliness and the humility that comes from understanding our appropriate place in the universe and instead explicitly treating ourselves as the pinnacle of creation. It is a refusal to watch for the limits of creation and behave righteously as the tillers of the soil. All of these thoughts and actions are sinful because they fundamentally alienate us from our neighbors, both human and non-human, from God, and ultimately from the people God desires for us to be. This feeds both types of hopelessness in profound ways. We become slothful when we believe that we are no longer called to do great things even in the midst of wicked problems, which can end in despair. And we grow more presumptive as we become more hubristic in our belief that our own ingenuity and technology can solve any problem of our making. Finally, Christians should view resisting climate change deniers as a public, hopeful expression of our faith. Not only should we disavow those who engage in the character assassination and humiliation of those who do the work of making climate science public and accessible, but we must also identify those who are only seeking to obscure the data in order to protect the status quo and their personal interests, which often includes the method by which they accumulate wealth.

11

The Church as a Beacon
of Hope: Part 2

I n *Laudato Si'*, Pope Francis argues that too frequently the type of environmental education our society prizes is more about the collection and
dissemination of information than it is about the creation of new behavior
through virtue formation. Indeed, we find ourselves in an era where we are
in need of a new type of "ecological citizenship."[1] We are in need of a cur-
riculum, as it were, that is as much about the establishment of virtue as it
is about accurate scientific knowledge. In this final chapter, let me propose
three ways in which the church might be a beacon of hope as it inspires and
supports a new brand of ecological citizenship that includes understanding
the best scientific knowledge we can produce.

Supporting Science

It is entirely unfortunate that so many American Protestant Christians, not
to mention the American public in general, believe that Christianity and
science are somehow in conflict with each other. This is no more evident
than in the more-than-century-long debate about the validity of the theory
of evolution. The so-called "creation versus evolution" debate has led far too
many well-meaning Christians to believe that their children will become
atheists if they accept that evolution is the correct theory explaining the rise
of biological complexity on this planet. What is often lost in this debate is
the difference between science and the interpretation of science. In the supposed controversy about evolution, famous and often media-savvy atheists
insist that the theory of evolution leads one to conclude rationally that there
is no purpose to the universe and consequently no such thing as God.[2] And

1. Pope Francis, *Laudato Si'*, 211.
2. E.g., Dawkins, *Selfish Gene*.

yet their conclusion is a philosophical interpretation of the science, one that they are perfectly entitled to, but not a necessary conclusion demanded by the scientific method. Christians must recognize that the difference between science and the interpretation of science is pivotal. While some interpret the scientific data and say there is no God, I and other Christians interpret the data and say that evolution is God's way of creating the richness of complexity that we see in this universe. An atheistic interpretation of evolution is no less valid than my theistic one, but neither of our interpretations is more or less justifiable because of the scientific method.

A similar situation has arisen with our understanding of climate science. Well-educated, fair-minded scientists, whose research has been peer-reviewed, which represents the best academics can do to guarantee informational accuracy, are telling us that our planet's climate is changing rapidly and that it is due overwhelmingly to anthropogenic causes. The strength of the scientific consensus on this topic is similar to that about evolution being the correct explanation for the rise of biological complexity. The findings of climate science represent our best explanation of the rising global temperature we currently observe as well as the best explanation for what we reasonably think we will encounter in the near and distant future. The climate change–denial industry in the United States, Australia, and other industrialized countries around the world operates in an analogous manner to that of the Christian evolution-denial industry. While climate change deniers argue that they are questioning the legitimacy of climate science and its findings, they are often really questioning the interpretations of the science. Climate science tells us that the climate is shifting and causing radical changes to the planet's hydrological cycles, ecosystem diversity, human health, etc., but the implications of the current and future consequences of this events are the actual concerns, whether explicitly stated or not, of those who promote climate change denial. Just as evolutionary biology cannot compel us logically to conclude that there is no purpose to the universe, climate science itself cannot prescribe our ethical, political, or economic responses to the radical changes we are causing to our planet and its many inhabitants. However, a reasonable interpretation of climate science demands that we change what we are doing—change it quickly, dramatically, and comprehensively. This is in fact what disturbs climate change deniers the most. Just as the ecological devastation during the time of Jeremiah called for a meaningful interpretation, climate science is providing us with the detailed observational data that needs interpreting. For Jeremiah, speaking on behalf of God, the devastation meant that the rich and powerful of Israel were being punished for disenfranchising the poor and the oppressed. For many Christian thinkers, including me, climate change fundamentally represents the failure to honor the cosmic covenant and to care meaningfully for the poor and oppressed. It is a failure on a global scale of an economy that is focused on maximizing the personal satisfaction of wants rather than needs instead of seeking sustainability and justice as its goals. It is a failure of an anthropomonist worldview that implicitly and explicitly declares that human concerns are the only ones that matter and human ingenuity can solve any problems that might come despite ecosystem collapse and biodiversity loss.

Christians must resist the coercion of climate change deniers who conflate climate science with potential policy implications and consequently demonize science in general and individual scientists in particular who toil diligently to explain how our planet functions.[3] Perhaps this is the reason that political ideology and party affiliation are more predictive of whether one agrees that climate change is happening and its consequences should be addressed seriously than one's religious identity, education, or other demographic factors like race.[4] Instead, we need to support the work of science vigorously by remembering that the alleged conflict American Christians perceive between faith and science belies a far richer story in Christian history. Many Christians from the beginning of the scientific revolution and the Enlightenment were seminal figures in the development and practice of the scientific method and Western science. In fact, many of the world's most important scientists have been Christians who led devout lives of discipleship. Galileo Galilei, Robert Boyle, Isaac Newton, Michael Faraday, Gregor Mendel, Asa Gray, Pierre Teilhard de Chardin, Max Planck, and Theodosius Dobzhansky are just some of the names of influential scientists since 1600 who identified themselves as believers.

The application and success of the scientific method has helped humanity comprehend how our planet and its varied ecosystems function in their multitudinous ways. While the scientific method is not the only way to understand how our planet works, its success is one of the staggering accomplishments of human civilization over the last 500 years. While the accumulation of data, seeing patterns within those data points, and the theorizing and testing of theories can be awe inspiring in itself, Christians like me and those mentioned above believe that the fact that the universe is itself orderly is more awesome than our ability to describe it mathematically or formulate theories about it. Our philosophical and theological

---

3. Oreskes and Conway, *Merchants of Doubt*.

4. Public Religion Research Institute and American Academy of Religion, "Believers, Sympathizers, and Skeptics."

interpretations about this order and what that might say about the Creator who is behind it are just as fascinating, if not more so.

Reflecting upon our observations and asking about whether or not there is a Creator behind this creation may be a trait unique to the *Homo* genus, something that we have been doing since we evolved to have the capacity to reflect upon the vastness of the cosmos and use symbols and metaphors to explain what we were contemplating. This is definitely the sense we get from the psalmist when he peered into the expanse of the stars and wondered, "what are human beings that you are mindful of them, mortals that you care for them?"[5] As we discussed previously, the link between knowing our place in the universe and the development of humility is critical. Basil of Caesarea exhorts us to go even further though in our reflections upon creation. "He [*sic*] magnifies the Lord who observes with a keen understanding and most profound contemplation the greatness of creation, so that from the greatness and beauty of creatures he may contemplate their Creator. The deeper one penetrates into the reasons for which things in existence were made and were governed, the more he contemplates the magnificence of the Lord and, as far as it lies in him, magnifies the Lord."[6] Centuries later, Thomas Aquinas echoes this argument by stating, "Any error about creation also leads to an error about God."[7] Our thoughts and beliefs about God and ourselves are shaped heavily by our interpretations of the observations of the world around us; they are shaped in our time period by the observations made by scientists using the scientific method. Christians, then, should be the first to support the rigorous examination of nature that the scientific method engages in because it allows us to comprehend God, creation, and ourselves more fully. Science can allow us to see the whole of creation more clearly. Science can also help us understand more fully the limits of creation, which we must grasp better if we are to live in such a way that we might appropriately serve creation. It is tragic, but unfortunately true, if climate change teaches us nothing else, that creation does have limits and there are profound consequences if those limits are exceeded. Moreover, keen observation through the scientific method can expand upon the observations of nature by the Israelite prophets that led them to believe in the cosmic covenant established by the just God who created the universe. By understanding how the planet functions, how the cosmic covenant is expressed, we can become better advocates for environmental justice for the poor and oppressed, who are disproportionately impacted by the ravages of anthro-

---

5. Ps 8:4.

6. Basil, *Homily* 16:3, quoted in Krueger, *Cloud of Witnesses*, 84.

7. Thomas Aquinas, *Summa Contra Gentiles* II.3.

pogenic climate change and environmental degradation. This is a significant way that our theological imaginary helps create a new social imaginary.

Implications of Sacramental Contemplation

The Christian affirmation that God created the universe and the subsequent belief that through the incarnation God became flesh in the person of Jesus of Nazareth are the basis for asserting that we exist in a sacramental universe. It is now time to examine what contemplation of our sacramental universe, as discussed in chapter 1, might actually do for us as Christians attempting to be witnesses of the hope this side of the resurrection.

It was typical for premodern Christian thinkers to be more sacramentally sensitive than those of us in the twenty-first century. The idea of seeing and comprehending a divine agent who sought to be known through the works of creation was commonplace for centuries. Even the father of the Protestant Reformation, who proclaimed "Sola Scriptura" as his theological battle cry, once said, "God writes the Gospel, not in the Bible alone, but also on trees, and in the flowers and clouds and stars."[8] Two medieval Christian theologians stand out as illustrative examples of the sort of Christian thought and spirituality that might help us become better at sacramental contemplation, even in a postmodern age. First, from Hugh of Saint Victor,

> This whole sensible world is like a book written by the finger of God, that is, created by the divine power, and individual creatures are like certain characters invented not by human judgment, but by divine choice to manifest and to signify in some way the invisible wisdom of God. But just as when unlettered people see an open book, they see characters, but do not know the letters, so foolish people and natural human beings, who do not perceive the things of God, see the external appearance in these visible creatures, but do not understand their inner meaning. But those who are spiritual persons can judge all things insofar as they consider the beauty of the work externally, but grasp within them how much the wisdom of the creator is to be admired.[9]

Second, from Saint Bonaventure,

8. Martin Luther, quoted in Krueger, *Cloud of Witnesses*, 273.

9. Hugh of Saint Victor, "Three Days of Invisible Light," quoted in Schaefer, *Theological Foundations*, 74–75.

Whoever, therefore, is not enlightened by such splendor of created things is blind; whoever is not awakened by such outcries is
deaf; whoever does not praise God because of all these effects is
dumb; whoever does not discover the First Principle from such
clear signs is a fool. Therefore, open your eyes, alert the ears
of your spirit, open your lips and apply your heart so that in
all creatures you may see, hear, praise, love and worship, glorify
and honor your God lest the whole world rise against you.[10]

The premodern lesson from these thinkers, as well as many others, is at least
threefold. One, the universe cries out that it is full of deeper meaning than
just the scientific storytelling done with mathematical formulas describing
the supposedly indisputable laws of nature. The universe itself points in the
distinct direction that it is in fact the creation of a Creator. Two, if we attune
ourselves closely enough to what our various senses are perceiving as we
walk through a forest or dive deep below the ocean's surface, then we may
become aware of the deeper mystery that dwells behind the created order.
Three, intentional reflection upon creation can open us to sacramental
contemplation. For Christians, especially, this should lead us to love and
worship more fully the Creator who gives life to the richness and depth of
this creation.

Building upon the insights of patristic and medieval Christian thinkers, Jame Schaeffer argues that the correct response to the Christian recognition of this sacramental universe is reverence.[11] Such reverential behavior
is not aimed at the creatures nor creation, but at the God whose presence is
mediated by the material world. Reverential behavior should aim to ensure
that creation, and all of its constituent members, no matter how big or small,
continues to mediate God's presence. This means that we should seek to
know as much about creation as possible so that we might avoid degrading
creation's capacity to tell us about God, which might include the preservation of species and ecosystems as well as the restraint of human development into undeveloped wildernesses. Scientific knowledge can thus help
us understand God more robustly through an examination of the divine
activity present in creation.

For Protestants like myself, the language of sacramentality may still
seem foreign, even if the concept seems intellectually palatable. Where
might we even start to recognize more fully God's sacramental presence in
creation? Relying on patristic and medieval teachings about the sacramental

10. Saint Bonaventure, Soul's Journey, 1.15, quoted in Schaefer, Theological Foundations, 78.

11. Ibid., 82–86.

nature of the universe, Schaffer contends that we can train ourselves to develop a sacramental sensibility through five complementary steps.[12] First,
we must actually be open to the possibility of a natural sacramental encounter with all creatures or landscapes we encounter. "Not one is seen,
touched, smelled, heard, or tasted without reference to God's active presence or the anticipation of revealing some aspect of God's character. Reactions of wonder, awe, astonishment, surprise, fascination, and curiosity over
other species, vistas, and systems need to be related to God."[13] Too many
Christians fear that the application of the scientific method will strip the
wonder or astonishment from us when we peer deeply into oceans or look
up into the stars and thus prevent us from seeing God, but the fact is that
science has the distinct ability to do just the opposite. The more we know
about the inner workings of the universe, the more awe inspiring it can
become. Second, to be sacramentally sensitive, one must start to become
aware of the relationship between oneself and the subject sensed. What does
it mean to observe the beauty of a sunset or smell the fragrance of a flower
or witness the majesty of a whale shark in the open sea? We must spend
time in serious reflection over these sorts of events in order to understand
what those encounters might do to us. "Feeling small and humble with the
greater reality before God is encouraged. Demonizing natural beings is
avoided. Pausing before taking action becomes routine."[14] Third, someone
who is sacramentally sensitive will seek out more information about the
creatures and the ecosystems that cause one to be drawn into the presence
of the Creator. We need to support scientific inquiry in order to increase
our faith in God. Scientific knowledge of creaturely life and the habitat in
which they live, no matter how elementary, helps us better to contextualize
our interactions with them as well as meditate upon the depth of experience
that this universe has to offer as it praises God. This will also allow us to
be more empathetic, like Job, who saw creation in a new light after gaining
more education about it from his vantage point in the whirlwind. Fourth,
sacramentally sensitive Christians should train their senses to develop the
skills needed to recognize and discern those things that impede our ability
to sense God's presence in creation. This will require an honest evaluation
of the human capacity to obscure creation's capacity to mediate God because we seem to be the only species capable of such unrighteousness.[15]
Learning to react appropriately to ecological abuse and degradation is an

12. Ibid., 86–89.
13. Ibid., 87.
14. Ibid.
15. Ps 104.

"indispensable" final step. Such reactions to environmental harm should include at least disgust, abhorrence, alarm, lament, and intolerance.[16] Schaffer contends that all five steps are essential and complementary in developing sacramental sensitivity.

While, on the surface, sacramental contemplation could appear to reflect an anthropocentric worldview, or even worse an anthropomonist one, I do not believe that is necessarily the case. Sacramental contemplation in the broadest sense as well as the sacramental sensitivity training outlined above should not make us more egotistical and self-centered, but instead should make us more humble, and powerfully so. The more we contemplate God's work in creation, the more likely we are to reflect upon our place in that creation. We should become more deeply aware of our interconnectedness and interdependence with the rest of creation. Humans do not and cannot stand alone. The more we ponder the idea that all of God's creatures are meant to mediate the glory of God in some measure or another, the more Christians should be compelled to protect the integrity of nonhuman creatures and ecosystems. Appreciation should propel us to meaningful care. In other words, sacramental contemplation should lead us to a theocentric worldview rather than an anthropocentric one. It should lead us to value what God values and to deplore what God deplores. This is why my scuba-diving adventure in the Maldives and the encounter with the whale shark were so impactful. It was the beginning of sacramental contemplation, the start of a new understanding of God and of my humble place in the universe.

Yet, herein lies a new challenge. Matching our new theological imaginary with proper new behavior may not be very difficult in the first four steps of Schaeffer's sacramental-sensitivity-training proposal. The final step, however, might be much more difficult. Humans only have finite pools of worry, and presently most of us do not really worry about climate change or species extinction demonstrably much at all, and if we do, then it is only if it is affecting us in our immediate life situations. It seems as if many people just do not have the psychological space to be disgusted by or even abhor the environmental ills of the world. Additionally, news-media outlets regularly practice overreaction to and oversensationalization of even the most pedestrian of events in order to attract viewers, which tends to make us jaded when a story of true significance is covered. This, too, prevents us from being genuinely alarmed or taking a sincere posture of lamentation because of environmental degradation or biodiversity loss. If sacramental contemplation can help develop within us a better sense of humility through an even deeper recognition of our interconnectedness and interdependence with

16. Schaffer, *Theological Foundations*, 88.

creation, I believe it is capable of realigning our worries and incorporating that indispensable fifth step that Schaeffer exhorts us to adopt. Perhaps Pope Francis speaks most illustratively to the latent possibility of this realignment: "Thanks to our bodies, God has joined us so closely to the world around us that we can feel the desertification of the soil almost as a physical ailment, and the extinction of a species as a painful disfigurement."[17] This is how profound our interconnectedness and interdependence with creation is, if only we are willing humbly to accept our place within it. Only then might we appropriately love what God loves and condemn what God condemns. In this way we might become more fully *imago Dei*. This truly makes for a hopeful Christian witness and the basis for Christians to be strong proponents of conservation and preservation efforts that seek to protect biodiversity.

Our Relationship to Technology

Whether it is the first stone wheel or the complex smartphone in our pockets, humans have always been fascinated with technology and what it can do for us. It makes our lives easier. It makes our lives faster. It makes our lives more convenient. It makes our lives better—at least that is what most of us choose to believe. These are just some of the relatively benign thoughts about technology that shape our social imaginary. But our social imaginary suggests something else about our collective view on technology. We often act as if any sort of technology represents progress, and that our technological successes far outweigh our failures. This view, however, is naive. The creation of technology may represent progress of some sort, but the usage of technology actually determines whether it is beneficial or destructive. Technology itself is ambiguous; it can be used for good or for ill. Understanding the atom allows us to create new cancer treatments or even possibly "clean" energy, but also nuclear weapons of mass destruction. While the steam engine opened the way to industrialization and the raising of the standard of living for many humans, it also started us down the road toward climate change and the effects it has and will have on countless humans and nonhumans and the rest of the planet. Our obsession with technology also manifests the very human tendency to exalt our successes and rationalize away our failures. We are quick to applaud our technological masterpieces and we swiftly forget our technological blunders. This sort of self-rationalization can be very hubristic behavior, which might be another form of human exceptionalism.

17. Pope Francis, *Evangelii Gaudium*, 167.

Additionally, our present social imaginary reflects a broad cultural belief held in the developed world at least that there is very little that technology cannot accomplish. When it comes to the current ecological crisis we often believe, or live like we believe, that if we only had the correct technology we could effectively mitigate or adapt to climate change seamlessly with little or no alteration of our current developed-world lifestyle. (But if we are being realistic, it is not just technology, but technology at a price we deem to be affordable, whatever that might be, that we are supposedly waiting for patiently.) This framing of environmental problems, however, is a failure to see them as they truly are: fundamentally moral and theological in character. Ellen Davis argues forcefully, "It is a moral and even theological crisis because it is occasioned in large part by our adulation and arrogant use of scientific technology, so that we make applications without rigorous critical regard for questions of compatibility with natural systems, of the integrity of the world that God has made."[18] Our desire to view the effects of climate change as only a lack of proper technology that could be available in the near future is a way to shift the examination of our personal and societal behavior to blaming scientists or government officials or the markets for not creating the sorts of technological wizardry that is supposedly needed for our present challenge. This shifting of blame and lack of self-examination alone should cause Christians to question whether or not this sort of behavior is sinful.

Do not hear me wrong: technology will play a large role in our efforts to mitigate (if that is still possible) and adapt to climate change, but we cannot wait for it as if it is the messiah that will deliver us from our ecological woes. We need a shift in our social imaginary in order to recognize the proper role of technology in our lives and in our efforts to mitigate and adapt to climate change. The shift in our social imaginary must also recognize that our veneration of technology prevents us from examining our personal and societal behavior in any considerable manner. In order to do this, we turn to two biblical stories that might help more carefully shape our theological imaginary and hence transform our social imaginary into a more hopeful daily Christian witness.

At the end of the primeval history found in the opening eleven chapters of Genesis comes the brief story commonly referred to as the Tower of Babel. The narrator begins the story by telling the audience that the peoples of the Earth, who spoke the same language, migrated from the east and settled in the land of Shinar. At that point, the narrator says, "Then they said, 'Come, let us build ourselves a city, and a tower with its top in the

18. Davis, *Scripture, Culture, and Agriculture*, 9.

heavens, and let us make a name for ourselves; otherwise we shall be scattered abroad upon the face of the whole earth.'"[19] This action leads to a rather direct divine response. God descends onto the scene and declares that from this point forward humans will speak different languages and God scatters them throughout the Earth. While this story is undoubtedly an etiology to explain why there are different languages and cultures throughout the planet, it is also a powerful theological statement about the relationship between the Creator and creatures. It would be easy to read this story and think it is about technological hubris and God's reaction toward humans striving to infiltrate divine space in the skies. The description of the tower reaching the heavens, though, is likely alluding to the height of the structure and not a depiction of an attempted invasion of the divine throne. However, what this story does seem to indicate is that humans are anxious about their position in creation. In Genesis 1, God commands humans to fill the Earth and in this story we see that humans are resistant to fulfilling the divine mandate. Instead of trusting that God has given them an appropriate vocation, humans decide not to fill the Earth, but instead to ensure their own security and prosperity by making a name for themselves in their technologically sophisticated stronghold. In essence, the story is a vivid example of humans failing to accept their God-given duties and consequently their creatureliness. Their use of the brick-building technology of their day signals a venture to make a name for themselves rather than a sincere effort to follow God's command and bring God glory. "The *unity* of peoples with isolationist concerns for self-preservation could promote any number of projects that would place creation in jeopardy. Their sin concentrates their energies on a creation-threatening task; even the finest creative efforts can subvert God's creational intentions. Although the text does not impugn cities, it does recognize that sin and its potential for disaster accompanies human progress of whatever sort."[20] While we are unquestionably creative creatures, human creativity mixed with anxiety about our creatureliness, especially when it comes to questioning God's vocation for us, can be a recipe for incredibly sinful behavior. The depiction of this sinful attitude and its consequences are especially relevant for our theological imaginary and its application to today's ecological crisis.

We have already looked at the Noah story from a variety of angles, but I believe it still has more to offer in shaping the contours of our theological imaginary. First of all, the flood story is a radical reminder that we are not the masters of our own destiny. "Humankind as God's creation cannot take

19. Gen 11:4.

20. Fretheim, "Book of Genesis," 413; italics in original.

for granted its own existence in the world; its existence is problematic and remains such in the presence of its creator. The creation decision can be revoked. The pre-history of the biblical flood narrative makes it even clearer that it is directed to the narrative of the creation of humans."[21] This message often seems lost on American Christians in light of our present ecological crisis. Second, while on the plain of Shinar humans use technology to make a name for themselves in opposition to the divine mandate, Noah builds the ark following God's command precisely. Noah does not seek to make a name for himself, but through his obedience honors the Creator by being a good creature and for this he is recognized as righteous. "According to the Old Testament the *saddiq* ('righteous person') does justice to a relationship in which he [*sic*] stands. . . . If man stands in right relation to God, i.e., believes, trusts God, then he is 'righteous.' Righteousness in this sense is not a juridical term of relation, but rather a theological one."[22] Third, the ark represents technology that serves not only Noah's needs and the needs of his family, but also those of nonhuman creatures that will be saved in God's floating conservation experiment during the flood. But more than this, Michael Northcott contends, "Against . . . theological and technological hubris, the Noah saga suggests that turning away from the ecologically destructive path on which humanity is headed requires humility and a preparedness to change direction in response to the clear signs of impending danger."[23] This story teaches us that while technology has its place, self-examination and behavior change are far more crucial in avoiding disaster.

These stories should have a profound impact on our theological imaginary and therefore modify our social imaginary if we listen carefully to what they are saying. In different ways, both stories come to a similar conclusion: human sin can irreparably alter the created order. Also, the juxtaposition between the uses of technology in each story could not be clearer. The comparison between the two stories leaves us with this rather pointed existential question: Do we use technology to "make a name for ourselves" and pursue what we ultimately desire, or is technology used in service of all members of creation? Our love of technology can quickly transform into a fascination with, and ultimately a love of, ourselves. We revel in our creativity by producing technology that reminds us of how truly gifted we can be as a species. In our more anxious moments, though, we seek to secure our future against uncertainty by creating things that make us feel safe. This reveling causes us to forget to be humble as we rationalize away our many failures

21. Westermann, *Genesis 1-11*, 393.

22. Rad, *Genesis*, 116.

23. Northcott, *Moral Climate*, 79.

and celebrate only our successes, while the anxiety-induced search for security causes us to hope in ourselves rather than in God. Our adoration of
technology prevents us from recognizing clearly the lessons of these two
stories. We are creatures who are created to honor God by fulfilling our
vocation. This calls for humility and recognition that creation is more than
just a staging ground for human endeavors. This is depicted explicitly in the
Noah account. If we are to be counted as "a herald of righteousness" like
Noah,[24] then we must not seek to make a name for ourselves but instead
take our proper place within creation and accept our creatureliness. Noah
was not just a paragon of righteousness, but of hopefulness as well. Noah
could have become overwhelmed by despair and lacked the courage to face
the challenge set before him and slipped into sloth, but he trusted in God
to deliver him. Placing his hope in God rather than in his own skill or the
technological sophistication of the ark cannot be overstated. Noah accepted
his role in the divine scheme and humbly changed his behavior to meet the
crisis with renewed strength and trust in God. This is a hopeful witness.

It is our love of technological wizardry and ultimately self-love of human potential that prevents us from discussing what is really needed in light
of our ecological crisis: behavior change. While technological solutions will
undoubtedly play a large role in climate change–mitigation and –adaptation strategies, we must not allow possible solutions in the future to deflect
our attention from present responsibilities. If humans really are creatures
who can see the creation whole, then we must not allow our fascination
with technology to prevent us from seeing the entirety of what needs to
be done. It is our lack of gratitude toward God for creating us to be part of
our interdependent created order that has started us down the road toward
ecological crisis, not merely a lack of "green" or "clean" technology that will
allow developed-world citizens to live excessively consumptive lifestyles. It
is our lack of humility in accepting the divine vocation God has for us that
has caused natural resources to be plundered indiscriminately, not the lack
of a proper pricing scheme of the commons. It is our inability to sacrifice
for the needs of others, both human and nonhuman, that has hastened
extinction and the loss of biodiversity around the planet, not the lack of
government funding for national parks and conservation hotspots. Just as
the people who built the Tower of Babel were using technology to secure
their wants rather than actively pursuing God's mandate to fill the Earth, we
too use technology to fill our desires instead of being the grateful, humble,
and sacrificial creatures God desires for us to be.

24. 2 Pet 2:5.

Finally, we must ask ourselves, does technological development and usage make us more or less hopeful? Does it help further foster our hope in God or in ourselves? There is no easy answer to this. The Tower of Babel story reminds us that it is easy to seek a name for ourselves and eventually come to rely on a security that centers on ourselves rather than God. This can make us believe that technology allows us to transcend our finite creatureliness and even give us an illusion of omnipotence.[25] This, however, is the beginning of the hopelessness of presumption, a self-deceptive reliance on a security that is not real. The story of Noah reminds us that it would be easy to fall into the hopelessness of despair, but trust in God can stimulate us to be courageous in the face of impending disaster. This trust can propel us into being the magnanimous creatures that God created us and yearns for us to be. While hope might involve the use of technology, it does not rely upon it. Hope relies upon the grace of God, and responding to that grace requires us to change our behavior, often radically, as it shapes us into more grateful, humble, and sacrificial creatures. As we see with Noah, placing our hope in God rather than ourselves is the only way that we may be deemed righteous and survive impending disaster.

25. For more on this in the development of intellectual history, see Noble, *Religion of Technology*.

Epilogue

O ne learns much about oneself when writing a book, and if it is not too
gratuitous I would like to share two such lessons at the close of this
work. Much of the work of writing this book was done in between two wonderful vacations. The first, as I mentioned in the introduction, took place at
the beginning of my sabbatical leave in 2015. The second occurred in 2016
to celebrate my fifteenth wedding anniversary. That trip took us to Iceland
and the Faroe Islands. As someone who is currently living through the worst
drought in California in more than one thousand years, I was immediately
struck by the beauty of the green foliage that covers much of the summer-
time landscape of Iceland and the Faroe Islands, especially compared to
much of the brown and gray areas of dead or dying plant life in southern
California. While I could go on about the vastness of the landscapes of these
islands, as I reflect upon the trip I continue to return to a series of scenes
that had less to do with the magnificent scope of these places and more to
do with some of its smallest members.

In both Iceland and the Faroe Islands, I saw an array of Lilliputian
flowers that continue to leave me in awe and inspire me to think deeply.
In one of the lava fields of Iceland, I saw tiny flowers revealing their colors
against the dark gray of the lava rocks. (The scientist in me kept looking
around wondering where exactly the pollinators for these tiny flowers were.)
Next to Skaftafellsjökull, the glacial tongue that extends outward through
Skaftafell, I again saw tiny flowers, smaller than my pinky nail, sprouting
up in between thawed sections of ice and along trails on the way to Svarti-
foss—white ones, violet ones, yellow ones, and pinkish bulb-like ones with
white tops. On our hike to Gásadalur village on Vágar, Faroe Islands, I saw
the same thing. This time purple flowers, much smaller than a dime, dotted
a mountainside that was bombarded by both sun and wind and seemed to
have more loose rocks than soil that would bring forth life.

While this trip was marked more by hiking and exploring above water,
we did have one unique underwater adventure. We dove in the 3°C waters

of the Silfra fissure in Þingvellir National Park in Iceland, which is the actual split between the North American and Eurasian tectonic plates. As a diver, I was immediately struck by the clarity of the water. The clear glacial water that feeds this fissure allows one to see more than 100 meters horizontally. (For those of you who are not divers, this sort of visibility does not exist in most places on this planet.) There happened to be some light rain the morning we dove and it was only then that I truly appreciated the clarity of the water. From 5 or so meters down, I rolled over to face the surface and watched individual drops of rain enter the water with enough velocity that they seemed to continue on for nearly a foot or more. The scene was breathtaking (do not fret my dive friends, I did not literally hold my breath); it was a scene of true natural splendor.

While tiny flowers may not seem like much in the grand scheme of things, or at least in comparison to my whale-shark siting in the Maldives, my mind has returned to the memory of them often. The reason for this I believe is simple. I was awestruck by this basic fact: even here, amidst rather seemingly inopportune surroundings near the Arctic circle, of all places, biological life was attempting to make its way, and it was succeeding in novel and beautiful ways. Rain falling into a open body of water is such a simple natural phenomenon, but one that was truly arresting, even as my index fingers and toes numbed from being in 3°C conditions. I am still struck by the beauty of this moment as I remember it now typing this sentence. As a Protestant, it may be hard for me to compute, but these represent actual steps of sacramental contemplation.

Many years ago, I heard a preacher say that as much as he would like to believe that he was delivering sermons that were tailored to the precise needs of his congregation, he was often actually preaching to an audience of one—himself. His sincere honesty initially struck me because I could not help thinking, "What are we paying you for if you are only preaching sermons meant for you?" After that thought passed, I realized more of what he meant. In the ebbs and flows of a personal walk with God, in concert with working intimately with a church family, a preacher's life often becomes the source for messages of exhortation, notes of encouragement, and moments of lamentation. It can also be a place where hints of skepticism or even doubt get worked out publicly in front of a church family rather than privately behind closed doors. After writing this book, I think I understand exactly what this preacher was talking about. Having grown up in a fantastically dysfunctional family, I was shaped by many forces to become skeptical, even cynical at times, about the decency of humans, the likelihood of human creativity being used in the service of others, and the actual reality of the good news of Christianity. Hope seemed either silly or so distant that it carried little meaningful existential weight. In many ways, this book is an exercise in me preaching to myself. I needed to figure out exactly what Christian hope was all about, even if I did not entirely realize it when I started the project. In the end, I have convinced myself, if you will, of the veracity of the Christian notion of hope in light of the resurrection of Christ. I am now convinced with complete clarity that hope is a confident expectation rather than a form of optimistic wishful thinking, and this allows me now to see divine grace more clearly. I am definitely not naive to the realities of the effects of climate change that are happening in the present and will continue well past my lifetime. I am terribly concerned about how those effects will continue to impact disproportionately "the least of these," who have little or no voice in our present society, but I am wholeheartedly hopeful that God will provide novel possibilities for a different future if we are only willing to listen to the call of divine grace and trust in God rather than ourselves.

Bibliography

Alkon, Alison Hope, and Julian Agyeman. "Introduction: The Food Movement as Polyculture." In *Cultivating Food Justice: Race, Class, and Sustainability*, edited by Alison Hope Alkon and Julian Agyeman, 1–20. Cambridge, MA: MIT Press, 2011.

Anderson, Sarah, ed. *Views from the South: The Effects of Globalization and the WTO on Third World Countries*. Milford, CT: Food First and the International Forum on Globalization, 2000.

Aquinas, Thomas. *Summa Theologica*. Translated by fathers of the English Dominican Province. 2nd and rev. ed. http://www.newadvent.org/summa/index.html.

Arnold, Bill T. *Genesis*. New Cambridge Bible Commentary. Cambridge: Cambridge University Press, 2009.

Arnold, Eberhart, ed. *The Early Christians in Their Own Words*. 4th ed. Farmington, PA: Plough, 1997.

Attfield, Robin. "Environmental Sensitivity and Critiques of Stewardship." In *Environmental Stewardship: Critical Perspectives, Past and Present*, edited by R. J. Berry, 76–91. London: T. & T. Clark, 2006.

Augustine. *Confessions*. Translated by Henry Chadwick. Oxford: Oxford University Press, 1991.

Avila, Charles. *Ownership: Early Christian Teaching*. Maryknoll, NY: Orbis, 1983.

Bagliani, Marco, et al. "A Consumption-Based Approach to Environmental Kuznets Curves Using the Ecological Footprint Indicator." *Ecological Economics* 65 (2008) 650–61.

Barbour, Ian G. *Religion and Science: Historical and Contemporary Issues*. New York: HarperOne, 1997.

Barrera, Albino. *Biblical Economic Ethics: Sacred Scripture's Teachings on Economic Life*. Lanham, MD: Lexington, 2013.

Barth, Karl. *Church Dogmatics*. Edited by G. W. Bromiley. Translated by J. W. Edwards et al. Edinburgh: T. & T. Clark, 1958.

Bartholomew I, Patriarch. *Cosmic Grace, Humble Prayer: The Ecological Vision of the Green Patriarch*. Edited by John Chryssavgis. Grand Rapids: Eerdmans, 2009.

Barton, John. "Reading the Prophets from an Environmental Perspective." In *Ecological Hermeneutics: Biblical, Historical and Theological Perspectives*, edited by David G. Horrell et al., 46–55. London: T. & T. Clark, 2010.

Bauckham, Richard. *The Bible and Ecology: Rediscovering the Community of Creation*. Waco, TX: Baylor University Press, 2010.

———. *God and the Crisis of Freedom: Biblical Contemporary Perspectives*. Louisville: Westminster John Knox, 2002.

Bauckham, Richard, and Trevor Hart. *Hope against Hope: Christian Eschatology at the Turn of the Millennium*. Grand Rapids: Eerdmans, 1999.

Beckwith, Roger T. "The Unity and Diversity of God's Covenants." *Tyndale Bulletin* 38 (1987) 93–118.

Bell, Daniel. *The Cultural Contradictions of Capitalism*. 20th anniversary ed. New York: Basic Books, 1996.

Bell, Daniel M., Jr. *The Economy of Desire: Christianity and Capitalism in a Postmodern World*. Grand Rapids: Baker Academic, 2012.

Bello, Walden. *Deglobalization: Ideas for a New World Economy*. New York: Zed, 2002.

Benne, Robert. *The Ethic of Democratic Capitalism: A Moral Reassessment*. Philadelphia: Fortress, 1981.

Bernard of Clairvaux, Saint. "On the Steps of Humility and Pride." In *Bernard of Clairvaux: Selected Works*, translated by G. R. Evans, 99–143. New York: Paulist, 1987.

Berry, Wendell. "The Gift of Good Land." In *The Art of the Commonplace: The Agrarian Essays of Wendell Berry*, edited by Norman Wirzba, 293–304. Washington, DC: Counterpoint, 2002.

———. "Waste." In *What Are People For?*, 126–28. Berkeley: Counterpoint, 1990.

Blanchard, Kathryn D., and Kevin J. O'Brien. *An Introduction to Christian Environmentalism: Ecology, Virtue, and Ethics*. Waco, TX: Baylor University Press, 2014.

Bloch, Ernst. *The Principle of Hope*. 3 vols. Cambridge, MA: MIT Press, 1986.

Boff, Leonardo. *Cry of the Earth, Cry of the Poor*. Translated by Phillip Berryman. Maryknoll, NY: Orbis, 1997.

Bonhoeffer, Dietrich. *Letters and Papers from Prison*. Edited by Eberhard Bethge. New York: Touchstone, 1997.

Bowe, John. *Nobodies: Modern American Slave Labor and the Dark Side of the New Global Economy*. New York: Random House, 2007.

Brown, Oli. *Migration and Climate Change*. Geneva: International Organization for Migration, 2008.

Brown, William P. *The Ethos of the Cosmos: The Genesis of Moral Imagination in the Bible*. Grand Rapids: Eerdmans, 1999.

———. *The Seven Pillars of Creation: The Bible, Science, and the Ecology of Wonder*. Oxford: Oxford University Press, 2010.

Brueggemann, Walter. *Genesis*. Louisville: Westminster John Knox, 2010.

———. *Theology of the Old Testament*. Minneapolis: Fortress, 1997.

Bryant, Bunyan, ed. *Environmental Justice: Issues, Policies, and Solutions*. Washington, DC: Island Press, 1995.

Bulgakov, Sergei. *Philosophy of Economy: The World as Household*. Translated and edited by Catherine Evtuhov. New Haven, CT: Yale University Press, 2000.

Bullard, Robert D. *Dumping in Dixie: Race, Class, and Environmental Quality*. Boulder, CO: Westview, 1994.

———. "Environmental Justice in the 21st Century." In *The Quest for Environmental Justice: Human Rights and the Politics of Pollution*, edited by Robert D. Bullard, 19–42. San Francisco: Sierra Club, 2005.

———. *The Quest for Environmental Justice: Human Rights and the Politics of Pollution*. San Francisco: Sierra Club, 2005.

Bullard, Robert D., et al. "Toxic Wastes and Race at Twenty, 1987–2007." https://www.nrdc.org/sites/default/files/toxic-wastes-and-race-at-twenty-1987-2007.pdf.

Buzby, Jean C., et al. "The Estimated Amount, Value, and Calories of Postharvest Food Losses at the Retail and Consumer Levels in the United States." http://www.ers.usda.gov/media/1282296/eib121.pdf.

Byrne, Brendan. "Creation Groaning: An Earth Bible Reading of Romans 8.18–22." In *Readings from the Perspective of Earth*, edited by Norman C. Habel, 193–203. The Earth Bible 1. Sheffield: Sheffield Academic, 2000.

———. *Romans*. Collegeville, MN: Liturgical, 1996.

Carmin, JoAnn, and Julian Agyeman. *Environmental Inequalities beyond Borders: Local Perspectives on Global Injustices*. Cambridge, MA: MIT Press, 2011.

Carolan, Michael. *The Real Cost of Cheap Food*. New York: Earthscan, 2011.

———. *Reclaiming Food Security*. New York: Routledge, 2013.

Cavanaugh, William T. *Being Consumed: Economics and Christian Desire*. Grand Rapids: Eerdmans, 2008.

Christian Aid. "Climate Justice for All." May 2015. http://www.christianaid.org.uk/Images/Climate-justice-for-all-May-2015.pdf.

———. "Human Tide: The Real Migration Crisis." https://www.christianaid.org.uk/Images/human-tide.pdf.

Chrysostom, John. *Homilies on Genesis 1–17*. Translated by Robert C. Hill. Washington, DC: Catholic University of America Press, 1986.

Clapp, Jennifer, and Peter Dauvergne. *Paths to a Green World: The Political Economy of the Global Environment*. Cambridge, MA: MIT Press, 2005.

Clement of Alexandria. *The Paedagogus (The Instructor)*. In vol. 2 of *Ante-Nicene Fathers*, edited by Alexander Roberts et al. Translated by William Wilson. Buffalo, NY: Christian Literature, 1885. http://www.newadvent.org/fathers/0209.htm.

Clough, David L. *On Animals*. New York: T. & T. Clark, 2012.

Cobb, John B., Jr. *Sustainablitiy: Economics, Ecology, and Justice*. Maryknoll, NY: Orbis, 1992.

Cohen, Stanley. *States of Denial: Knowing about Atrocities and Suffering*. Cambridge: Polity, 2001.

Cole, Luke W., and Sheila R. Foster. *From the Ground Up: Environmental Racism and the Rise of the Environmental Movement*. New York: New York University Press, 2001.

Commission for Racial Justice, United Church of Christ. *Toxic Wastes and Race in the United States*. New York: United Church of Christ, 1987.

Common, Mick, and Sigrid Stagl. *Ecological Economics: An Introduction*. Cambridge: Cambridge University Press, 2005.

Conradie, Ernst M. "The Road Towards an Ecological Biblical and Theological Hermeneutics." *Scriptura* 93 (2006) 305–14.

———. "Towards an Ecological Hermeneutics: A Review Essay of the Earth Bible Project." *Scriptura* 85 (2004) 123–35.

———. "What on Earth Is an Ecological Hermeneutics?: Some Broad Parameters." In *Ecological Hermeneutics: Biblical, Historical and Theological Perspectives*, edited by David G. Horrell et al., 295–311. London: T. & T. Clark, 2010.

Cook, Christopher D. *Diet for a Dead Planet: Big Business and the Coming Food Crisis*. New York: New Press, 2006.

Cox, Ronald. *By the Same Word: Creation and Salvation in Hellenistic Judaism and Early Christianity.* New York: de Gruyter, 2007.

———. "Why It All Matters: Appreciating the Universal Scope of Colossians 1.15–20." *Leaven* 21.3 (2013). http://digitalcommons.pepperdine.edu/leaven/vol21/iss3/5/.

Crenshaw, James L. "When Form and Content Clash: The Theology of Job 38:1—40:5." In *Creation in the Biblical Traditions,* edited by Richard J. Clifford and John J. Collins, 70–84. Catholic Biblical Quarterly Monograph Series 24. Washington, DC: Catholic Biblical Association of America, 1992.

Cummans, Jared. "What Is Corn Used For?: 13 Surprising Uses of Corn." June 24, 2015. http://commodityhq.com/investing-ideas/13-ways-corn-is-used-in-our-everyday-lives/.

Daily, Gretchen C. *Nature's Services: Societal Dependence on Natural Ecosystems.* Washington, DC: Island Press, 1997.

Daly, Herman. *Beyond Growth: The Economics of Sustainable Development.* Boston: Beacon, 1996.

Daly, Herman E., and John B. Cobb. *For the Common Good: Redirecting the Economy toward Community, the Environment, and a Sustainable Future.* Boston: Beacon, 1989.

Daly, Herman E., and Joshua Farley. *Ecological Economics: Principles and Applications.* Washington, DC: Island Press, 2004.

Davis, Ellen F. *Scripture, Culture, and Agriculture: An Agrarian Reading of the Bible.* Cambridge: Cambridge University Press, 2009.

Dawkins, Richard. *The Selfish Gene.* Oxford: Oxford University Press, 1976.

DeWitt, Calvin B., and Robert Nash. "Christians and the Environment: How Should Christians Think about the Environment?" http://www.equip.org/articles/christians-and-the-environment-how-should-christians-think-about-the-environment/.

Dietz, Rob, and Dan O'Neill. *Enough Is Enough: Building a Sustainable Economy in a World of Finite Resources.* San Francisco: Berrett-Koehler, 2013.

Donlon, Diana. "Food and Climate: Connecting the Dots, Choosing the Way Forward." Washington, DC: Center for Food Safety, 2014. http://www.centerforfoodsafety.org/files/foodclimate_51242.pdf.

Douglas, Mary. *In the Active Voice.* London: Routledge and Kegan Paul, 1982.

Dunn, James D. G. *The Epistles to the Colossians and to Philemon: A Commentary on the Greek Text.* Grand Rapids: Eerdmans, 1996.

Dyer, Keith D. "When Is the End Not the End?: The Fate of Earth in Biblical Eschatology (Mark 13)." In *The Earth Story in the New Testament,* edited by Norman C. Habel and Vicky Balabanski, 44–56. The Earth Bible 5. Sheffield: Sheffield Academic, 2002.

Ekins, Paul. *Economic Growth and Environmental Sustainability: The Prospects of Green Growth.* London: Routledge, 2000.

Elliott, John H. *1 Peter.* Anchor Bible 37b. New York: Random House, 2000.

Elton, Sarah. *Consumed: Food for a Finite Planet.* Chicago: University of Chicago Press, 2013.

Environmental Protection Agency. "Agriculture." https://www.epa.gov/agriculture.

———. "Environmental Justice." http://www.epa.gov/environmentaljustice/.

Environmental Working Group. "The United States Farm Subsidy Information." https://farm.ewg.org/region.php?fips=00000.

Eriksson, Ralf, and Jan Otto Andersson. *Elements of Ecological Economics*. London: Routledge, 2010.

Essay, Majid, et al. "Towards an Integrated Framework for Development and Environment Policy: The Dynamics of Environmental Kuznets Curves." *World Development* 29.8 (2001) 1421–34.

Ferguson, Everett. *Early Christians Speak: Faith and Life in the First Three Centuries*. Vol. 2. 3rd ed. Abilene, TX: Abilene Christian University Press, 2002.

Feuerbach, Ludwig. *The Essence of Christianity*. Translated by George Eliot. New York: Harper and Row, 1957.

Figueres, Christiana. "Why Women Are the Secret Weapon to Tackling Climate Change." *CNN.com*, March 6, 2014. http://www.cnn.com/2014/03/06/world/why-women-are-the-secret/.

Finn, Daniel K. *Christian Economic Ethics: History and Implications*. Minneapolis: Fortress, 2013.

Foer, Jonathan. *Eating Animals*. New York: Little, Brown, 2009.

Food and Agriculture Organization of the United Nations. "Livestock's Long Shadow." http://www.fao.org/docrep/010/a0701e/a0701e00.htm.

Foreman, Christopher H., Jr. *The Promise and Peril of Environmental Justice*. Washington, DC: Brookings Institution, 1998.

Fretheim, Terence E. "The Book of Genesis." In vol. 1 of *New Interpreter's Bible*. Nashville: Abingdon, 1994.

Friedman, Benjamin M. *The Moral Consequences of Economic Growth*. New York: Knopf, 2005.

Friedman, Milton. *Capitalism and Freedom*. Chicago: University of Chicago Press, 1982.

———. *Essays in Positive Economics*. Chicago: University of Chicago Press, 1953.

Friends of the Earth. "A Citizen's Guide to Climate Refugees." https://www.foe.org.au/sites/default/files/CitizensGuide2007.pdf.

———. "Healthy Planet Eating: How Lower Meat Diets Can Save Lives and the Planet." https://www.foe.co.uk/sites/default/files/downloads/healthy_planet_eating.pdf.

Gold, Mark. "The Global Benefits of Eating Less Meat." Petersfield, UK: Compassion in World Farming Trust, 2004.

Goldenberg, Suzanne. "US Congressman Cites Biblical Flood to Dispute Human Link to Climate Change." *Guardian*, April 10, 2013. http://www.theguardian.com/environment/blog/2013/apr/11/republican-biblical-flood-climate-change.

Goodland, Robert, and Jeff Anhang. "Livestock and Climate Change." *World Watch* 22.6 (2009) 10–19.

Gottlieb, Robert, and Anupama Joshi. *Food Justice*. Cambridge, MA: MIT Press, 2010.

Gregory the Pope. *The Books of the Morals*. London: J. G. F. and John Rivington, 1844. http://www.lectionarycentral.com/GregoryMoraliaIndex.html.

Gunders, Dana. "Wasted: How America Is Losing Up to 40 Percent of Its Food from Farm to Fork to Landfill." NRDC Issue Paper, August 2012. https://www.nrdc.org/sites/default/files/wasted-food-IP.pdf.

Gustavsson, Jenny, et al. "Global Food Losses and Food Waste: Extent, Causes and Prevention." http://www.fao.org/docrep/014/mb060e/mb060e.pdf.

Gutiérrez, Gustavo. *On Job: God-Talk and the Suffering of the Innocent*. Translated by Matthew J. O'Connell. Maryknoll, NY: Orbis, 1988.

———. *A Theology of Liberation*. Translated and edited by Sister Caridad Inda and John Eagleson. Maryknoll, NY: Orbis, 1998.

Habel, Norman C. "'Is the Wild Ox Willing to Serve You?': Challenging the Mandate to Dominate." In *The Earth Story in Wisdom Traditions*, edited by Norman C. Habel and Shirley Wurst, 179–89. The Earth Bible 3. Sheffield: Sheffield Academic, 2000.

Hall, Douglas John. *Imaging God: Dominion as Stewardship*. Grand Rapids: Eerdmans, 1986.

———. *The Steward: A Biblical Symbol Come of Age*. Grand Rapids: Eerdmans, 1990.

Hamilton, Clive. *Requiem for a Species: Why We Resist the Truth about Climate Change*. Washington, DC: Earthscan, 2010.

Harrison, Peter. "Having Dominion: Genesis and the Mastery of Nature." In *Environmental Stewardship: Critical Perspectives, Past and Present*, edited by R. J. Berry, 17–31. London: T. & T. Clark, 2006.

Hart, John. *Sacramental Commons: Christian Ecological Ethics*. Lanham, MD: Rowman and Littlefield, 2006.

Hartman, Laura. *The Christian Consumer: Living Faithfully in a Fragile World*. Oxford: Oxford University Press, 2011.

Haught, John F. *The Promise of Nature: Ecology and Cosmic Purpose*. New York: Paulist, 1993.

Hauter, Wenonah. *Foodopoly: The Battle Over the Future of Food and Farming in America*. New York: New Press, 2012.

Hawken, Paul, Amory Lovins, and L. Hunter Lovins. *Natural Capitalism: Creating the Next Industrial Revolution*. Boston: Little, Brown, 1999.

Hayek, Friedrich A. *The Road to Serfdom*. Chicago: University of Chicago Press, 1972.

Hayhoe, Katharine, and Andrew Farley. *A Climate for Change: Global Warming Facts for Faith-Based Decisions*. New York: FaithWords, 2009.

Heal, Geoffrey. *Nature and the Marketplace: Capturing the Value of Ecosystem Services*. Washington, DC: Island Press, 2000.

Herzfeld, Noreen. *In Our Image: Artificial Intelligence and the Human Spirit*. Minneapolis: Fortress, 2002.

Hiebert, Theodore. "The Human Vocation: Origins and Transformations in Christian Traditions." In *Christianity and Ecology: Seeking the Well-Being of Earth and Humans*, edited by Dieter T. Hessel and Rosemary Redford Ruether, 135–54. Cambridge, MA: Harvard University Press, 2000.

Hill, Peter J., and John Lunn. "Markets and Morality." *Journal of Religious Ethics* 35 (2007) 627–53.

Hiuser, Kris, and Matthew Barton. "A Promise Is a Promise: God's Covenantal Relationship with Animals." *Scottish Journal of Theology* 67 (2014) 340–56.

Holt-Giménez, Eric. "Food Security, Food Justice, or Food Sovereignty?: Crises, Food Movements, and Regime Change." In *Cultivating Food Justice: Race, Class, and Sustainability*, edited by Alison Hope Alkon and Julian Agyeman, 309–30. Cambridge, MA: MIT Press, 2011.

Horrell, David G. "Biblical Vegetarianism?: A Critical and Constructive Assessment." In *Eating and Believing: Interdisciplinary Perspectives on Vegetarianism and Theology*, edited by David Grummet and Rachel Muers, 44–59. New York: T. & T. Clark, 2008.

Horrell, David G., et al. *Greening Paul: Reading the Apostle in a Time of Ecological Crisis*. Waco, TX: Baylor University Press, 2010.

Horsely, Richard A. *Covenant Economics: A Biblical Vision of Justice for All*. Louisville: Westminster John Knox, 2009.

Hulme, Mike. *Why We Disagree about Climate Change: Understanding Controversy, Inaction and Opportunity*. Cambridge: Cambridge University Press, 2009.

Intergovernmental Panel on Climate Change. "Fifth Assessment Report (AR5)." http://ipcc.ch/report/ar5/.

Irenaeus. *Against Heresies*. In vol. 1 of *Ante-Nicene Fathers*, edited by Alexander Roberts et al. Translated by Alexander Roberts and William Rambaut. Buffalo, NY: Christian Literature, 1885. http://www.newadvent.org/fathers/0103533.htm.

Jackson, Tim. *Prosperity without Growth: Economics for a Finite Planet*. Washington, DC: Earthscan, 2009.

Jensen, Robert. *We Are All Apocalyptic Now: On the Responsibilities of Teaching, Preaching, Reporting, Writing, and Speaking Out*. Robert William Jensen, 2013.

Jewett, Robert. *Romans: A Commentary*. Minneapolis: Fortress, 2007.

Jung, L. Shannon. *Food for Life: The Spirituality and Ethics of Eating*. Minneapolis: Fortress, 2004.

———. *Sharing Food: Christian Practices for Enjoyment*. Minneapolis: Fortress, 2006.

Kareiva, Peter, et al., eds. *Natural Capital: Theory and Practice of Mapping Ecosystem Services*. Oxford: Oxford University Press, 2011.

Kittel, Gerhard, ed. *Theological Dictionary of the New Testament*. Translated by Geoffrey W. Bromiley. 10 vols. Grand Rapids: Eerdmans, 1967.

Krueger, Frederick, ed. *A Cloud of Witnesses: The Deep Ecological Legacy of Christianity*. Eugene, OR: Wipf and Stock, 2002.

Kuznets, Simon. "Economic Growth and Income Inequality." *American Economic Review* 45 (1955) 1–28.

Lappé, Anna. *Diet for a Hot Planet: The Climate Crisis at the End of Your Fork and What You Can Do about It*. New York: Bloomsbury, 2010.

Leopold, Aldo. *A Sand County Almanac and Sketches Here and There*. Oxford: Oxford University Press, 1989.

Levenstein, Harvey. *Paradox of Plenty: A Social History of Eating in Modern America*. New York: Oxford University Press, 1993.

Levin, Kelly, et al. "Overcoming the Tragedy of Super Wicked Problems: Constraining Our Future Selves to Ameliorate Global Climate Change." *Policy Sciences* 45 (2012) 123–52.

Linville, P. W., and G. W. Fischer. "Preferences for Separating and Combining Events: A Social Application of Prospect Theory and the Mental Accounting Model." *Journal of Personality and Social Psychology* 60 (1990) 5–23.

Linzey, Andrew. *Animal Theology*. Urbana: University of Illinois Press, 1994.

Linzey, Andrew, and Tom Regan, eds. *Compassion for Animals: Readings and Prayers*. London: SPCK, 1988.

Lovins, L. Hunter, and Boyd Cohen. *Climate Capitalism: Capitalism in the Age of Climate Change*. New York: Hill and Wang, 2011.

Loya, Melisssa Tubbs. "'Therefore the Earth Mourns': The Greivance of the Earth in Hosea 4:1–3." In *Exploring Ecological Hermeneutics*, edited by Norman C. Habel and Peter Trudinger, 85–90. Atlanta: Society of Biblical Literature, 2008.

Lymbery, Philip, and Isabel Oakeshott. *Farmageddon: The True Cost of Cheap Meat*. New York: Bloomsbury, 2014.

Macquarrie, John. *Christian Hope*. New York: Seabury, 1978.

Mallett, Robyn K. "Eco-Guilt Motivates Eco-Friendly Behavior." *Ecopsychology* 4 (2012) 223–31.

Maniates, Michael. "Individualization: Plant a Tree, Buy a Bike, Save the World?" In *Confronting Consumption*, edited by Thomas Princen et al., 43–66. Cambridge, MA: MIT Press, 2002.

Marglin, Stephen A. *The Dismal Science: How Thinking Like an Economist Undermines Community*. Cambridge, MA: Harvard University Press, 2008.

Marlow, Hilary. *Biblical Prophets and Contemporary Environmental Ethics: Re-Reading Amos, Hosea, and First Isaiah*. Oxford: Oxford University Press, 2009.

McDuff, Mallory. *Natural Saints: How People of Faith Are Working to Save God's Earth*. Oxford: Oxford University Press, 2010.

————. *Sacred Acts: How Churches Are Working to Protect Earth's Climate*. Gabriola, BC: New Society Publishers, 2012.

McFague, Sallie. *Blessed Are the Consumers: Climate Change and the Practice of Restraint*. Minneapolis: Fortress, 2013.

————. *Life Abundant: Rethinking Theology and Economy for a Planet in Peril*. Minneapolis: Fortress, 2001.

————. *Models of God: Theology for an Ecological, Nuclear Age*. Minneapolis: Fortress, 1987.

————. *A New Climate for Theology: God, the World, and Global Warming*. Minneapolis: Fortress, 2008.

————. *Super, Natural Christians: How We Should Love Nature*. Minneapolis: Fortress, 1997.

McKenzie, Steven L. *Covenant*. St. Louis: Chalice, 2000.

McKibben, Bill. *The Comforting Whirlwind: God, Job, and the Scale of Creation*. Grand Rapids: Eerdmans, 1994.

————. *Deep Economy: Economics as If the World Mattered*. Oxford: Oneworld, 2007.

————. *Eaarth: Making a Life on a Tough New Planet*. New York: Times Books, 2010.

Meeks, M. Douglas. *God the Economist: The Doctrine of God and Political Economy*. Minneapolis: Fortress, 1989.

Mekonnen, M. M., and Hoekstra, A. Y. "The Green, Blue and Grey Water Footprint of Farm Animals and Animal Products." Delft: UNESCO-IHE Institute for Water Education, 2010.

Méndez-Montoya, Angel F. *The Theology of Food: Eating and the Eucharist*. West Sussex, UK: Wiley-Blackwell, 2012.

Michaels, J. Ramsey. *1 Peter*. Word Biblical Commentary 49. Waco, TX: Word, 1988.

Millennium Institute. "Global Food and Nutrition Scenarios." March 15, 2013. http://www.un.org/en/development/desa/policy/wess/wess_bg_papers/bp_wess2013_millennium_inst.pdf.

Miller, Vincent J. *Consuming Religion: Christian Faith and Practice in a Consumer Culture*. New York: Continuum, 2003.

Moltmann, Jürgen. *Ethics of Hope*. Translated by Margaret Kohl. Minneapolis: Fortress, 2012.

————. *Theology of Hope*. Translated by James W. Leitch. London: SCM, 2002.

Moo, Jonathan A., and Robert S. White. *Let Creation Rejoice: Biblical Hope and Ecological Crisis*. Downers Grove, IL: IVP Academic, 2014.

Murray, Robert. *The Cosmic Covenant: Biblical Themes of Justice, Peace and the Integrity of Creation*. London: Sheed and Ward, 1992.

Næss, Arne. *Ecology, Community and Lifestyle: Outline of an Ecosophy*. Translated and edited by David Rothenberg. Cambridge: Cambridge University Press, 1989.

Nash, James A. "Ethics and the Economics-Ecology Dilemma: Toward a Just, Sustainable, and Frugal Future." *Theology and Public Policy* 6 (1994) 33–63.

———. *Loving Nature: Ecological Integrity and Christian Responsibility*. Nashville: Abingdon, 1991.

———. "On the Subversive Virtue: Frugality." In *Ethics of Consumption: The Good Life, Justice, and Global Stewardship*, edited by David A. Crocker and Toby Linden, 416–36. Landham, MD: Rowman and Littlefield, 1997.

National Geographic. "The Hidden Water We Use." http://environment. nationalgeographic.com/environment/freshwater/embedded-water/.

Nellemann, Christian, et al., eds. "The Environmental Food Crisis: The Environment's Role in Averting Future Food Crises." http://www.grida.no/files/publications/ FoodCrisis_lores.pdf.

Nelson, Robert H. "The Theology of Economics." In *Faithful Economics: The Moral Worlds of a Neutral Science*, edited by James W. Henderson and John Pisciotta, 89–107. Waco, TX: Baylor University Press, 2005.

Newsom, Carol A. "Common Ground: An Ecological Reading of Genesis 2–3." In *The Earth Story in Genesis*, edited by Norman C. Habel and Shirley Wurst, 60–72. The Earth Bible 2. Sheffield: Sheffield Academic, 2000.

Nixon, Rob. *Slow Violence and the Environmentalism of the Poor*. Cambridge, MA: Harvard University Press, 2011.

Noble, David F. *The Religion of Technology: The Divinity of Man and the Spirit of Invention*. New York: Penguin, 1997.

Norgaard, Kari Marie. *Living in Denial: Climate Change, Emotions, and Everyday Life*. Cambridge, MA: MIT Press, 2011.

Northcott, Michael S. *The Environment and Christian Ethics*. Cambridge: Cambridge University Press, 1996.

———. "Eucharistic Eating, and Why Many Early Christians Preferred Fish." In *Eating and Believing: Interdisciplinary Perspectives on Vegetarianism and Theology*, edited by David Grummet and Rachel Muers, 232–46. London: T. & T. Clark, 2008.

———. *A Moral Climate: The Ethics of Global Warming*. Maryknoll, NY: Orbis, 2007.

Novak, Michael. *The Spirit of Democratic Capitalism*. New York: Simon and Schuster, 1982.

Novatian. "On the Jewish Meats." In vol. 5 of *Ante-Nicene Fathers*, edited by Alexander Roberts et al. Translated by Robert Ernest Wallis. Buffalo, NY: Christian Literature, 1886. http://www.newadvent.org/fathers/0512.htm.

O'Brien, Kevin J. *An Ethics of Biodiversity: Christianity, Ecology, and the Variety of Life*. Washington, DC: Georgetown University Press, 2010.

O'Donovan, Oliver. *Resurrection and Moral Order: An Outline for Evangelical Ethics*. Grand Rapids: Eerdmans, 1994.

Ogle, Maureen. *In Meat We Trust: An Unexpected History of Carnivore America*. Boston: Houghton Mifflin Harcourt, 2013.

Olley, John. "Mixed Blessings for Animals: The Contrasts of Genesis 9." In *The Earth Story in Genesis*, edited by Norman C. Habel and Shirley Wurst, 130–39. The Earth Bible 2. Sheffield: Sheffield Academic, 2000.

Oreskes, Naomi, and Erik M. Conway. *Merchants of Doubt: How a Handful of Scientists Obscured the Truth on Issues from Tobacco Smoke to Global Warming*. New York: Bloomsbury, 2011.

Oxfam America. "Lives on the Line: The Human Cost of Cheap Chicken." https://www. oxfamamerica.org/static/media/files/Lives_on_the_Line_Full_Report_Final.pdf.

Page, Ruth. *God and the Web of Creation*. London: SCM, 1996.

Palmer, Clare. "Stewardship: A Case Study in Environmental Ethics." In *Environmental Stewardship: Critical Perspectives, Past and Present*, edited by R. J. Berry, 63–75. London: T. & T. Clark, 2006.

Patel, Raj. *Stuffed and Starved: The Hidden Battle for the World Food System*. Brooklyn: Melville House, 2012.

Pellow, David N. *Resisting Global Toxics: Transnational Movements for Environmental Justice*. Cambridge, MA: MIT Press, 2007.

Pellow, David Naguib, and Robert J. Brulle. *Power, Justice, and the Environment: A Critical Appraisal of the Environmental Justice Movement*. Cambridge, MA: MIT Press, 2005.

Person, Raymond F., Jr. "The Role of Nonhuman Characters in Jonah." In *Exploring Ecological Hermeneutics*, edited by Norman C. Habel and Peter Trudinger, 85–90. Atlanta: Society of Biblical Literature, 2008.

Pew Commission on Industrial Farm Animal Production. "Putting Meat on the Table: Industrial Farm Animal Production in America." http://www.pewtrusts.org/~/media/legacy/uploadedfiles/peg/publications/report/pcifapfinalpdf.pdf.

Pieper, Josef. *Faith, Hope, Love*. San Francisco: Ignatius, 2012.

Pollan, Michael. *In Defense of Food: An Eater's Manifesto*. New York: Penguin, 2008.

———. *The Omnivore's Dilemma: A Natural History of Four Meals*. New York: Penguin, 2006.

Pope Francis. *Evangelii Gaudium: Apostolic Exhortation on the Proclamation of the Gospel in Today's World*. http://w2.vatican.va/content/dam/francesco/pdf/apost_exhortations/documents/papa-francesco_esortazione-ap_20131124_evangelii-gaudium_en.pdf.

———. *Laudato Si': On Care for Our Common Home*. http://w2.vatican.va/content/francesco/en/encyclicals/documents/papa-francesco_20150524_enciclica-laudato-si.html.

Prose, Francine. *Gluttony: The Seven Deadly Sins*. New York: Oxford University Press, 2003.

Public Religion Research Institute, and American Academy of Religion. "Believers, Sympathizers, and Skeptics: Why Americans Are Conflicted about Climate Change, Environmental Policy, and Science." https://www.aarweb.org/sites/default/files/pdfs/Annual_Meeting/2014/2014PRRI-AAR-ClimateChangeSurvey.pdf.

Rad, Gerhard von. *Genesis: A Commentary*. Translated by John H. Marks. Philadelphia: Westminster, 1961.

Rahner, Karl. *Theological Investigations*. Vol. 10, *Writings of 1965–67 (2)*. Translated by David Bourke. London: Darton, Longman and Todd, 1973.

Reichenbach, Bruce R., and V. Elving Anderson. "Tensions in a Stewardship Paradigm." In *Environmental Stewardship: Critical Perspectives, Past and Present*, edited by R. J. Berry, 112–25. London: T. & T. Clark, 2006.

Richards, Timothy J., and Geoffrey Pofahl. "Pricing Power by Supermarket Retailers: A Ghost in the Machine?" *Choices: The Magazine of Food, Farm, and Resource Issues* 25.2 (2010). http://www.choicesmagazine.org/magazine/article.php?article=126.

Rittel, Horst W. J., and Melvin M. Webber. "Dilemmas in a General Theory of Planning." *Policy Sciences* 4 (1973) 155–69.

Roberts, Paul. *The End of Food*. Boston: Mariner, 2009.

Robinson, Mary. "Why Women Are World's Best Climate Change Defense." *CNN.com*, http://www.cnn.com/2011/12/09/opinion/mary-robinson-women-climate/.

Rothenberg, Daniel. *With These Hands: The Hidden World of Migrant Farmworkers Today*. Berkeley: University of California Press, 1998.

Sandler, Ronald, and Phaedra C. Pezzullo, eds. *Environmental Justice and Environmentalism: The Social Justice Challenge to the Environmental Movement*. Cambridge, MA: MIT Press, 2007.

Santmire, H. Paul. "Partnership with Nature According to the Scriptures: Beyond the Theology of Stewardship." *Christian Scholar's Review* 32.4 (2003).

————. *The Travail of Nature: The Ambiguous Ecological Promise of Christian Theology*. Minneapolis: Fortress, 1985.

Schaefer, Jame. *Theological Foundations for Environmental Ethics: Reconstructing Patristic and Medieval Concepts*. Washington, DC: Georgetown University Press, 2009.

Schlosser, Eric. *Fast Food Nation: The Dark Side of the All-American Meal*. New York: Mariner, 2012.

Schmemann, Alexander. *The Eucharist: Sacrament of the Kingdom*. Translated by Paul Kachur. Crestwood, NY: St. Vladimir's Seminary Press, 1987.

————. *For the Life of the World: Sacraments and Orthodoxy*. Rev. ed. Crestwood, NY: St. Vladimir's Seminary Press, 1973.

Schumpeter, Joseph A. *Capitalism, Socialism, and Democracy*. New York: Harper, 1950.

Scrinis, Gyorgy. "On the Ideology of Nutritionism." *Gastronomica: The Journal of Food and Culture* 8 (2008) 39–48.

Shipler, David. *The Working Poor: Invisible in America*. New York: Knopf, 2004.

Shiva, Vandana. *Earth Democracy: Justice, Sustainability, and Peace*. Cambridge, MA: South End, 2005.

————. *Soil Not Oil: Environmental Justice in an Age of Climate Crisis*. Cambridge, MA: South End, 2008.

Smith, Adam. *An Inquiry into the Nature and Causes of the Wealth of Nations*. Chicago: University of Chicago Press, 1976.

Southgate, Christopher. *The Groaning of Creation: God, Evolution, and the Problem of Evil*. Louisville: Westminster John Knox, 2008.

————. "Protological and Eschatological Vegetarianism." In *Eating and Believing: Interdisciplinary Perspectives on Vegetarianism and Theology*, edited by David Grummet and Rachel Muers, 247–65. New York: T. & T. Clark, 2008.

————. "Stewardship and Its Competitors: A Spectrum of Relationships between Humans and the Non-human Creation." In *Environmental Stewardship: Critical Perspectives, Past and Present*, edited by R. J. Berry, 185–95. London: T. & T. Clark, 2006.

Spencer, Nick, et al. *Chrisianity, Climate Change, and Sustainable Living*. Peabody, MA: Hendrickson, 2009.

Steffen, Will, et al. "The Anthropocene: Are Humans Now Overwhelming the Great Forces of Nature?" *Ambio* 36.8 (2007) 614–21.

Steiman, Adina. "The Truth about Protein." *Men's Health*, April 7, 2015. http://www.menshealth.com/nutrition/protein-facts.

Stern, David, et al. "Economic Growth and Environmental Degradation: The Environmental Kuznets Curve and Sustainable Development." *World Development* 24.7 (1996) 1151–60.

Stern, Nicholas. *The Economics of Climate Change.* Cambridge: Cambridge University Press, 2007.

Stuart, Tristram. *Waste: Uncovering the Global Food Scandal.* New York: Norton, 2009.

Taylor, Charles. *Modern Social Imaginaries.* Durham, NC: Duke University Press, 2004.

Temple, William. *Nature, Man and God.* London: Macmillan, 1934.

Tepper, Rachel. "World's Meat Consumption: Luxembourg Eats the Most per Person, India the Least." *Huffington Post*, May 3, 2012. http://www.huffingtonpost.com/2012/05/03/world-meat-consumption_n_1475760.html#s934899&title=THE_MOST_1.

Theokritoff, Elizabeth. "Creation and Priesthood in Modern Orthodox Thinking." *Ecotheology* 10 (2005) 345–50.

———. *Living in God's Creation: Orthodox Perspectives on Ecology.* Crestwood, NY: St. Vladimir's Seminary Press, 2009.

Thompson, Charles D., Jr., and Melinda Wiggins, eds. *The Human Cost of Food: Farmworkers' Lives, Labor, and Advocacy.* Austin: University of Texas Press, 2002.

Tillich, Paul. *Dynamics of Faith.* New York: Harper, 1957.

Tocqueville, Alexis de. *Democracy in America and Two Essays on America.* Translated by Gerald E. Bevan. New York: Penguin, 2003.

United Nations. "Women, Gender Equality and Climate Change." http://www.un.org/womenwatch/feature/climate_change/.

United Nations Framework Convention on Climate Change. "Copenhagen Accord." http://unfccc.int/documentation/documents/advanced_search/items/6911.php?priref=600005735#beg.

United States Department of Agriculture. "Food Prices and Spending." http://www.ers.usda.gov/data-products/ag-and-food-statistics-charting-the-essentials/food-prices-and-spending.aspx#.U7r_01ZYXfN.

———. "Profiling Food Consumption in America." http://www.usda.gov/factbook/chapter2.pdf.

———. "Supertracker." https://supertracker.usda.gov/.

Vendituoli, Monica. "Agribusiness." *OpenSecrets.org*, https://www.opensecrets.org/lobby/background.php?id=A&year=2014.

Vischer, Lukas. "Listening to Creation Groaning: A Survey of Main Themes of Creation Theology." In *Listening to Creation Groaning*, edited by Lukas Vischer, 11–31. Geneva: Centre International Réformé, John Knox, 2004.

Washington, Haydn, and John Cook. *Climate Change Denial: Heads in the Sand.* London: Earthscan, 2011.

Watson, Francis. "In the Beginning: Irenaeus, Creation and the Environment." In *Ecological Hermeneutics: Biblical, Historical and Theological Perspectives*, edited by David G. Horrell et al., 127–39. London: T. & T. Clark, 2010.

Webb, Stephen H. *Good Eating.* Grand Rapids: Brazos, 2001.

——. *On God and Dogs: A Christian Theology of Compassion for Animals.* New York: Oxford University Press, 1998.

Weber, Elke U. "Experience-Based and Description-Based Perceptions of Long-Term Risk: Why Global Warming Does Not Scare Us (Yet)." *Climate Change* 77 (2006) 103–20.

Weinfeld, Moshe. "'Justice and Righteousness': The Expression and Its Meaning." In *Justice and Righteousness: Biblical Themes and Their Influence*, edited by Henning Graf Reventlow and Yair Hoffman, 228–46. Sheffield: JSOT Press, 1992.

Wenham, Gordon J. *Genesis 1–15.* Word Biblical Commentary 1. Waco, TX: Word, 1987.

Wesley, John. "The General Deliverance." Wesley Center for Applied Theology, 1999. http://wesley.nnu.edu/john-wesley/the-sermons-of-john-wesley-1872-edition/sermon-60-the-general-deliverance/.

Westermann, Claus. *Creation.* Translated by John J. Scullion. Philadelphia: Fortress, 1974.

——. *Genesis 1–11: A Continental Commentary.* Translated by John J. Scullion. Minneapolis: Fortress, 1984.

White House. "Fixing Our Broken Immigration System: The Economic Benefits to Agriculture and Rural Communities." https://www.whitehouse.gov/sites/default/files/uploads/ag-rural-report-07292013.pdf.

White, Lynn. "The Historical Roots of Our Ecologic Crisis." *Science* 155 (1967) 1203–7.

Winne, Mark. *Closing the Food Gap: Resetting the Table in the Land of Plenty.* Boston: Beacon, 2008.

Wirzba, Norman. *Food and Faith: A Theology of Eating.* Cambridge: Cambridge University Press, 2011.

——. *The Paradise of God: Renewing Religion in an Ecological Age.* Oxford: Oxford University Press, 2003.

——. "The Touch of Humility: An Invitation to Creatureliness." *Modern Theology* 24 (2008) 225–44.

Woodwell, George M. *A World to Live In: An Ecologist's Vision for a Plundered Planet.* Cambridge, MA: MIT Press, 2016.

Wright, N.T. *Surprised by Hope: Rethinking Heaven, the Resurrection, and the Mission of the Church.* New York: HarperOne, 2008.

Young, Alistair. *Environment, Economy, and Christian Ethics: Alternative Views on Christians and Markets.* Minneapolis: Fortress, 2015.

Young, Richard Alan. *Is God a Vegetarian?: Christianity, Vegetarianism, and Animal Rights.* La Salle, IL: Open Court, 1999.

Zizioulas, John. "Priest of Creation." In *Environmental Stewardship: Critical Perspectives, Past and Present*, edited by R. J. Berry, 273–90. London: T. & T. Clark, 2006.

Index of Authors

Index of Subjects

ecological sin as rejection of,
100–105
God's care of, 20–21
goodness of, 25–27
human knowledge of, 97–98
human stewardship of, 71–80,
82–90
incarnation and, 27–29
reverence for, 211–14
sacramentalism of, 29
science and, 207–10
creation care
church as model of, 191–92
ecological sin and, 102–5
foundation of, 68–69
human vocation for, 81–90
for nonhuman creatures, 20–21
resurrection and, 53–69
terminology of, 16
creation *vs.* evolution controversy,
climate change denial and, 5–6,
70, 206–10
crucifixion of Jesus, injustice of, 55–56
culture
eating rituals and, 164–65
ecological sin and, 102–5
food and, 146–50, 156, 162–63
neoclassical economics and, 123–26

daily life, resurrenction's significance in,
63–67
despair
failure of food system and, 161–63
hope *vs.,* 62–63
neoclassical economics and, 124–26
resurrection as answer to, 63–67
disconnectedness, principle of, climate
change denial and, 11
distributive justice
eating habits and, 185–89
neoclassical economics and, 120–22,
124–26
divine sovereignty, denial of climate
change and, 4–6

Earth Bible series, eco-justice principles
promoted by, 11n26
eating habits
culture and rituals surrounding,
164–65
Eucharist ritual and, 18
in Genesis, 151
hope and, 18, 164–72, 184–89
meat in diet and, 172–83
ecological citizenship, 206
ecological disorder, Paul's references to,
48–49
ecological economic model, 106–7,
127–34
ecological sin, 100–105
food wastefulness as, 156–61
proposed concept of, 17
economic growth
American Christian presumptions
concerning, 64–67
Christian faith and, 17–18
as cultural idol, 106–26
ecological goals and, 127–34
hopelessness and, 122–26
talents parable linked to, 72
ecosystem monetization, neoclassical
economic model and, 119–20
Endangered Species Act, 197
environmentalism
justice and, 41–44, 198–201
moral and theological issues in, 6–8
pantheism and, 11
Environmental Protection Agency
(EPA), 42
ethics, economics and, 113–22
Eucharist
food production and ritual of,
162–63
hopeful eating based on, 18, 164–72
Orthodox interpretation of, 85
political and economic dimensions
of, 166–72, 186–89
as sacrament, 29, 33
evangelicalism, American Protestantism
and, 19–20
evolutionary theory, Christian resistance
to, 5–6, 70, 206–10
Executive Order 12898, 197